What do Entrepreneurs Create?

Understanding Four Types of Ventures

H. Morris

Professor of Entrepreneurship and Social Innovation, Keough School of Global Affairs, University of Notre Dame, South Bend, Indiana, USA

Donald F. Kuratko

The Jack M. Gill Distinguished Chair of Entrepreneurship, Professor of Entrepreneurship, and Executive and Academic Director, Johnson Center for Entrepreneurship and Innovation, Indiana University, Bloomington, Indiana, USA

 Edward Elgar
PUBLISHING

Cheltenham, UK • Northampton, MA, USA

Published by
Edward Elgar Publishing Limited
The Lypiatts
15 Lansdown Road
Cheltenham
Glos GL50 2JA
UK

Edward Elgar Publishing, Inc.
William Pratt House
9 Dewey Court
Northampton
Massachusetts 01060
USA

Paperback edition 2021

A catalogue record for this book
is available from the British Library

Library of Congress Control Number: 2019951889

This book is available electronically in the **Elgar**online
Business subject collection
DOI 10.4337/9781789900224

Printed on elemental chlorine free (ECF)
recycled paper containing 30% Post-Consumer Waste

ISBN 978 1 78990 021 7 (cased)
ISBN 978 1 78990 022 4 (eBook)
ISBN 978 1 80088 841 8 (paperback)

Typeset by Columns Design XML Ltd, Reading

Printed and bound in the USA

Contents

List of figures   vi
List of tables   vii
List of boxes   viii
About the authors   ix
Preface   xi

 1 The entrepreneurial journey: intention versus emergence   1

 2 Venture types: what entrepreneurs actually create   17

 3 Survival ventures: just getting by   36

 4 Lifestyle ventures: seeking stability   50

 5 Managed growth ventures: learning to fly   66

 6 Aggressive growth ventures: changing the world   85

 7 A resource-based perspective on venture types   101

 8 How ventures develop unique identities   122

 9 The fit between type of venture and entrepreneur   136

10 Types within types   151

11 Why all ventures matter: toward a portfolio perspective   166

12 Venture types, public policy and ecosystem support   189

Index   211

Figures

1.1 The process perspective on entrepreneurship 4

1.2 The emergent nature of venture creation 9

2.1 Comparing four types of ventures in the same industry 29

2.2 Comparing technology usage in different types of entrepreneurial ventures 30

3.1 Common characteristics of survival ventures 40

3.2 Elements contributing to the commodity trap 42

4.1 Common characteristics of lifestyle ventures 53

5.1 Determinants of growth and venture types 71

6.1 Hockey stick growth pattern 90

6.2 Entrepreneurial newness framework 91

6.3 Innovation diffusion curve and the chasm 93

7.1 Characterizing the resource portfolios of different venture types 109

7.2 The resource portfolio, resource attributes and bundling processes for entrepreneurial ventures 114

7.3 The resource portfolio, resource attributes, bundling processes and leveraging processes for entrepreneurial ventures 116

8.1 Entrepreneurial identity and the four types of ventures 124

8.2 Shared and unique identity descriptors for venture types 127

9.1 Entrepreneurial characteristics and the four types of ventures 145

11.1 A portfolio perspective on venture types 183

12.1 Examples of support needs at different stages of development 206

Tables

2.1	Classifications of ventures by scholars	20
2.2	Four types of entrepreneurial ventures	25
3.1	Literacy challenges for survivalist entrepreneurs	45
5.1	Key characteristics of managed growth firms	73
7.1	Characterizing the resource portfolios of venture types	105
7.2	VRIO framework applied to resource portfolios of venture types	110
9.1	Critical competencies involved in venture creation and growth	140
10.1	Sub-categories of survival ventures	152
10.2	Sub-categories of lifestyle ventures	155
10.3	Sub-categories of managed growth ventures	158
10.4	Sub-categories of aggressive growth ventures	161
11.1	Balancing objectives across the venture types	180
12.1	Supporting entrepreneurship with both public policy and community action	193
12.2	Examples of public policies addressing needs of the four venture types	200
12.3	Community programs addressing needs of the four venture types	202

Boxes

1.1   Properties of emergence in new venture creation   7
4.1   Common myths about lifestyle ventures   56
4.2   Major challenges confronting lifestyle ventures   60
11.1 Why survival, lifestyle and managed growth ventures matter   170

About the authors

Michael H. Morris is Professor of Entrepreneurship and Social Innovation at the Keough School of Global Affairs at the University of Notre Dame. Prior to that he held distinguished entrepreneurship chairs at the University of Florida, Oklahoma State University, and Syracuse University. The entrepreneurship programs he has built at different universities have received international recognition. Dr. Morris is a pioneer in curricular innovation and experiential learning. His outreach efforts have facilitated the development of thousands of start-up ventures, and he has launched three ventures of his own. Professor Morris is the Director of the Experiential Classroom, which shares best practices in entrepreneurship education with faculty from around the globe. He also works to bring entrepreneurship empowerment to those operating under conditions of adversity, and annually coordinates the Entrepreneurship Empowerment in South Africa Program. He has authored 13 books and published over 130 articles in peer-reviewed journals. He co-edits the Prentice-Hall Entrepreneurship Series, and is editor emeritus of the *Journal of Developmental Entrepreneurship*. Dr. Morris is a Past President of the United States Association for Small Business and Entrepreneurship (USASBE). He has been awarded the Academy of Management's Dedication to Entrepreneurship Award, the Leavey Award from the Freedoms Foundation for impacting private enterprise education, and the Entrepreneurship Educator of the Year Award from USASBE. A former Fulbright Scholar, he earned his PhD in marketing from Virginia Tech in 1983.

Donald F. Kuratko is the Jack M. Gill Distinguished Chair of Entrepreneurship; Professor of Entrepreneurship; Executive and Academic Director, Johnson Center for Entrepreneurship & Innovation, The Kelley School of Business, Indiana University, Bloomington. Dr Kuratko is a prominent scholar and national leader in the field of entrepreneurship, having published over 200 articles on aspects of entrepreneurship and corporate entrepreneurship. Professor Kuratko has authored or co-authored 30 books, including one of the leading entrepreneurship textbooks, *Entrepreneurship: Theory, Process, Practice*, 11th edition

(Cengage Publishers, 2020). In addition, Dr Kuratko has been a consultant on corporate innovation and entrepreneurial strategies to a number of major corporations. Under Professor Kuratko's leadership and with one of the most prolific entrepreneurship faculties in the world, Indiana University's Entrepreneurship Program has consistently been ranked as the #1 university for entrepreneurship research by the Global Entrepreneurship Productivity Rankings; #1 university for Global Entrepreneurship Research in the *Journal of Small Business Management* 12-year analysis for entrepreneurship research productivity, and the #1 Graduate and Undergraduate Business School for Entrepreneurship (Public Institutions) by *U.S. News & World Report*. Professor Kuratko has been named one of the Top 25 Entrepreneurship Scholars in the world and was recipient of the Karl Vesper Entrepreneurship Pioneer Award for his dedication to developing the field of entrepreneurship. He was honored by the National Academy of Management with the Entrepreneurship Mentor Award for his exemplary mentorship to the next generation of entrepreneurship.

Preface

What do entrepreneurs create? This book attempts to address this question and establish why it is so critical for our understanding of entrepreneurship. Entrepreneurs create a wide variety of businesses. However, most of the research and teaching in entrepreneurship fails to distinguish the different types of ventures created by entrepreneurs, resulting in significant confusion and misdirection by both entrepreneurs and those attempting to foster entrepreneurship (economic development professionals, public policy experts, community organizations, universities). Further, the entrepreneur may or may not have a clear idea of what kind of business they want to create, as the entrepreneurial journey is an emergent one – what entrepreneurs actually create often differs markedly from what they originally intended.

An overwhelming emphasis has been placed by many observers on explosive growth ventures such as Facebook, Google, Amazon, Uber and Airbnb. Yet, while important, these businesses represent less than 1 percent of start-ups. This book distinguishes four types of new ventures: survival, lifestyle, managed growth and aggressive growth.[1] Each type is discussed in some detail in terms of its underlying nature and characteristics. Further, the resources, skills and capabilities necessary for success with each type are explored, with implications drawn. A wide range of examples of each are provided.

We investigate a number of issues that arise based on this typology of ventures. Examples include an exploration of reasons for why ventures of one type rarely change to become a different type, and how entrepreneurs can determine the appropriate type of venture they should pursue. Further, for communities to realize the real potential of entrepreneurship, we introduce what we call the "portfolio" concept. Here, emphasis is placed on encouraging development of a balanced mix or portfolio of survival, lifestyle, managed growth and aggressive growth ventures. The portfolio perspective recognizes the value and interdependencies among the four types, and the importance of balancing risks, investments and different kinds of outcomes. We also investigate sub-categories that exist within each venture type, and how the characteristics of these sub-categories impact venture emergence. For public policy makers, economic development professionals, educators and others trying to foster entrepreneurship at a local, regional or national level, the implications of the four types of ventures for policy and ecosystem development are highlighted.

ORGANIZATION

The chapter sequence in *What do Entrepreneurs Create? Understanding Four Types of Ventures* is systematically organized around understanding the unique nature of the entrepreneurial journey and the particular aspects of this journey when pursuing four different types of new ventures: survival, lifestyle, managed growth and aggressive growth. What follows is a brief synopsis of what each chapter entails.

In Chapter 1, the nature of the entrepreneurial journey is explored to illustrate how ventures organically emerge. Each venture has a purpose and mission, develops a culture and values that guide its operations, plans for the future, reacts to threats and opportunities, and attempts to ensure long-term viability. It takes risks and makes mistakes. It can be creative, developing new products and services, and looking for ways to improve its internal ways of doing things. It nurtures an image in the marketplace and within the communities where it operates. Accomplishing all of this is the work of the entrepreneur. Usually with insufficient resources, he or she must overcome obstacles, demonstrate tenacity, and constantly solve new problems. In the end, most ventures are created in the face of adversity, and it is the entrepreneur who has a vision, addresses the critical implementation risks, makes the necessary adjustments, and keeps a venture going through the inevitable ups and downs that occur.

The types of ventures that emerge from the entrepreneurial journey are examined in Chapter 2. A typology is introduced that distinguishes four categories of early stage ventures: survival, lifestyle, managed growth and aggressive growth. The typology builds upon past attempts at classifying entrepreneurial firms, while also addressing some of the shortcomings in these earlier efforts. The commonalities among the ventures in each of the four categories are considered as well as some of the major differences between the types. The chapter illustrates the path-dependent nature of the decisions and resource commitments surrounding each type of venture that make it difficult, though not impossible, for ventures to progress from one category to another.

The single largest category of start-up ventures is survival businesses, and they are the focus of Chapter 3. The term survival is used to describe a venture that struggles to stay in business on a continuous basis. It can also be referred to as a "hand-to-mouth" venture in the sense that, at best, just enough revenue is generated to pay bills and cover expenses, including paying the entrepreneur (but often less than he or she might earn working for someone else). However, little to nothing is left over to reinvest in the business. It is quite difficult to ever get ahead with these types of businesses. Instead, there is an ongoing struggle just to keep up. Hence, both the venture and the entrepreneur do little more than survive or get by.

Lifestyle ventures represent the second most common form of start-up, and are the focus of Chapter 4. They include the locally owned and operated bar, hardware store, day care center, hair salon, machining shop or copy business. More than a survival business, which exists on a hand-to-mouth basis, the lifestyle venture can be relatively profitable. It affords the entrepreneur a decent living, and so supports a lifestyle for them and their families. Sometimes referred to as "mom and pop operations," they are small in size, independent, usually full-time operations with employees, often family-owned, with limited capacity. The lifestyle entrepreneur seeks incremental increases in sales and profits, but without meaningful expansion of the scope of operations or significant increases in the employee base. Thus, any growth occurs within a fairly fixed set of parameters. Entrepreneurs frequently establish these types of businesses around their specific skills, interests or knowledge base.

Chapter 5 focuses on managed growth ventures. Here, the entrepreneur seeks sustained growth and ongoing expansion of the business, but they also strive to achieve this growth in a deliberate and controlled manner. Importantly, with this type of venture, the entrepreneur is not trying simply to increase sales revenue from current operations, or improve profits by reducing costs, which is common in many lifestyle ventures. Rather, the objective is to expand the nature and scope of the business. Managed growth can be accomplished in a number of ways. It could involve steadily adding new locations, expanding one's current territory or market reach, entering new markets, creating new products or revenue drivers, developing entirely new lines of business, or acquiring another firm. Frequently, it involves some combination of these approaches.

Aggressive growth ventures are explored in Chapter 6. These are often disruptive businesses that change markets, industries, societies, and, sometimes, the world. Although fewer in number, they create a disproportionate number of patents, jobs and wealth in society, and can enhance the global competitiveness of a nation. Aggressive growth ventures can generate huge returns to founders and investors, but also represent significant risk. They are often trying to create a market that does not exist, or significantly change how people address a particular need. They require extraordinary amounts of resources to fuel growth, which leads them to rely heavily on large equity investments from outside parties. As a result, the founder(s) must generally be willing to give up a substantial amount of ownership. These are especially volatile ventures, with high stress levels, and intense demands placed on the founding team and early stage employees.

A resource-based perspective on the venture types is introduced in Chapter 7. It focuses on the kinds of resources each category of venture tends to have, and the manner in which these resources are deployed. It is argued that resources determine what the entrepreneur is able to create, and what the venture is able to become. They provide the means for experimentation, risk-taking and development of proactive approaches that enable growth. As such, one of the most significant challenges confronting entrepreneurial ventures is the determination of how resources can best be used to achieve sustainability. For each venture type the configuration of the resource portfolio, the properties of these resource configurations, and the bundling and leveraging processes involved when managing resources are investigated.

Chapter 8 is concerned with identity. People tend to develop identities that reflect how they see themselves at a fundamental or core level. Identities also emerge at the organizational level. Based on their inter-actions over time, the people that make up an organization come to develop a set of beliefs regarding what is central, distinctive and enduring about a business. The role played by identity in the four venture types is explored in this chapter. Attention is first devoted to the entrepreneurial identity of the founder, and how this might influence the tendency to develop a survival, lifestyle, managed growth or aggressive growth venture. Considered also is the likelihood that this is a two-way relation-ship, with outcomes from each venture type serving to affect the founder's identity. The chapter then looks at the concept of organizational identity, illustrating how a number of the underlying characteristics that define the venture types are key determinants of the kind of organ-izational identity that emerges. Finally, the importance of identity in establishing and maintaining the legitimacy of each type of venture is examined.

The question, "how do entrepreneurs decide what type of venture they should create?" is addressed in Chapter 9. Consideration is given to the issue of fit between the type of venture being created and the nature of the individual who starts and runs the business. The personality, ambitions, experiences, risk tolerance, values, time horizons, skills and other characteristics of the individual can influence how he or she builds the business and what it becomes. The chapter also examines how some of the unique attributes of entrepreneurs and the considerations they confront impact the entrepreneur's decision process for a specific type of venture.

In Chapter 10, sub-categories of each venture type are identified. The four venture categories do not represent a continuum where ventures simply vary by degree. Each venture type is a unique category of enterprise with a unique identity. The differences between any two types tend to be much greater than the differences among the businesses of a given type. However, the ventures that make up each category are not homogeneous. Within each of the four venture types one encounters considerable variance. As a result, types within types can be identified. The challenge becomes one of placing these businesses into subcategories that enable us to better understand how they function. This chapter explores the underlying differences among ventures of a given type, and draws implications from these sub-categories.

The relative contributions of each of the four venture types are assessed in Chapter 11. Relationships and interdependencies among the four types are investigated and the disproportionate benefits produced by aggressive growth ventures are tied to these interdependencies. A series of arguments are presented regarding the need to encourage all four types of ventures. Based on these arguments, the adoption of a portfolio perspective is advocated. As with a financial portfolio, risks and returns to society will be maximized when there is a balance across the portfolio of ventures. Implications are drawn for venture portfolios that are unbalanced, or over-emphasize a particular type of venture.

In our final chapter, attention is devoted to identifying ways that public policies and support initiatives at the community (or local ecosystem) level can be developed in tandem to foster a balanced portfolio of venture types. Ongoing gaps in policies and programs to foster venture creation are identified. Key policy levers and community support elements that could be used to facilitate entrepreneurship are then identified. The elements of a more holistic policy and community action framework are described – one that reflects the needs and challenges of the different venture types over their stages of development.

CONTRIBUTIONS OF THE BOOK

This book was created to explore the significance of differences in the kinds of businesses created by entrepreneurs. It addresses a critical shortcoming in much of the research, teaching and economic development work that deals with entrepreneurship. This shortcoming concerns the tendency to treat entrepreneurial start-ups generically, or alternatively to place an overwhelming emphasis on extremely high growth ventures, or gazelles, to the exception of other kinds of start-ups.

Our hope, in the chapters to come, is to facilitate a fundamental rethinking of entrepreneurial activity and how it is manifested. Instead of the general theories of entrepreneurship, we lay a foundation for developing theories of different kinds of entrepreneurial ventures. Instead of insights into entrepreneurs and entrepreneurial ventures as a group, we produce insights into the underlying nature, functioning and requirements for success of each of our four types of ventures. We seek to highlight the interdependencies among these four venture types, and advocate adoption of a portfolio approach when developing entrepreneurial ecosystems and designing policies and programs to foster entrepreneurship. As the reader navigates these pages, we hope he or she comes to appreciate the distinctiveness of survival, lifestyle, managed growth and aggressive growth businesses, the reasons why each represents a critical component of the entrepreneurial landscape, and how collectively they drive the global entrepreneurial revolution.

Michael H. Morris, South Bend, Indiana
Donald F. Kuratko, Bloomington, Indiana

NOTE

1. We recognize that entrepreneurs also start non-profits and social ventures, as well as corporate ventures, but our focus is on new for-profit entities.

1. The entrepreneurial journey: intention versus emergence

UNDERSTANDING ENTREPRENEURSHIP

The distinguishing characteristic of an entrepreneur is that he or she creates a venture (Gartner, 1988). The key is that an operating entity actually gets launched. It may subsequently fail or succeed, grow or not grow, and last months, years or many decades. It may be well planned or somewhat accidental, high-tech or relatively low-tech, privately or publicly owned, and formally registered or operating beneath the radar. In fact, one of the most remarkable aspects of entrepreneurial ventures is how diverse they are.

What exactly does it mean to create a venture? Many potential entrepreneurs fail to understand the distinction between an interesting product idea and a functioning business, or more basically, the difference between innovation and entrepreneurship. Innovation is coming up with an idea (and even developing a prototype or working model) for a new app that enables people to schedule hair appointments at thousands of different salons, a snow plow with a unique blade that removes twice as much snow, or a better designed knee replacement joint. It takes entrepreneurship to translate the innovation into a business, get the venture up and running, and make it sustainable.

So, what does a business look like? A business has customers and an ability to address their needs and collect money from them. New customers are continually acquired and existing ones receive ongoing marketing communications. It typically has employees who need to be supervised, evaluated and compensated. It has suppliers with whom terms have to be negotiated, orders placed, the logistics of delivery and returns coordinated, and payments made. It has operations, where inputs are turned into products or services, quality is managed and inventory is maintained. It must keep accounting records, maintain legal protection and insure itself against unforeseen developments. And, of course, a business never stops running.

More importantly, a venture is organic – it is a living, breathing thing. It has a purpose and mission. It develops a culture and values that guide its operations. It plans for the future, reacting to threats and opportunities, and attempting to ensure long-term viability. It takes risks and makes mistakes. It can be creative, developing new products and services and looking for ways to improve its internal ways of doing things. It nurtures an image in the marketplace and within the communities where it operates.

Accomplishing all of this is the work of the entrepreneur. Usually with insufficient resources, he or she must overcome obstacles, demonstrate tenacity, and constantly solve new problems. As we shall see, most ventures are created in the face of adversity, and it is the entrepreneur who has a vision, addresses the critical implementation risks, makes the necessary adjustments, and keeps a venture going through the inevitable ups and downs that will occur.

VENTURE CREATION AS A JOURNEY

Anyone can start a venture. In one sense venture creation is relatively simple. Consider the farmer's wife who makes attractive quilts. She has her nephew create a website, registers her business as a sole proprietorship, does some social media marketing, and begins making sales. In another sense, it can be quite complex. An entrepreneur who has developed a novel drug that treats kidney stones must try to get patent protection, which can be denied, has to go through expensive clinical trials to obtain regulatory approval, typically must raise millions of dollars from equity investors to cover ongoing research and development costs, has to establish large-scale production and distribution capabilities, and is subject to relatively strict product liability laws should the product have any adverse side effects.

Regardless of how basic or complicated the venture is, a variety of steps are involved and these are implemented over time. This reality has led entrepreneurship scholars to adopt what can be called the "process perspective" (McMullen and Dimov, 2013; Shane, 2003). In essence, entrepreneurship is conceptualized as a set of stages that unfold over a prolonged period. This is critical, as it allows for the fact that these steps can be managed and the process can be learned. Further, as a manageable process, it can be applied by anyone and in a wide variety of contexts.

Although there are different conceptualizations of the entrepreneurial process, Figure 1.1 provides an illustration of the principal stages involved. The process begins with the identification of a market opportunity. Opportunities derive from forces in the external environment creating a gap or opening for something new. This gap or opening represents an unmet need. Then a business idea is formulated and it typically centers around a new product or service offering. The business idea captures a unique value proposition for capitalizing on the opportunity. A business model is next developed where one translates the innovative product or service concept into the essence of a business. The business model provides a basic architecture or design of the business and how it will make money. With this business model in mind, the entrepreneur determines the necessary financial, physical, human, relational, intellectual and technological resources necessary to actually launch a venture. He or she does not usually have most of these resources, and so must develop creative approaches to acquiring them through bootstrapping, leveraging and financing activities. Then comes the actual launch of the business where operations are set up and the entrepreneur begins addressing the marketplace. Here, adjustments are being made as the individual figures out what works in practice and comes to better understand the market opportunity. At this point, the entrepreneur must learn how to be a manager, formalize various aspects of operations, and, if he or she wants to grow, develop the necessary infrastructure. Eventually, there is a need to pursue some kind of exit strategy, such as selling the business, passing it on to a family member or other party, or simply shutting it down and selling off the assets.

The process as presented in Figure 1.1 appears to be a fairly straightforward, linear set of steps or stages. Yet, in reality, venture creation tends to be anything but linear. It is messy, chaotic and ambiguous. The entrepreneur gets to a particular stage and encounters obstacles and new information that necessitate adjustments to decisions made in a previous stage. Aspects of different stages are pursued in tandem, and ongoing adjustments are made to decisions from earlier stages.

As a result, the venture creation process should be approached as a journey. This journey is one where the path is not well marked, there are lots of twists and turns, and the ultimate course taken depends on key decisions made by the entrepreneur along the way (Morris et al., 2012). The founder of a business is constructing reality as he or she goes. It is an experience filled with uncertainty and encounters with novelty, or things with which the entrepreneur has little previous experience, particularly early on. The days are long and tend to be filled with highs and lows surrounding extended periods of hard work and little result. In a sense, the entrepreneur is equivalent to an actor in a play where there is no script or director.

Three critical things happen when someone tries to launch a business: (a) the entrepreneur makes a number of mistakes; (b) there is resistance

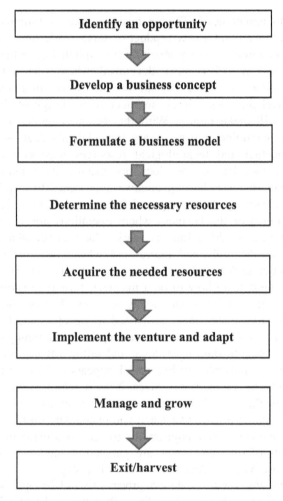

Figure 1.1   The process perspective on entrepreneurship

to the new venture; and (c) unexpected developments impact the business. As the venture unfolds, many of the entrepreneur's initial assumptions and expectations (often captured in a business plan) prove to be wrong. Costs are higher, the market smaller, customers more demanding, logistics more complex. Based on faulty or incomplete information, wrong interpretations and errant judgments, multiple mistakes are made. Despite best efforts, the entrepreneur ends up pricing too high or low, emphasizing products or services that are not the ones desired by the market, targeting the wrong customers, selecting an inappropriate location, buying the wrong piece of equipment or technology, operating at the wrong hours, and not hiring the right kinds of employees – among many other errors.

At the same time, a person creating a new venture deals with various sources of resistance, and tends to underestimate what it will take to overcome these obstacles and establish a successful operation. There can also be resistance from competitors, customers, suppliers, regulators, distributors, financiers, and even family members and friends. For example, requests for funding might be rejected by over a dozen banks, competitors attempt to undercut the new business by running specials and spreading poor word of mouth, and the entrepreneur may be encouraged to get a stable job by family members who grow weary of the long hours and limited revenue.

On top of this, all sorts of unplanned events take place that impact the business. A roof leak during a rainstorm results in the spoilage of (uninsured) inventory worth thousands of dollars, the first employee hired suddenly quits and starts a competing business, a random connection made at a social event leads to a sizeable new customer account, a distributor that had agreed to carry the entrepreneur's product decides instead to work with a competing firm. Changes can happen in the regulatory, economic and technological environments that positively or adversely affect the venture.

These developments indicate that the entrepreneurial journey is an unpredictable, often tumultuous one, where the entrepreneur controls much less than one might imagine. The key to what becomes of the venture lies in how the entrepreneur deals with mistakes, resistance and unexpected developments. Entrepreneurship is a learning journey. Entrepreneurs who learn quickly from mistakes and are able to adapt to ongoing developments on a timely basis are the ones who achieve the most success. Further, in attempting to chart a path and make corrections, it becomes important to experiment and engage in trial and error – reinforcing the importance of learning what works and what does not, making appropriate adjustments, and moving on. The nature of the journey also makes clear that entrepreneurs succeed because of tenacity and perseverance as they outlast the sources of resistance.

THE EMERGENT NATURE OF NEW VENTURES

The journey we have described has important implications. Perhaps the most important of these is the emergent nature of entrepreneurship (Morris and Webb, 2015). Emergence means that what one starts out to create is not what is actually created. Rather, as the entrepreneur undertakes the myriad tasks involved in pursuing an entrepreneurial idea, something that is distinctively different tends to emerge.

Venture creation involves an unceasing dynamic as the individual copes with unfolding events, many of which are unpredictable and uncontrollable. A multitude of novel events are encountered by the entrepreneur in the early years of a venture (often on a daily basis). They produce ongoing incongruities and changing realities, such that continual flux and encounters with novelty become essential characteristics of the entrepreneurial experience (Schindehutte and Morris, 2009). As such, entrepreneurship is a creative process, yet one in which the initially conceived idea for the venture can be reinforced or radically disrupted through subsequent sparks of creativity that are stimulated by internal and external developments.

As disruptions interrupt the everyday operations in a venture, they clash with any sense of order that has been achieved by the entrepreneur. In trying to bring order to their circumstances, entrepreneurs are forced to continually reweave their webs of beliefs and habits of action to accommodate new experiences (Tsoukas and Chia, 2002). Although they seek to establish routines and stability, entrepreneurs are forced to improvise and adapt as new developments create changing demands and opportunities. Unfolding events introduce variety which feeds individual learning and exploratory behavior. Learning, in turn, is instrumental in the individual's ability to adapt. Improvisational and adaptive behaviors serve to generate new events or realities. In this way, the entrepreneurial experience becomes a crucible involving the confluence of change, improvisation, learning, adaptation and ongoing challenges to one's assumptions, perceptions and beliefs.

Emergence differs from growth, evolution, or the pursuit of a new direction by the venture. It instead represents the establishment of a new type of order (Lichtenstein, 2014). Order is being created out of instability and change, where novel and coherent structures and patterns are derived during the process of self-organization (Goldstein, 1999). The venture is in the process of becoming something it was not before. Emergence might involve changes that lead to growth or decline or simply the reshaping of the new venture without any real effect on size. Similarly, emergence does not necessarily unfold through a pre-determined set of stages (e.g., birth, growth, maturity and decline) but is more random (Aldrich and Ruef, 2006). More specifically, the emergence perspective asserts that the properties of emergence (Box 1.1) are fundamental to the understanding of subsequent order creation within new ventures.

BOX 1.1   PROPERTIES OF EMERGENCE IN NEW VENTURE CREATION

Irreversibility: Emergence occurs based on experiences as they unfold and accumulate. New experiences are continually added, creating an increasingly nuanced and interconnected process of emergence. The unique combination of events defining a particular entrepreneur's experience leaves an indelible stamp, where it is impossible to return to a pre-emergent state.

Adaptive tension: A large variety of unexpected and uncontrollable events combine with ongoing intrinsically based disruptions that create instability in entrepreneurs' lives and lead them to seek change as a means of adjusting back to a more stable state.

Presence of nonlinear change and feedback, where small inputs can produce large outcomes: The occurrence of small, random events has the potential to be amplified and, based on feedback received, fundamentally shift the entrepreneur's path of emergence.

Surprise, where non-obvious or unexpected behaviors come from the object in question: Ventures produce and interact with a stream of unpredictable, surprise events, both positive and negative. Also, moments of sudden insight, or instinctual or improvisational acts, can be instrumental in affecting outcomes.

Reciprocal interactions between micro-level events and behaviors and emergent macro-structures: A wide mix of internal and external variables constantly interact at micro-, meso and macro-levels to produce a venture that often differs markedly from what was originally intended. Emergence and the subsequent behaviors of those involved can radically shape the structures in which they are embedded and create new structures.

Co-evolution among components of the system and increasing complexity: Co-evolution occurs (a) among the components that form the opportunity, the venture or the entrepreneur, and (b) as a result of the interplay among the emergent opportunity, venture and entrepreneur.

Supervenience of resultant structure over components: The novel structure that surfaces through emergence can establish order for the various components (i.e., individuals, routines/activities, interactions, etc.) that initially came together to form the resultant structure.

Source: Adapted from Morris and Webb (2015).

When launching a new venture, three core elements are emerging: the business model, the opportunity and the entrepreneur. Consider a venture that is five years old and doing quite well on various performance indicators. Then draw a simple comparison between the business model of this successful venture and the business as described in the original business plan written for the venture. The result will almost always be more difference than similarity. The principal product being sold, target audiences generating the most revenue, positioning and pricing approach, financial structure of the firm, kinds of employees needed, locational requirements, marketing and distribution approaches, and much more are likely to change. Again, the entrepreneur is correcting mistakes, overcoming obstacles, and dealing with unanticipated developments. He or she is experimenting and seeing what works and what does not.

In addition, the underlying opportunity that supports the venture tends to emerge, and this is tied to the so-called "corridor principle" (Ronstadt, 1988). In the process of pursuing a perceived opportunity, the entrepreneur is likely to become aware of additional opportunities that would never have been apparent had he or she not begun the journey in the first place. In a sense, the pursuit of opportunity begets recognition of other opportunities. By starting the venture, interacting with market forces, learning from what does not work, and experimenting with alternative approaches, the entrepreneur is able to discover where the real opportunity lies. This discovery process suggests that opportunities tend to emerge. Consider an example. An entrepreneur starts a cleaning business and initially perceives that the opportunity lies with the residential market. While some inroads are made with this market, it proves to be too crowded or insufficiently profitable. Yet, based on new information that becomes available because the entrepreneur is interacting with stakeholders in the marketplace, he or she is able to determine that the real opportunity may lie with cleaning offices, warehouses or government buildings. As a result, the entrepreneur starts to provide cleaning services to office buildings. Eventually, he or she discovers that medical offices represent an especially attractive niche. Then, additional insights suggest that, with some training and certification, the company can charge a lot more by specializing in dealing with clean up and disposal of bio-waste and hazardous materials (hazmat). Ultimately, the entrepreneur realizes that it might be more lucrative to actually provide the bio-waste and hazardous materials training to hospital employees and others. With time, experience, continued experimentation, learning and adaptation, a more attractive and viable opportunity has emerged.

As the opportunity and the business model emerge, so too does the entrepreneur. The evidence suggests that entrepreneurs are not born – people do not have some sort of genetic predisposition to start ventures (Bird, 1989; Morris, 1998). Much of what is required is learned. It certainly helps to have passion, a strong work ethic, and to be organized. One must also be open to change, and have the ability to learn and adapt. The entrepreneur is learning how to make sense of developments as they occur, to tolerate ambiguity, and to manage when surrounded by uncertainty. He or she is learning the many different roles that have to be played as a venture unfolds (e.g., salesperson, money manager, service provider, supervisor, record keeper, delegator, planner, organizer, innovator and so on). In the end, just as the entrepreneur creates a venture, over time the venture is creating the entrepreneur (Morris et al., 2012). By being immersed in the experience, one is being formed into an entrepreneur.

Figure 1.2 illustrates the concept of emergence. Here, the entrepreneur starts with an idea for a new venture. Building on his or her past experiences, knowledge base, assumptions and beliefs, the research they engage in, and interactions with others, they develop intentions and expectations. In short, they have some concept of what they are trying to create, what will be required, and what sort of outcomes might be realized. Once the venture is launched, the entrepreneur is exposed, in varying degrees, to the many characteristics of the entrepreneurial journey that we have described (e.g., ambiguity, novelty, unexpected events, new opportunities). The question becomes how these developments are interpreted and responded to. The combination of these ongoing responses together with the dynamic interactions between external developments and internal resources/conditions influence what is emerging in terms of opportunities, the business model and the entrepreneur.

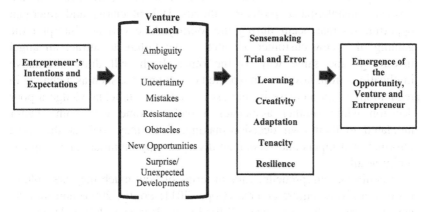

Figure 1.2   The emergent nature of venture creation

EVERY ENTREPRENEURIAL JOURNEY IS UNIQUE

Two people who start the same type of venture at the same time and with the same resources are likely to create very different types of businesses.

Even if they have similar skills and capabilities, the outcomes will still diverge. It is not just about differences in performance, but in the very nature of the venture being created. And no two people will experience the entrepreneurial journey in the same way.

There is a path dependency in the manner in which a venture unfolds. Hundreds of critical decisions and actions are taken as a venture takes form, with little consistency among entrepreneurs in the order in which things are done. Decisions and actions (or inactions) at certain points in time impact future developments, often in unexpected ways. Hence, when one starts a venture, a decision to sign a two-year lease on a building or pursue a particular market segment will affect a range of subsequent developments both within and outside the venture (e.g., obstacles created, resources available, opportunities uncovered), and delimit certain future choices. Even if subsequently modified, every decision has a permanent imprint on the emerging venture. The same dependency can apply to actions taken or not taken. The entrepreneur who finds the willpower to call on one more bank after rejections from ten others, or attend one more networking function despite being exhausted, can find these simple acts profoundly redirect the pathway of the venture.

Further, every entrepreneur is unique based on how he or she processes and responds to the pressures, resource constraints, misdirection and mistakes, unanticipated problems, threats, lack of clarity and emergent opportunities that occur during the journey. One will not interpret the gaining of a new customer account or the failure to attract an angel investor in the same way as the other. Each will draw alternative implications from novel or unexpected developments, such as a change in regulations or an increase in interest rates. One will acknowledge a poor decision while another associates a bad outcome with some factor unrelated to their own decision-making. Both may look at the same informational inputs and recognize divergent opportunities, or no opportunity at all.

In addition, entrepreneurs vary in terms of how much they are able to learn in a given venture context (Cope, 2011; Politis, 2008) and they do not all learn in the same ways (Minniti and Bygrave, 2001). Moreover, some are more willing to experiment and are better able to draw lessons from trials and failures (Sarasvathy, 2009). The same is true for the individual's relative rigidity or flexibility when it comes to adapting aspects of the venture over time. Schindehutte and Morris (2001) demonstrate how entrepreneurs vary in their capacity to adapt, how much they actually adapt, and the strategies relied upon to adapt.

Lastly, a critical factor explaining how people respond to the many events occurring as a venture emerges is the development of an entrepreneurial mindset. McGrath and MacMillan (2000) describe this mindset as an ongoing focus on recognizing opportunities and pursuing the most attractive ones with passion and discipline The mindset represents a way of both thinking and acting (Haynie et al., 2010; Ireland et al., 2009). From an attitudinal perspective, the person believes they are able to effect change in their environment. They tend to be optimistic, and recognize that, even in dire circumstances, the world is filled with opportunities. They believe that most anything can be improved, done better or enhanced in some way. Individuals embrace change and new approaches, and are tolerant of failure. With regard to behavior, the mindset includes an action orientation, where the individual is willing to pursue new, innovative approaches. They persevere in the face of obstacles, and continually adapt to these obstacles and emerging opportunities. They are not big risk-takers, but instead are adept at mitigating and managing risks. They understand the importance of leveraging resources, creatively finding ways to bootstrap, using other people's resources, and recognizing things as resources that others do not.

Individuals vary in how much they demonstrate an entrepreneurial mindset, and this affects how their ventures emerge. Importantly, the mindset is something that can be developed and nurtured. It is enhanced with practice – by doing entrepreneurial things all the time. Arguably, it declines with lack of practice. The adverse circumstances encountered as a venture unfolds represent a key incentive for thinking and acting in entrepreneurial ways. The extent to which this mindset is manifested can dramatically alter the pathways open to the venture.

MAKING SENSE OF THE DIVERSITY

Entrepreneurs start businesses for many reasons. They can be motivated by a drive for independence, a need for achievement, a quest for income or wealth, or a desire to contribute to one's community, among other factors. Some are pushed into entrepreneurship by necessity and others are pulled by the attractiveness of an opportunity (Block et al., 2015). There are those who deliberately seek to be entrepreneurs, and those who find themselves starting what become successful ventures almost by accident (Shah and Tripsas, 2007). We can also distinguish one-time entrepreneurs from those with experience in starting multiple ventures (Sarasvathy, 2009). And there are those who wish to see a new business through to its maturity, while others are speculative entrepreneurs who find they are better at getting the venture established and then exiting early on (Bruce, 2016).

However, regardless of their motives or intentions at the outset, things change as the venture emerges. The business takes on shapes and forms that depart from what the entrepreneur originally had in mind. Sometimes expectations are exceeded, and other times outcomes fall short of what was hoped for. What started as a high-end pastry bar becomes a supplier of desserts to two- and three-star restaurants. A venture launched with a technology to detect potentially unsafe chemicals in research laboratories subsequently emerges as a company that sells kits to police departments for use in bomb detection. In addition, a venture is always a work in progress. Unlike a painting created by an artist or a bridge built by an engineer, a business is never completed. It continues to emerge, resulting in ongoing changes in resource requirements and performance outcomes.

The picture we are describing is one of diversity, with every venture emerging in its own idiosyncratic way. Consider the differences between someone who launches a unique type of retail toy store that eventually grows to three locations in different cities in Great Britain and Elon Musk's launch of Tesla, the US-based automobile company seeking to create a more sustainable energy future. Both are entrepreneurial ventures, but they have relatively little in common. Not only are the risks and returns surrounding these two ventures dramatically different, but so too are their structures, resource requirements, sources of investment, relative reliance on technology, management styles, growth potential, market impact, and much more.

The reality of this diversity and these differences makes entrepreneurship a more difficult subject to research and understand. If every entrepreneurial journey is unique, how are we able to draw any general conclusions about such fundamental questions as:

- How can the venture start-up rate be increased?
- What skills, capabilities and resources does it take to create a sustainable venture?
- Why do most ventures start small and stay small?
- What drives the level of innovation that occurs in a new business?
- Why do new ventures fail?
- What is the role of entrepreneurship in economic development?

Definitive answers to these and other basic questions have eluded scholars for many decades. What is true for some ventures may not hold for many others. One result of this state of affairs is the relatively widespread dissemination of a number of myths and misconceptions regarding entrepreneurship (e.g., regarding venture success rates, who can be an entrepreneur, the nature of entrepreneurial risk-taking, the social and economic impacts of entrepreneurship) despite the lack of evidence to support the underlying beliefs.

We believe the key to sorting out the tremendous diversity among entrepreneurial ventures and making progress in addressing many of the basic questions about venture creation lies in distinguishing general categories or types of ventures. Specifically, we argue that ventures will emerge as one of four general types. We will label these types as *survival, lifestyle, managed growth* and *aggressive growth* ventures. As we shall see in the chapters to come, each has a number of defining characteristics that make it possible to draw general conclusions about the ventures that fall into the category in spite of the uniqueness that characterizes every venture.

In exploring these four types of ventures, we seek to demonstrate how core commonalities among ventures within a given category outweigh the significant differences between those in different categories. Further, the four types do not represent a continuum, suggesting the differences are less ones of degree and instead go to the essence of the business itself. It thus becomes necessary to treat each category as a separate kind of entrepreneurship. In a sense, then, attempts at producing a general theory of entrepreneurship must give way to theories of different types of ventures.

CONCLUSIONS

When historians look back on the twenty-first century, they may well label it the "age of entrepreneurship," a time when more ventures were started than at any other time in history.

On any given day, thousands of new ventures are created across the globe, each with its own unique development path and identity. This chapter has examined the emergent nature of new venture creation, and identified factors contributing to the fact that no two ventures, and no two entrepreneurs, are alike. This diversity has important implications for our ability to explain and predict many aspects of the venture creation process.

An interesting question then becomes how much will we have learned about entrepreneurship, its true nature, and how to facilitate it in a range of contexts by the end of the century. A beginning point in ensuring real progress is made is the question "what do entrepreneurs create?" The fact that they create everything from the corner hotdog stand to SpaceX and Instagram leaves us in a difficult position, particularly when it comes to developing the kinds of insights that advance theory, help entrepreneurs to be successful, and support development of public policies that encourage entrepreneurial behavior. Much of what we know about entrepreneurship depends entirely on the type of venture under question. Thus, a research finding regarding the cognitive processes employed by entrepreneurs, the role of networks in successful new business formation, how firms overcome the liability of newness, what makes a business model sustainable, the effectiveness of different resource leveraging approaches, and hundreds of other questions will not likely apply equally to every venture, and may only be relevant for a relatively small percentage of entrepreneurial firms.

To address this challenge and make sense of the significant diversity among ventures, this book introduces a typology that distinguishes four types of entrepreneurial firms. Venture type thus becomes a key contextual variable that drives how entrepreneurship theory and practice should be approached. In the chapters to come, we provide the underpinnings for development of the typology, and dedicate attention to an in-depth examination of each type. The tendency of ventures of a given type to develop a kind of shared identity is explored, and efforts are devoted to establishing reasons why a business of one type tends to not evolve into a different type over time. Issues of fit between types of entrepreneurs and types of ventures are probed. The diversity among firms of a given type is also acknowledged, with sub-groups of ventures identified for each category. Interdependencies among the four types of ventures are then reviewed, and the concept of a "new venture portfolio" is introduced as a guide in fostering economic development. Finally, we draw implications from the venture portfolio for ongoing theory development, management practice and the formulation of public policy.

REFERENCES

Aldrich, H.E. and Ruef, M.E. (2006). *Organizations Evolving*. Thousand Oaks, CA: Sage.

Bird, B.J. (1989). *Entrepreneurial Behavior*. New York: Scott Foresman & Company.

Block, J.H., Kohn, K., Miller, D., and Ullrich, K. (2015). Necessity entrepreneurship and competitive strategy. *Small Business Economics*, *44*(1), 37–54.

Bruce, R. (2016). Are you a fundamental or a speculative entrepreneur. *Forbes Magazine*, July 19. Accessed January 15, 2019 at https://www.forbes.com/

sites/robinbruce/2016/07/19/are-you-a-fundamental-or-speculative-entrepreneur/
#247ec7437a3d.

Cope, J. (2011). Entrepreneurial learning from failure: An interpretative phenomenological analysis. *Journal of Business Venturing, 26*(6), 604–623.

Gartner, W.B. (1988). "Who is an entrepreneur?" is the wrong question. *American Journal of Small Business, 12*(4), 11–32.

Goldstein, J. (1999). Emergence as a construct: History and issues. *Emergence, 1*, 49–72.

Haynie, J.M., Shepherd, D.A., Mosakowski, E., and Earley, P.C. (2010). A situated metacognitive model of the entrepreneurial mindset. *Journal of Business Venturing, 25*(2), 217–229.

Ireland, R.D., Covin, J.G., and Kuratko, D.F. (2009). Conceptualizing corporate entrepreneurship strategy. *Entrepreneurship Theory Practice, 33*(1), 19–46.

Lichtenstein, B.B. (2014). *Generative Emergence: A New Discipline of Organizational, Entrepreneurial and Social Innovation.* New York: Oxford University Press.

McGrath, R.G. and MacMillan, I.C. (2000). *The Entrepreneurial Mindset: Strategies for Continuously Creating Opportunity in an Age of Uncertainty,* Vol. 284. Cambridge, MA: Harvard Business Press.

McMullen, J.S. and Dimov, D. (2013). Time and the entrepreneurial journey: The problems and promise of studying entrepreneurship as a process. *Journal of Management Studies, 50*(8), 1481–1512.

Minniti, M. and Bygrave, W. (2001). A dynamic model of entrepreneurial learning. *Entrepreneurship Theory and Practice, 25*(3), 5–16.

Morris, M.H. (1998). *Entrepreneurial Intensity: Sustainable Advantages for Individuals, Organizations, and Societies.* Westport, CT: Greenwood Publishing Group.

Morris, M.H. and Webb, J.W. (2015). Entrepreneurship as emergence. In *The Oxford Handbook of Creativity, Innovation, and Entrepreneurship: Multilevel Linkages.* New York: Oxford University Press, pp. 457–476.

Morris, M.H., Schindehutte, M., and Pryor, C. (2012). *Entrepreneurship as Experience: How Events Create Ventures and Ventures Create Entrepreneurs.* Cheltenham, UK and Northampton, MA, USA: Edward Elgar Publishing.

Politis, D. (2008). Does prior start-up experience matter for entrepreneurs' learning? A comparison between novice and habitual entrepreneurs. *Journal of Small Business and Enterprise Development, 15*(3), 472–489.

Ronstadt, R. (1988). The corridor principal and entrepreneurial time. *Journal of Business Venturing, 3*(1), 31–40.

Sarasvathy, S.D. (2009). *Effectuation: Elements of Entrepreneurial Expertise.* Cheltenham, UK and Northampton, MA, USA: Edward Elgar Publishing.

Schindehutte, M. and Morris, M.H. (2001). Understanding strategic adaptation in small firms. *International Journal of Entrepreneurial Behavior & Research, 7*(3), 84–107.

Schindehutte, M. and Morris, M.H. (2009). Advancing strategic entrepreneurship research: The role of complexity science. *Entrepreneurship Theory and Practice, 33*(2), 241–276.

Shah, S.K. and Tripsas, M. (2007). The accidental entrepreneur: The emergent and collective process of user entrepreneurship. *Strategic Entrepreneurship Journal*, *1*(1–2), 123–140.

Shane, S.A. (2003). *A General Theory of Entrepreneurship: The Individual-Opportunity Nexus*. Cheltenham, UK and Northampton, MA, USA: Edward Elgar Publishing.

Tsoukas, H. and Chia, R. (2002). On organizational becoming: Rethinking organizational change. *Organization Science*, *13*, 567–582.

2. Venture types: what entrepreneurs actually create

INTRODUCTION

Entrepreneurs create a wide array of businesses. Their ventures include everything from Uber and Facebook to a regional financial services firm and a local counseling service. Arguably, differences among many of these firms can be greater than the things they share in common. Ventures vary in numerous ways, including how much they take risks, are market-driven, innovate, attempt to expand, rely on outside capital, are productive with resources, involve family members, incorporate new technologies, and generate rents, among others. In fact, there is so much diversity in what gets created that it becomes difficult to draw meaningful conclusions about the underlying nature and characteristics of entrepreneurial firms.

This diversity creates significant problems for those who want to pursue, understand or support entrepreneurship. Consider a few examples:

- Nascent entrepreneurs – for someone thinking about starting a business, it can be difficult to grasp what is required in terms of resources, skills and effort when ventures can vary so much.
- Researchers – for those attempting to theorize about entrepreneurship, the ability to conduct research where patterns are identified and generalizations can be drawn is quite problematic when there is more disarray than commonality among ventures.
- Resource providers – the ability of financiers and others to predict the amount and types of resources required for business success is made much more complicated by the wide variability among ventures.
- Public policy makers – the impacts of policies in general, and particularly of policies meant to facilitate entrepreneurial activity, are likely to vary considerably depending on the diversity among the ventures affected.

- Communities – as communities work to develop supportive entrepreneurial ecosystems, the elements that are relevant in supporting
  certain ventures may fail to serve many other ventures.

Given this diversity, there is ample room for confusion regarding what
we are talking about when we discuss entrepreneurial start-ups. There
clearly is no single prototype of the entrepreneurial venture. But it is also
not true that all ventures are completely different from one another. A
more fruitful path might involve some sort of middle ground, where we
focus on the commonalities that exist among sub-groups, or general
categories, of ventures.

Our purpose in this chapter is to introduce a typology that distinguishes four categories of early stage ventures: survival, lifestyle, managed growth and aggressive growth. The typology builds upon past
attempts at classifying entrepreneurial firms, while also addressing some
of the shortcomings in these earlier efforts. We consider the commonalities among the ventures in each of the four categories, and explore some
of the major differences between the types. We then argue that the
path-dependent nature of the decisions and resource commitments surrounding each type of venture make it difficult, though not impossible,
for ventures to progress from one category to another. Implications are
drawn from the typology for how entrepreneurship is approached by a
variety of different stakeholders.

TYPOLOGIES: PAST ATTEMPTS TO CAPTURE
ENTREPRENEURIAL FIRMS

Gartner (1988) defines entrepreneurship as the act of organization
creation. This broad and inclusive perspective suggests an entrepreneur is
not just someone who creates a disruptive firm built around radically new
innovation and rapidly scales the enterprise (e.g., Schumpeter, 1934;
Shane, 2009). It allows for the creation and development of new ventures
of all types. This inclusive perspective is consistent with the views of a
large number of scholars (e.g., Davidsson, 2005; Klyver et al., 2008;
Mintzberg, 1989; Reynolds and Curtin, 2009), but it also creates some
challenges.

Using this broader delineation, the entrepreneurial context includes
emerging firms that may or may not grow, do or do not innovate, are
self-funded or rely on outside finance, and vary considerably in their
economic impact. This approach produces such a diverse mix of ventures
that it makes it difficult to generalize across the entrepreneurial context.

Consider just a few basic questions about entrepreneurship: "why do ventures fail and at what rate?"; "how do entrepreneurs process information and make decisions?"; "what are the key roles played by the founder in achieving venture success?"; "how do networks and social capital explain venture outcomes?"; and "how do ventures exit from the market?" The answers to these and many other questions will differ significantly across the population of ventures.

However, there may be general categories or types of ventures that share some critical characteristics, and these commonalities have implications for the requirements, capabilities, behaviors and performance of ventures within a given category. Stated differently, while it may not be possible to draw insights or conclusions that apply to all entrepreneurial ventures, we may find common tendencies or patterns exist among particular types of firms. The question then becomes one of determining how best to group or categorize the diverse mix of ventures created by entrepreneurs.

The term 'typology' refers to the study of types, while a particular typology is an attempt to classify phenomena (e.g., plants, people, countries, symbols) according to type. There have been various attempts by scholars to classify types of entrepreneurial firms over the years. Table 2.1 provides a summary of some of the key attempts. Although some of these were proposed 40 or more years ago, it would not appear that they have had much influence on how we think about entrepreneurship.

Underlying each of the typologies presented in Table 2.1 are one or more variables used to group firms. For instance, some observers emphasize the nature of planning and strategy within the firm, such as the extent to which the company is more rigid or adaptive (Smith and Miner, 1983), proactive or reactive (Miles et al., 1978; Miller, 1983). Others stress the amount of emphasis placed on innovation (Miller and Friesen, 1977), or whether the venture is more high-tech or low-tech (Roberts, 1991). And still others categorize firms based on the types of goals they pursue (Parsons, 1956), the payoffs or potential returns from the venture (Vesper, 1990; Webster, 1977), the firm's structure, complexity and workflows (e.g., Haas et al., 1966; Pugh et al., 1969), whether it is family-owned or not (Glueck, 1980), and how involved it is in export or international activity (Oviatt and McDougall, 1994).

However, the most prevalent approach stresses both the growth orientation (low/moderate/high) and relative sophistication (i.e., simple versus complex) of the firm. Thus, in Table 2.1 there are typologies that include categories of craft/promotion/administrative (Filley and Aldag, 1978),

Table 2.1   Classifications of ventures by scholars

Authors	Categories of Ventures	Classification Criteria
Parsons (1956)	Oriented to economic goals/Political goals/Integrative/Pattern maintenance	Function to society
Haas et al. (1966)	Class 1–10	Business type, technology, size (99 variables)
Pugh et al. (1969)	Bureaucracy: Full/Nascent full/Workflow/Nascent workflow/Pre-workflow/Personnel/as well as Implicitly structured	1. Structuring of activities 2. Concentration of authority 3. Line control of workflow
Liles (1974)	Marginal/Interesting (size and growth to come)/High potential (rapid growth)	Size and growth potential
Stanworth and Curran (1976)	Craftwork/Classic entrepreneurial/Managerial	Motives and drivers
Webster (1977)	Large payoff-many principals/Small payoff-few principals/Large payoff-few principals	Four-P Index, the perceived payoff per principal
Miller and Friesen (1977)	Adaptive-moderate dynamism/Adaptive-extreme dynamism/Dominant firm/Giant under fire/Entrepreneurial firm/Innovator	Intelligent rationality, heterogeneity, dynamism, centralization/temperament (proactivism, risk-taking)
Filley and Aldag (1978)	Craft/Promotion/Administrative	Goals, leadership, structure, staff, functional development, innovation, risk-taking
Glueck (1980)	Family business ventures/Entrepreneurial ventures	Strategic priorities, goals, hiring and other management practices
Miles et al. (1978)	Defenders/Analyzers/Prospectors/Reactors	Configuration of technology, structure, strategy and process
Dunkelberg and Cooper (1982)	Craft firm/Seeking Independence/Growth-oriented	Aggressiveness
Miller (1983)	Simple firms/Planning firms/Organic firms	Environment, structure, decision-making style, strategy and entrepreneurship

Authors	Categories of Ventures	Classification Criteria
Ronstadt (1982)	Lifestyle/Small-profitable/ High growth	Growth
Smith and Miner (1983)	Rigid/Adaptive	Customer mix, product mix, production method and facilities, markets, change plans
Carland et al. (1984)	Small business/Entrepreneurial venture	Launch of new goods, production methods, markets, supply sources, reorganization
Vesper (1990)	Low-pay, stably/High-pay, stably/High growth	Growth, capitalization, industrial sector, technological type and degree of innovation
Julien (1990)	Micro/Small/Medium	Size in revenues or employees
Sexton and Bowman-Upton (1991)	Marginal small/Lifestyle small/Successful small/High growth	Propensity for growth, ability to manage growth
Roberts (1991)	High-tech/Non-high-tech	Technological orientation
Rizzoni (1991)	Static-sheltered/Traditional/ Dominated/ Technology-based/New technology-based	Market and competitive factors, technological innovation
Oviatt and McDougall (1994)	Domestic/Export-import/ Multinational trader, Geographically focused/Global start-up	International activities and number of countries involved
Kunkel (2001)	Independent/Corporate	Context of entrepreneurial behavior
Hisrich and Peters (1998)	Lifestyle/Foundation/High potential gazelle	Growth orientation

lifestyle/small-profitable/high growth (Ronstadt, 1982), craft/seeking independence/growth-oriented (Dunkelberg and Cooper, 1982), simple/ planning/organic (Miller, 1983), marginal small/lifestyle small/successful small/high growth (Sexton and Bowman-Upton, 1991), low-pay, stably/ high-pay, stably/high growth (Vesper, 1990), and lifestyle/foundation/ high potential gazelle (Hisrich and Peters, 1998). The specific categories in these seven typologies have significant overlap and generally range from small, simple enterprises that do not attempt to expand or grow to more complex enterprises that seek aggressive growth.

TOWARD A STANDARD TYPOLOGY OF ENTREPRENEURIAL VENTURES

It is possible to synthesize the various perspectives found in Table 2.1 and produce a standard typology for use by entrepreneurs, educators, scholars, financiers, entrepreneurial support organizations and public policy makers. Our focus is on ventures in their emergent stages (Morris et al., 2012). This is the time period over which a new venture is conceptualized and created, mistakes are made, learning occurs, adjustment and adaptation take place, and a sustainable business model can take root. Hence, we are concentrating on ventures from inception through the point at which they become sustainable or fail, and have settled on a particular growth mode (e.g., no growth, steady growth, rapid growth). Further, the venture is typically in its first five or so years of existence.

In developing the typology, our objective was to be parsimonious in the number of categories included while at the same time identifying venture types that are meaningfully different. We sought categories that were, for the most part, mutually exclusive while also being collectively exhaustive. Further, we emphasize categories that appear more consistently across the different attempts at venture classification in Table 2.1. In selecting the factors that define each category, we consider 14 underlying variables:

- annual growth rate
- time horizon
- critical resources
- managerial focus
- management style
- management skills
- entrepreneurial orientation
- technology investment
- liability of smallness
- source of finance
- company structure
- economic motives
- reward emphasis
- exit approach.

These variables cover multiple dimensions of the enterprise, including aspects of strategy, structure and management. Importantly, the inclusion of firm growth remains central, but we believe the growth that occurs is likely a by-product of some of the other 12 variables. These other variables are suggested by particular typologies in Table 2.1, and/or by contemporary research in entrepreneurship (e.g., Boso et al., 2013; Bradley et al., 2011; Covin and Slevin, 1989; Langlois, 2007; Naldi and Davidsson, 2013; Perez-Luno et al., 2011). As such, the proposed typology represents a synthesis and extension of these earlier approaches.

The result is a typology consisting of four types of ventures. They include:

- *Survival Ventures*: Provide basic subsistence for the entrepreneur and his or her family, in effect allowing for little more than a hand-to-mouth type of existence. The business may or may not be formally registered, and typically has no premises, very few assets, no business banking relationship, and operates on a cash or barter basis. As the business exists to provide for basic personal financial needs, once costs are covered there is generally no capacity to reinvest into the venture. Launch of the business is often necessity-driven, and the business generally operates in highly competitive, price-based and largely undifferentiated markets.

  (Examples: lawncare service, handyman, mobile automobile detailer, roadside fruit stand, small craft maker, personal trainer, Uber driver, hotdog vendor, dog walker, Airbnb host, home-based childcare or laundry service.)

- *Lifestyle Ventures*: Provide a relatively stable income stream for owners based on a workable business model and a maintenance approach to management. Relatively modest reinvestments are made to maintain competitiveness in a local market where the firm is embedded. The venture typically has premises, usually a single location, and employees, but does not seek meaningful expansion or growth. The number of employees remains relatively constant. Given limited capacity, it is difficult for the venture to achieve economies in operations.

  (Examples: local bar or restaurant, hair salon, hardware store, auto repair shop, toy store, independent movie theatre, small accounting firm, local taxi company, owner of a single franchise.)

- *Managed Growth Ventures*: Have a workable business model and seek stable growth over time, as reflected in occasional launches of new products or new lines of business, periodic entry into new markets, a steady expansion of facilities, locations and staff, and

development of a strong local and regional brand. Ongoing rein-
vestment in the business and continuous but controlled growth
guide ongoing business development.

(Examples: custom boat manufacturer, third-party logistics company, charter jet business, multi-location walk-in medical clinic,
regional law firm, real estate company, marketing agency, or auto
dealership.)

- *Aggressive Growth Ventures*: Referred to as gazelles, these are often
  technology-based ventures with strong innovation capabilities that
  seek exponential growth and are funded by equity capital. Launch
  of the venture is opportunity-driven, with the founders (often a
  team) seeking to transform industries and create new markets. The
  focus is typically national or international and the firms often
  become candidates for initial public offerings or acquisition.

  (Examples: Amazon, Applied Optoelectronics, Avedro, Baidu,
  Eventbrite, FITBIT, Facebook, LinkedIn, Nexeon, Restore Health
  SpaceX, Under Armour.)

The four types are further detailed in Table 2.2. Here, each venture type
is characterized based on the 14 underlying variables mentioned above.
Two of the categories experience relatively little growth or expansion,
while the other two grow but to differing degrees. The inclusion of the
survival category reflects the fact that a number of typologies include a
simple, low-pay, craft, micro or marginal category, and is based on the
growing interest in informal ventures and businesses operated by those in
severely resource-constrained conditions (e.g., Hall et al., 2012; Sutter
et al., 2019; Webb et al., 2009). Not only do such ventures provide
subsistence to sizeable numbers of people in both developed and developing economies, but they often produce a meaningful proportion of a
country's GDP (Commission on the Private Sector and Development,
2004; Prahalad, 2005).

Surveys of the emerging venture landscape suggest that survival and
lifestyle businesses may constitute as much as 85 percent of the new
ventures in developed economies, reinforcing the idea that most new
businesses start small and stay small (Dennis, 2014; Kauffman Foundation, 2019). Aggressive growth firms represent only about 1 percent of
start-ups. However, the managed growth and aggressive growth firms
together produce a disproportionate amount of job and wealth creation
(Birch, 1987; Malchow-Møller et al., 2011).

Table 2.2   Four types of entrepreneurial ventures

	Survival	Lifestyle	Managed Growth	Aggressive Growth
Annual growth rate	nominal	< 5%	10–15%	> 20%
Time horizon	day to day	weekly, monthly	1–3 years	2–5 years
Key resources	few, physical, simple, formative	simple, physical utilitarian, robust	complex, physical and intangible, robust	complex, intangible, instrumental, robust
Management focus	selling whatever I have	maintenance of working business	incremental strategic growth	scalability model
Management style	reactive	tactical	strategic	strategic and proactive
Entrepreneurial orientation	very low	low	moderate	high
Technology investment	none	limited	moderate	high
Liability of smallness	significant	significant	less significant	not significant
Source of finance	self	self, family and friends, bank	self, family and friends, bank, private investors	bank, angel investors, venture capital and private equity firms, public markets
Exit approach	shut down	shut down, sell, transfer	sell, merge, transfer	sell, merge, go public
Management skills	making, selling	operational skills, basic management	planning, strategizing, delegating, leveraging	planning, innovation, cash flow management, negotiation
Structure	little to none	simple	functional, centralized	functional; product and market-based
Economic motives	sustain oneself, one's family	income substitution	wealth creation	wealth creation
Reward emphasis	weekly income taken from business	salary, bonus	salary, performance incentives, equity	equity, capital gain

CONTRASTING THE FOUR TYPES OF VENTURE

Differences certainly exist among ventures within a given category, and we will explore these further in Chapter 10. However, differences between the categories are more significant and have greater implications. The underlying variables that define each category, when combined, produce a unique and distinctive quality. This uniqueness is apparent when we examine ventures from each category operating within the same industry. Consider four examples of cleaning companies.

Clara's Cleaning

Clara runs a small cleaning business from her home that focuses on residential customers in her local community. The business is a sole proprietorship, and Clara is the only formal employee, doing much of the cleaning herself, and using her personal vehicle to get to jobs. She relies on family members and friends when she has more work and needs help. Having very little equipment of her own, Clara uses the mops, vacuum cleaners and supplies of her clients and rents some equipment. The business serves about seven customers a week, but does not have contracts with any of them. Customers pay in cash or by personal check. New accounts all come from word of mouth referrals, as little formal marketing is done. She does her own bookkeeping, although her records tend to be quite incomplete. She carries no business insurance and does not have a business bank account. Clara does not pay herself a salary, but takes money out of the business for personal use when she can. Limited revenue forces Clara to clean homes during the day, and work at a part-time job in the evenings.

Mainstreet Commercial Cleaners

Operating out of a single location in a mid-sized city, Mainstreet concentrates on cleaning offices, retail stores and commercial buildings. Many of the clients sign month-to-month or six-month contracts. The company has 15 employees, including an office manager/bookkeeper, and offers them basic healthcare benefits. It owns two vans and a mix of basic cleaning equipment and supplies. Much of the cleaning work is done in the early morning, evenings and on weekends. Marketing efforts include a company website and business Facebook page, brochures that are mailed to local businesses, testimonials from satisfied customers, and attendance by the owner at numerous business networking events. The company carries liability insurance and coverage for its vehicles and equipment. It has a business banking account, and all customers pay by check or electronically. The business generates a consistent but moderate profit in a fairly competitive environment. In addition to earning a decent salary, the owner is able to periodically replace or upgrade equipment, and takes money out of the business in good years. While the founder occasionally considers adding a third van and more cleaning crews, he is not certain the local market would support this.

Bio-clean Medical and Health Specialists

BMHS offers specialized cleaning and sanitizing services to hospitals, medical clinics and doctors' offices. Started and initially financed by three partners, and certified as a woman-owned and veteran-owned business, over ten years the company has grown from a single location in the founders' hometown to locations in seven cities located throughout the region. Growth has been financed from retained earnings and bank debt. The company and its employees have multiple certifications, including those addressing the handling of hazardous materials, and they receive ongoing training. It employs a patient-centered cleaning approach, and adapts to the established cleaning protocols of the different medical facilities being served. BMHS employs a total of 120 people. There are 7–9 cleaning teams operating out of each of its locations, with teams specializing in particular types of facilities or jobs. The company has a fleet of trucks and vans, and an array of basic and specialty equipment, materials and supplies are inventoried at each location. The company has built a strong regional brand. Marketing efforts include a coordinated mix of personal selling, ads in healthcare publications, appearances at regional trade shows and conferences, and a strong online presence. The company has invested in technology to support job performance and a number of administrative functions within the company.

Merry Maids

Founded in Omaha, Nebraska, to provide cleaning services for residential customers, the company offers a wide range of traditional and specialty services tailored to individual client requests. The founder and his family members created the Merry Maids unique operating system which focuses on professionalism, consistency and a personal touch. They also set the business up using a franchising model tailored to residential cleaning. Today, the company has the largest home cleaning franchise network in the world, with more than 1400 franchises in ten countries. It employs over 8000 cleaning professionals, and cleans more than 300,000 residences per month. The company prides itself on the use of branded, eco-friendly equipment and cleaning products. Franchises are independently owned and operated, with Merry Maids providing extensive training, mentoring, marketing and financing support, as well as an intranet for communications. The company has developed proprietary software that integrates all facets of a franchisee's business operations, including office management, scheduling, payroll, bookkeeping, goal setting and performance tracking. As with many aggressive growth ventures, the company was an attractive acquisition candidate and was purchased by ServiceMaster.

Distinct aspects of each of these businesses are summarized and compared in Figure 2.1. As a survival venture, Clara's Cleaning is unique in in its degree of resource scarcity, which makes it problematic for the owner to have premises, hold much inventory, hire full-time employees, achieve volume in production, realize meaningful profits, reinvest in the business, incorporate technology and innovate. Alternatively, the distinctiveness of Mainstreet Commercial Cleaners lies in the maintenance of a simple and relatively fixed business model. Operations center on a small market niche, the company employs basic physical assets, and, when effectively maintained, the business owner is afforded a decent lifestyle. The managed growth model reflected in Bio-clean Medical and Health Specialists is unique in its planned and controlled approach to uncovering and exploiting new opportunity, with supportive infrastructure developed parallel to expansion. Merry Maids stands apart based on its proprietary value proposition and its abilities to leverage technology, achieve consistency and efficiency in value delivery, and develop the kind of infrastructure that lends itself to rapid scaling of the enterprise.

As is evidenced in these four examples, as we move from the survival to the aggressive growth venture, we can generally observe the business transform from being:

- highly labor intensive to less labor intensive
- reliant on simple, physical resources to employing complex, intangible resources
- undifferentiated to well differentiated
- less entrepreneurial to more entrepreneurial.

Some of this is due to technology, which plays a distinct role in each type of venture. With the survival venture, technology has at best a nominal role, and is largely absent from most facets of the business. Alternatively,

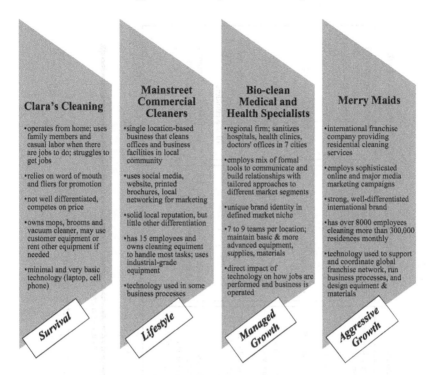

Clara's Cleaning

• operates from home; uses family members and casual labor when there are jobs to do; struggles to get jobs

• relies on word of mouth and fliers for promotion

• not well differentiated, competes on price

• owns mops, brooms and vacuum cleaner, may use customer equipment or rent other equipment if needed

• minimal and very basic technology (laptop, cell phone)

Survival

Mainstreet Commercial Cleaners

• single location-based business that cleans offices and business facilities in local community

• uses social media, website, printed brochures, local networking for marketing

• solid local reputation, but little other differentiation

• has 15 employees and owns cleaning equiment to handle most tasks; uses industrial-grade equipment

• technology used in some business processes

Lifestyle

Bio-clean Medical and Health Specialists

• regional firm; sanitizes hospitals, health clinics, doctors' offices in 7 cities

• employs mix of formal tools to communicate and build relationships with tailored approaches to different market segments

• unique brand identity in defined market niche

• 7 to 9 teams per location; maintain basic & more advanced equipment, supplies, materials

• direct impact of technology on how jobs are performed and business is operated

Managed Growth

Merry Maids

• international franchise company providing residential cleaning services

• employs sophisticated online and major media marketing campaigns

• strong, well-differentiated international brand

• has over 8000 employees cleaning more than 300,000 residences monthly

• technology used to support and coordinate global franchise network, run business processes, and design equiment & materials

Aggressive Growth

Figure 2.1   Comparing four types of ventures in the same industry

the products or services of aggressive growth ventures often represent technological breakthroughs, while process technology is instrumental in making possible the scalability of the business. Figure 2.2 illustrates how technology can affect critical activity areas within the four venture types.

An interesting question concerns levels of efficiency within each type of venture. Some would argue that survival and lifestyle ventures are inefficient while managed growth and (especially) aggressive growth ventures are highly efficient (Shane, 2009). The reality may be more complex, particularly as survival and lifestyle ventures are often able to stretch their limited resources and use them in novel ways, while also serving market niches that would be too expensive (or inefficient) for larger or more scalable firms to serve. We will further address this issue in Chapter 11.

	Survival	Lifestyle	Managed Growth	Aggressive Growth
Operations & logistics	• Mostly manual labor, little to no equipment	• Mix of manual labor and basic equipment use	• Shrinking labor component, use of more sophisticated equipment, some automation	• Automated or outsourced production; electronic data interchange with value chain
Financial transactions	• Cash	• Cash and electronic	• Cash and electronic	• Electronic
Accounting & financial management	• Mostly paper-based	• Some paper, but mostly electronic	• Electronic	• Electronic and integrated across enterprise
Customer interactions	• Personal	• Personal and online (e.g., social media & website)	• Increased use of customer relationship management (CRM) systems	• Interactive (online) and through CRM systems
Market feedback	• In-person feedback from customers	• Personal interactions, paper surveys, online complaints	• Online surveys of suppliers, customers, employees	• Real-time electronic market feedback, online surveys of all stakeholders
Human resource management	• Little to no hiring, reliance on family members and informal systems	• Most HR functions manually done with use of simple electronic databases; some online recruitment	• Use of electronic systems for recruiting, payroll, benefits	• Automation of all human resource management functions
	Low	Low to medium		High

Level of technology

Figure 2.2 *Comparing technology usage in different types of entrepreneurial ventures*

DOES ONE TYPE OF VENTURE EVOLVE INTO ANOTHER TYPE?

Some might be tempted to view the four categories as a logical continuum along which a given venture can move over time. The question therefore arises as to whether ventures tend to evolve from one type to another (e.g., from lifestyle to managed growth). While it certainly does happen, we believe this tendency is more the exception than the rule. Instead, ventures of a given type tend to remain that type.

A venture can be thought of as a portfolio of resources. Resources have properties, such as how valuable, rare and easy to copy or transfer they are (Barney and Clark, 2007). The nature of the resources the entrepreneur is able to acquire and deploy differ significantly across our four venture types, as we shall explore in more depth in Chapter 7. As a result, they serve to delimit what the venture can become, and the opportunities the entrepreneur is able to exploit. There is a path dependency involved, such that once a commitment is made to certain kinds of resources, the possibilities for the venture are restricted, as are the kinds of resources the organization is able to subsequently acquire or exploit. The resources determine not only what the venture is able to accomplish, but also the way things are done, and the underlying nature of the organization. Thus, once the venture has committed to a resource path, it struggles to recognize, understand, acquire and/or exploit the kinds of resources that would enable it to become a different type of venture.

From another perspective, as a venture emerges, it takes on a certain identity. Organizational identity captures what is central, distinctive and enduring about a business (Albert and Whetten, 1985). It impacts how decisions are made, the company's ability to change and its growth trajectory (He and Brown, 2013; Shah and Tripsas, 2007). Further, once established, organizations strive to maintain their identities (Gagliardi, 1986). There is some evidence that different identities are associated with each of our four venture categories (Morris et al., 2016). If so, this would work against a venture evolving from one type to another. We will further examine the importance of organization identity in Chapter 8.

Conceptually, the distance to be traveled in moving from one type of venture to another gets greater as we move from survival to lifestyle, managed growth and then aggressive growth. Alternatively, while one can imagine a circumstance where a lifestyle venture declines to the point that it is really more of a survival venture, in general we believe a given venture thrives or fails as a particular type.

CONCLUSIONS

It is impossible to draw general insights or conclusions about entrepreneurial ventures as a whole. They represent a diverse population, and no two ventures are alike. Yet, there are categories of ventures that share critical characteristics, and these categories offer promise for advancing how we research, support, facilitate and pursue entrepreneurship. In this chapter we have introduced a typology that distinguishes survival, lifestyle, managed growth and aggressive growth ventures based on 14 underlying characteristics. While there is considerable variability within each category, the differences between the categories are core to the nature and functioning of each venture type.

Our typology allows for an inclusive approach, suggesting that entrepreneurship is concerned with the act of creating a venture, regardless of what actually gets created. While all ventures represent change (to individuals, families, communities, markets, industries), they do not necessarily have to be disruptive, highly innovative or scalable. As such, the typology eliminates the need to pursue debates concerning differences between small businesses and an entrepreneurial firm, as all start-ups are to some degree entrepreneurial. In addition, it is consistent with the idea that what entrepreneurs set out to create often differs from what actually emerges.

In considering these venture categories, it is critical to note that they do not differ from one another simply by degree, but rather, represent four unique types of businesses. Further, most ventures are likely to remain a given type over time rather than evolve from one type to another. As we shall see in subsequent chapters, this uniqueness has important implications for the skills and resources required, nature of operations, critical support needs, and outcomes produced for each type of venture. We begin, however, by examining each venture type in more detail.

REFERENCES

Albert, S. and Whetten, D.A. (1985). *Organizational Identity: Research in Organizational Behavior*. Greenwich, CT: JAI Press.

Barney, J.B. and Clark, D. (2007). *Resource-based Theory: Creating and Sustaining Competitive Advantage*. New York: Oxford University Press.

Birch, D.G. (1987). *Job Creation in America: How Our Smallest Companies Put the Most People to Work*. Urbana, IL: University of Illinois at Urbana-Champaign's Academy for Entrepreneurial Leadership Historical Research Reference in Entrepreneurship.

Boso, N., Story, V.M., and Cadogan, J.W. (2013). Entrepreneurial orientation, market orientation, network ties, and performance: Study of entrepreneurial firms in a developing economy. *Journal of Business Venturing*, *28*(6), 708–727.

Bradley, S., Wiklund, J., and Shepherd, D. (2011). Swinging a double-edged sword: The effect of slack on entrepreneurial management and growth. *Journal of Business Venturing*, *26*(5), 537–554.

Carland, J.W., Hoy, F., Boulton, W.R., and Carland, J. (1984). Differentiating entrepreneurs from small business owners: A conceptualization. *Academy of Management Review*, *9*(2), 354–359.

Commission on the Private Sector and Development (2004). *Making Business Work for the Poor*. New York: United Nations Development Programme.

Covin, J.G. and Slevin, D.P. (1989). Strategic management of small firms in hostile and benign environments. *Strategic Management Journal*, *10*(1), 75–87.

Davidsson, P. (2005). What is entrepreneurship? *Researching Entrepreneurship*, *1*(1), 1–16.

Dennis, W.J. (2014). *Profile of American Small Businesses and Their Owners*. Washington, DC: National Federation of Independent Businesses Research Foundation.

Dunkelberg, W.C. and Cooper, A.C. (1982), Entrepreneurial typologies. In K.H. Vesper (ed.), *Frontiers of Entrepreneurship Research*. Wellesley, MA: Babson Center for Entrepreneurial Studies, pp. 1–15.

Filley, A. and Aldag, R. (1978). Characteristics and measurement of an organizational typology. *Academy of Management Journal*, *2*(4), 578–591.

Gagliardi, P. (1986). The creation and change of organizational cultures: A conceptual framework. *Organization Studies*, *7*(2), 117–134.

Gartner, W.B. (1988). Who is an entrepreneur? is the wrong question. *American Journal of Small Business*, *12*(4), 11–32.

Glueck, W.F. (1980). *Business Policy and Strategic Management*. New York: McGraw-Hill.

Haas, J.E., Hall, R.H., and Johnson, N.J. (1966). Toward an empirically derived taxonomy of organizations. In R.V. Bowers (ed.), *Studies on Behavior in Organization*. Athens, GA: University of Georgia Press, pp. 157–180.

Hall, J., Matos, S., Sheehan, L., and Silvestre, B. (2012). Entrepreneurship and innovation at the base of the pyramid: A recipe for inclusive growth or social exclusion? *Journal of Management Studies*, *49*(4), 785–812.

He, H. and Brown, A.D. (2013). Organizational identity and organizational identification: A review of the literature and suggestions for future research. *Group & Organization Management*, *38*(1), 3–35.

Hisrich, R.D. and Peters, M.P. (1998). *Entrepreneurship*, 4th edn. Boston, MA: McGraw-Hill/Irwin.

Julien, P.A. (1990). Vers une Typologie Multicritères des PME (Moving toward multicriteria SMEs). *Revue Internationale P.M.E.*, *3*(3–4), 411–425.

Kauffman Foundation (2019). *Kauffman Entrepreneurship Indicators*. Kansas City: Kauffman Foundation. Accessed March 15, 2019 at https://indicators.kauffman.org/.

Klyver, K., Hindle, K., and Meyer, D. (2008). Influence of social network structure on entrepreneurship participation – a study of 20 national cultures. *International Entrepreneurship and Management Journal*, 4(3), 331–347.

Kunkel, S.W. (2001). Toward a typology of entrepreneurial activities. *Academy of Entrepreneurship Journal*, 7(1), 75–90.

Langlois, R.N. (2007). The entrepreneurial theory of the firm and the theory of the entrepreneurial firm. *Journal of Management Studies*, 44(7), 1107–1124.

Liles, P. (1974). Who are the entrepreneurs? *MSU Business Topics*, 22(1), 5–14.

Malchow-Møller, N., Schjerning, B., and Sørensen, A. (2011). Entrepreneurship, job creation and wage growth. *Small Business Economics*, 36(1), 15–32.

Miles, R.E., Snow, C.C., Meyer, A.D., and Coleman, H.J. (1978). Organizational strategy, structure, and process. *Academy of Management Review*, 3(3), 546–562.

Miller, D. (1983). The correlates of entrepreneurship in three types of firms. *Management Science*, 29(7), 770–791.

Miller, D. and Friesen, P.H. (1977). Strategy-making in Context: Ten empirical archetypes. *Journal of Management Studies*, 14(3), 253–280.

Mintzberg, H. (1989). *Mintzberg on Management: Inside Our Strange World of Organizations*. New York: Free Press.

Morris, M.H., Pryor, C.G., and Schindehutte, M. (2012). *Entrepreneurship as Experience: How Events Create Ventures and Ventures Create Entrepreneurs*. Cheltenham, UK and Northampton, MA, USA: Edward Elgar Publishing.

Morris, M.H., Neumeyer, X., Jang, Y., and Kuratko, D.F. (2016). Distinguishing types of entrepreneurial ventures: An identity-based perspective. *Journal of Small Business Management*, 56(3), 453–474.

Naldi, L. and Davidsson, P. (2013). Entrepreneurial growth: The role of international knowledge acquisition as moderated by firm age. *Journal of Business Venturing*, 29(6), 687–703.

Oviatt, B.M. and McDougall, P.P. (1994). Toward a theory of international new ventures. *Journal of International Business Studies*, 25(1), 45–64.

Parsons, T. (1956). Suggestions for a sociological approach to the theory of organizations. *Administrative Science Quarterly*, 1(1), 63–85.

Perez-Luno, A., Wiklund, J., and Cabrera, R.V. (2011). The dual nature of innovative activity: How entrepreneurial orientation influences innovation generation and adoption. *Journal of Business Venturing*, 26(5), 555–571.

Prahalad, C.K. (2005). *The Fortune at the Bottom of the Pyramid, Eradicating Poverty through Profits*. Upper Saddle River, NJ: Wharton School Publishing.

Pugh, D.S., Hickson, D.J., and Hinings, C.R. (1969). An empirical taxonomy of structures of work organizations. *Administrative Science Quarterly*, 14(1), 115–126.

Reynolds, P.D. and Curtin, R.T. (eds) (2009). *New Firm Creation in the United States: Initial Explorations with the PSED II Data Set*, Vol. 23. New York: Springer Science & Business Media.

Rizzoni, A. (1991). Technological innovation and small firms: A taxonomy. *International Small Business Journal*, 9(3), 31–42.

Roberts, E.B. (1991). *Entrepreneurs in High Technology: Lessons from MIT and Beyond*. New York: Oxford University Press.

Ronstadt, R. (1982). *Entrepreneurship*. Dover, MA: Lord Publishing.

Schumpeter, J.A. (1934). *The Theory of Economic Development: An Inquiry into Profits, Capital, Credit, Interest, and the Business Cycle*, Vol. 55. Piscataway, NJ: Transaction Publishers.

Sexton, D.L. and Bowman-Upton, N.B. (1991). *Entrepreneurship: Creativity and Growth*. New York: Macmillan.

Shah, S.K. and Tripsas, M. (2007). The accidental entrepreneur: The emergent and collective process of user entrepreneurship. *Strategic Entrepreneurship Journal*, *1*(1–2), 123–140.

Shane, S. (2009). Why encouraging more people to become entrepreneurs is bad public policy. *Small Business Economics*, *33*(2), 141–149.

Smith, N. and Miner, J. (1983). Type of entrepreneur, type of firm, and managerial motivation: Implications for organizational life cycle theory. *Strategic Management Journal*, *4*(4), 325–340.

Stanworth, M.J.K. and Curran, J. (1976). Growth and the small firm – an alternative view. *Journal of Management Studies*, *13*(2), 95–110.

Sutter, C., Bruton, G., and Chen, J. (2019). Entrepreneurship as a solution to extreme poverty: A review and future research directions. *Journal of Business Venturing*, *34*(1), 197–214.

Vesper, K.H. (1990). *New Venture Strategies*. Englewood Cliffs, NJ: Prentice-Hall.

Webb, J., Tihanyi, L., Ireland, R.D., and Sirmon, D. (2009). You say illegal, I say legitimate: Entrepreneurship in the informal economy. *Academy of Management Review*, *34*(3), 492–510.

Webster, F.A. (1977). Entrepreneurs and ventures: An attempt at classification and clarification. *Academy of Management Review*, *2*(1), 54–61.

3. Survival ventures: just getting by

A CONTINUOUS STRUGGLE

The single largest category of start-up ventures is survival businesses. The term survival is used to describe a venture that struggles to stay in business on a continuous basis. It can also be referred to as a "hand-to-mouth" venture in the sense that, at best, just enough revenue is generated to pay bills and cover expenses, including paying the entrepreneur (but often less than he or she might earn working for someone else). However, little to nothing is left over to reinvest in the business. It is quite a challenge to ever get ahead with these types of businesses. One is always struggling just to keep up. Hence, both the venture and the entrepreneur do little more than survive or get by.

It is difficult to determine the number of survivalist ventures, as many are unregistered or otherwise do not get captured in statistical databases. In the United States, one indicator is the number of sole proprietorships. Over 26 million sole proprietorships currently exist, and they constitute about 71 percent of all businesses (Internal Revenue Service, 2018). While some of these may be lifestyle ventures, the large majority are likely survivalists.

Survivalist ventures take a variety of forms. Among others, they include (a) vendors who sell an array of goods (e.g., fresh vegetables, prepared foods, crafts, clothing) on the street or at public forums such as fairs and farmers' markets; (b) people with skills related to a basic trade (e.g., house painting, massage or graphic design) or that have knowledge related to some task (e.g., tour guide, math tutor, disk jockey) that they try to build a business around; (c) providers of less-skilled but broadly demanded tasks (e.g. cleaning homes, lawn care, dog walking); (d) those with a hobby or personal interest (e.g., sewing quilts, selling things on e-Bay, designing creative screen savers for phones) that find others will pay them for their product or service; and (e) individuals owning an under-utilized asset (e.g., person who has a van and decides to provide transport services; someone who is homebound but offers call center services to small businesses). They also include a large number of ventures that

operate in the informal sector. These are unregistered, unlicensed businesses that provide both legitimate and illicit goods and services.

In this chapter, we take an in-depth look at the nature and operations of
survival ventures. We first explore the question of whether survivalists
are really entrepreneurs. The underlying characteristics of these ventures
are then examined, with a focus on aspects they have in common and
elements that many tend to share. Detailed attention is then devoted to
what is arguably their most common problem, which we label the
commodity trap. In addition, consideration is given to the role of
technology in these businesses. As a substantial proportion of the survival
ventures in many developing countries can be found in the informal
sector, the unique challenges of operating below the radar are investigated. Finally, essential factors for sustaining a survival venture over time
are discussed.

WHAT MAKES THIS ENTREPRENEURSHIP?

In Chapter 1, we defined an entrepreneur as someone who starts a
business. Yet, there are those who would question whether people who
start survival businesses are really entrepreneurs. They would argue that
these are people who create a job for themselves, but little more. To
appreciate what makes them entrepreneurs, let us consider examples of
three survivalist ventures.

First, there is the case of the handyman who provides an array of
simple repair and maintenance services to homeowners. He will fix a
broken doorbell, install some shelves, paint a room, or complete other
tasks depending on the needs of the customer. He owns or leases a truck
and some tools, and rents equipment for any bigger or more complex
tasks. If materials are needed, he either instructs the customer what to
buy or purchases items himself and gets reimbursed. He bills customers
based on the estimated time it will take to complete the work, with the
principal cost being the labor of the entrepreneur. Revenue is tied to how
many hours the entrepreneur is able to work, and how many jobs he can
find. He probably works alone, or with an assistant, but is not able (or not
willing) to build an employee base.

As a second example, consider an individual who launches a personal
tutoring business. She focuses on math and science tutoring, and targets
children from middle- and upper-class families. Most of her clients come
from referrals. Tutoring sessions are typically held at the student's home,
to which the entrepreneur drives. Sessions last ninety minutes, and she
charges per session. She has developed problem sets and exercises for the

student to work on between tutoring sessions. She owns a computer and
has acquired an array of books and learning materials.

Our third survivalist is a street vendor that sells coffee and muffins
from a mobile cart. The cart is colorful and has heating capabilities and a
small refrigerator. The entrepreneur has a permit that allows him to locate
the cart in any of three different areas within the city. The location
chosen varies by day of the week and time of the day. It is a cash
business that does not accept credit cards. The customer base tends to be
people who work near the location of the cart, and includes a number of
regulars. He bakes the muffins at home, and sources ingredients, coffee,
paper cups and other supplies from warehouse clubs such as Costco or
Sam's Club.

In all three cases, the primary operations of the business are performed
by the entrepreneur. In each instance, the ability to make a profit is
limited by capacity and, for the handyman and street vendor, relatively
high unit costs. It is our position that all three individuals should be
considered entrepreneurs for at least seven reasons:

- Each recognized an opportunity and developed the capacity to
  capitalize on that opportunity.
- Each was willing to accept the opportunity costs associated with
  running their own enterprise rather than pursuing a job (possibly
  with benefits) or some other path.
- Each assumed the financial, reputational and psychological risks
  associated with venture failure, the amount of which, in relative
  terms, can be quite high for these individuals.
- With no guarantee of revenue or payment, each of the entrepreneurs
  must generate more money than they are spending to sustain the
  venture over time, and owes taxes on any profits.
- Each develops a business reputation or brand, assumes responsibility for delivery of value to a customer, and directly suffers the
  consequences of mistakes or quality problems that undermine the
  value proposition.
- Actions taken on behalf of the business have legal consequences.
- Lastly, it is possible that all three of them had much bigger plans
  when they launched their enterprises, but found that the venture
  never became more than a survival business.

The motives of our handyman, tutor and street vendor may or may not
differ, but once they are on the entrepreneurial path, they share a journey
of uncertainty, ambiguity, self-reliance and independence. In all three
cases, the business requires more of them than simply performing the

jobs of fixing, teaching or selling. Decisions must continually be made, risks taken, resources acquired, value delivered and records kept.

Ultimately, the person who launches a survival venture has a dream to build something that does not exist, just as do those of the entrepreneurs who create high growth firms such as Uber or SpaceX. They pursue the venture with no safety net, and do not know where the business will go or whether it will succeed. They can demonstrate levels of passion, tenacity and work ethic and experience levels of independence and autonomy similar to any other entrepreneur. The fact that what emerges is small, vulnerable, generates few jobs and makes relatively little money does not change the entrepreneurial nature of the undertaking, especially in the early days of the venture.

UNDERLYING CHARACTERISTICS OF SURVIVAL VENTURES

Although considerable diversity exists within the universe of survival ventures, they share critical characteristics that contribute to their basic nature (Figure 3.1). To begin with, they depend on the entrepreneur to run the business, but to also be the primary person doing the work of the business. The work tends to be labor intensive. The entrepreneur is unable or unwilling to incorporate expensive equipment or available technologies that could reduce unit costs. As the revenue that comes in each week must be used to pay the expenses necessary to operate each week, it is hard to get ahead. A lack of cash makes it difficult to purchase raw materials or supplies in bulk quantities, which further contributes to higher unit costs. There is no money to reinvest in the business or to innovate. This combination of factors also puts significant capacity constraints on the business.

Survival ventures do not tend to have permanent premises. Many of these ventures are either home-based, the entrepreneur operates from a stall or stand, or he or she travels to the customer site. Marketing efforts are generally very basic and there is heavy reliance on word of mouth. There is little market segmentation or targeting, as the entrepreneur tends to see everyone as a potential customer.

In addition, these are often cash-based businesses, unable to take credit cards or engage in electronic funds transfers. This can complicate the abilities to track revenues and expenses and minimize employee theft. To a greater or lesser degree, many of these entrepreneurs mix personal finances with business finances, and some run their household and business out of a single bank account. When such characteristics are

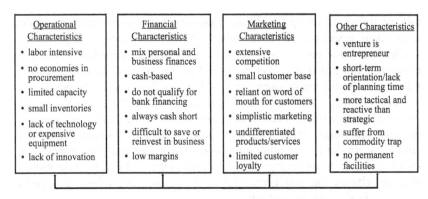

Operational Characteristics	Financial Characteristics	Marketing Characteristics	Other Characteristics
• labor intensive	• mix personal and business finances	• extensive competition	• venture is entrepreneur
• no economies in procurement	• cash-based	• small customer base	• short-term orientation/lack of planning time
• limited capacity	• do not qualify for bank financing	• reliant on word of mouth for customers	• more tactical and reactive than strategic
• small inventories	• always cash short	• simplistic marketing	• suffer from commodity trap
• lack of technology or expensive equipment	• difficult to save or reinvest in business	• undifferentiated products/services	• no permanent facilities
• lack of innovation	• low margins	• limited customer loyalty	

Figure 3.1   Common characteristics of survival ventures

combined with a general lack of assets, qualifying for loans or a credit facility from banks can be problematic.

Scarcity is a core aspect of the survival venture – scarcity of money, labor, inventory, time and customers. Scarcity can serve to limit the entrepreneur's cognitive bandwidth. Shah and co-authors (2012) demonstrate how those with scarce resources tend to focus more exclusively on accomplishing the most pressing tasks at hand and ignoring other critical tasks – even where doing so may take away from the ability to accomplish larger goals. Immediate problems loom so large in one's consciousness that they consume a disproportionate amount of one's time, effort and limited financial resources. In effect, a lack of resources together with financial instability leaves the entrepreneur with less time to plan or focus on strategic issues. Quick operational decisions have to be made on a real-time basis, often with less regard to the implications for a range of other decisions or longer-term impacts. The survivalist is thus forced by conditions to have a short-term orientation (Mani et al., 2013). Further, there is less time for ideation and less room for innovation.

As the survivalist entrepreneur is usually scrambling to get by, the managerial approach tends to be more reactive and tactical than strategic (Tirado, 2015). It is harder to focus on a bigger vision or larger goals, or to understand how key decisions impact one another and must be coordinated. With reactive management the entrepreneur can become a victim of circumstances. An extensive amount of time is spent on responding to emergencies or critical demands from customers, suppliers, employees, or some unforeseen development. Being reactive suggests a lack of planning or preparation for events. The entrepreneur fails to anticipate developments so that any negative consequences or costs can be minimized (or any benefits can be fully capitalized upon). Moreover, he or she often fails to understand the root cause of the development, which means any solution or response only addresses symptoms. The underlying problem remains and will eventually manifest itself again in similar or new ways.

In a related vein, the survivalist is often a micromanager. They are often unable to hire people (and especially qualified people), and so rely on temporary labor or family members and friends to help out. As a result, they have to be able to do everything in the business themselves. They are involved in negotiation with suppliers, producing the product or service, doing marketing, keeping the books, raising money, cleaning equipment, and dealing with customer complaints. These realities can turn the entrepreneur into a micromanager. Preoccupied with all these tasks, he or she does not develop the bandwidth to think and act strategically.

Like most entrepreneurs, the survivalist will engage in a trial-and-error approach in order to figure things out, particularly in the early days of the venture. Prices are modified, operating hours or locations are changed, a promotion is run, or some other change is made to see if it stimulates sales or reduces costs. However, with survival ventures, these experiments may be more random than systematic, do not reflect particular goals, and can be inconsistent with other decision areas in the business. There are no clear criteria for determining whether or not the tactic worked. Alternatively, the entrepreneur may observe something another business is doing and try to mimic the approach, without considering differences in context. Although such tactical moves sometimes result in a positive outcome, they often waste time and money, send mixed or inconsistent messages to customers, confuse employees, and produce other negative outcomes. All too often tactics are attempted, do not appear to produce results, and are discarded, with no real learning taking place as to why the approach did or did not work.

Finally, the complete dependence of the venture on the entrepreneur has additional implications. If the entrepreneur is ill, has to travel, experiences a family emergency or is otherwise unavailable, the business simply may not operate. Similarly, this dependence limits the exit strategies available to survival ventures. Most are not sold or transferred to successors, but instead are simply shut down, and any assets are disposed of or given away.

THE COMMODITY TRAP

A critical aspect of most survival ventures can be traced to what we might call "the commodity trap" (Figure 3.2) It starts with having a business that is by and large selling something that is not meaningfully different from what many others in the same market are selling. A lawncare business or street vendor provides goods or services quite similar to any number of competitors. If customers see little difference, they opt to buy from whomever has the lowest price or is the most convenient to patronize. They have no loyalties, and effectively view the purchase as a commodity.

Firms in these conditions may feel forced to compete on price rather than on some other basis – and this is almost always a losing proposition. Margins are squeezed as firms attempt to undercut one another in order to retain or gain customers. Meanwhile, operating costs tend to be high

Figure 3.2   Elements contributing to the commodity trap

because of the small scale and lack of technology in the business, and this further reduces margins. The picture is even bleaker if the firm is operating in a relatively saturated market, where growth opportunities are limited. With smaller margins, the entrepreneur has little to reinvest in the business. The failure to reinvest can lead the business to only become more of a commodity, especially if other firms are trying new and different things.

A continuing downward cycle where costs keep rising and margins keep declining will lead to the demise of the business. The goal must be to achieve meaningful and sustainable differentiation. This means offering something unique that creates value for the broader market, or specializing in the particular needs of a smaller market niche. Either approach can represent a real challenge for the survivalist, as money and time are required, as well as an in-depth understanding of customers, competitors, supplier capabilities and available technologies. Discipline is also important, as once a source of differentiation is identified, the venture's value proposition and marketing efforts must be redesigned around this difference. Unfortunately, concerns that any changes might alienate existing customers often lead to inaction by the entrepreneur.

THE LITERACY CHALLENGE

Another factor that keeps many survival ventures from escaping the commodity trap, achieving sustainable profits, or becoming lifestyle or growth companies involves the literacy shortcomings of the entrepreneur. Morris et al. (2018) discuss five key literacies that would seem particularly relevant in a survivalist context. Briefly, they can be defined as follows:

- *Functional literacy*: The abilities to read and write, use numbers, interpret images and graphs, understand and communicate effectively, gain and integrate knowledge, and solve mathematical problems that come into play in every facet of business operations.
- *Financial literacy*: The ability to make financially responsible decisions, including knowledge of how to save, manage credit and debt obligations, prepare budgets, manage cash flow, and separate business from personal financial transactions.
- *Technological literacy*: An awareness and appreciation for the significance of key technologies impacting a business, the ability to use these technologies, and an understanding of the issues raised by their use.

- *Economic literacy*: Appreciating how markets work, the implications for business decisions of changes in supply and demand conditions, the impact on the business of new or changing public policies, how to capitalize on economic incentives and disincentives, and how to determine the costs and benefits of alternative courses of action.
- *Business literacy*: Understanding the basics of administration and record-keeping, organizing business operations, selling, hiring and other critical business tasks, while mastering the terminology and techniques necessary for dealing with suppliers, bankers, distributors, lawyers, employees and other stakeholders.

Further, the five literacies interact with one another. Functional literacy makes possible the other four. Financial and business literacies can contribute to economic literacy, and hence the ability to properly react to changes in supply and demand conditions. And technological literacy interacts with financial and business literacy to affect how cost competitive the firms is, its value proposition and ongoing investment decisions.

Many survival entrepreneurs have limitations in all five of these areas. As a result, they can struggle with everything from calculating the size of the market and understanding business models to communicating with key stakeholders, incorporating technology into the business and managing cash flows. Table 3.1 provides a more detailed set of examples regarding how literacy problems impact the survivalist when performing a wide variety of entrepreneurial tasks. The end result is reduced managerial capacity. The entrepreneur is less able to make decisions that are timely, well formulated or based on the full range of relevant considerations. The ability to think and act strategically becomes problematic.

SURVIVALISTS AND THE INFORMAL SECTOR

Survival ventures are quite common in the informal sector. This sector includes businesses that are not registered in the national accounts and not subject to formal rules of contract, licensing, labor practices, inspection, reporting and taxation. They are believed to contribute well over half the GDP in some lesser developed countries (Morris et al., 1996). There is a growing pattern around the world of people with severely limited resources starting unregistered businesses, building something that is sustainable, and making a living (Banerjee and Duflo, 2007). In the process, hundreds of millions of people have been pulled out of poverty (Abraham, 2012).

Table 3.1 Literacy challenges for survivalist entrepreneurs

Type of Literacy	Sample Challenges
Functional literacy	Struggle to conduct market research, create business plans, calculate size of market opportunities, determine feasibility of the business; Challenges in communicating with stakeholders in oral or written form; Difficulty in interpreting regulations, written instructions, or a contract or lease; Reduced ability to set prices that cover costs and generate acceptable margins, determine correct shipping volumes, inventory levels and procurement requirements, properly prepare invoices or bids, pay employees and suppliers correct amounts, record expenses and revenues and determine profit, measure operational efficiencies, or analyse patterns in data.
Financial literacy	Difficulties in knowing how to save, manage credit and debt obligations, and separate business from personal financial transactions; Struggles in determining how much money is needed to start the business or what breakeven sales levels are at any point in time; Problems in budgeting and cash flow management; Difficulties in knowing when to pay bills, how much to pay, and how to negotiate payment deadlines; Lower resilience to disruptive financial events; Inability to raise funds.
Economic literacy	Challenges in understanding how supply and demand conditions affect the entrepreneur's position in the marketplace and the implications for a variety of decision areas (e.g., pricing, making investments in the businesses, determining inventory and staffing levels); Reduced understanding of how changes in interest rates, inflation, unemployment rates, trade barriers and tax policy impact the business; Less ability to assess costs and benefits surrounding key business decisions.
Business (non-financial) literacy	Reduced abilities to communicate with key stakeholders and incorporate key business concepts into ongoing decision-making,
Technological literacy	Inability to incorporate technology into products and services being developed and sold to customers; Inefficiencies within the business due to failure to incorporate technologies into various facets of operations.

Source: Adapted from Morris et al. (2018).

Some of the informal sector opportunities are criminal in nature, such as ventures centered on the drug trade, prostitution, money laundering, car theft, gun sales and credit card fraud. However, the large majority involve unregistered or unlicensed businesses that provide goods and services available in the traditional marketplace, but operate informally or in the underground economy. They include everything from home-based hair salons, small restaurants and tour guides to dress makers, construction businesses and website developers. In a study of the underground economy in the inner city, Venkatesh (2006) describes a vibrant business community consisting of a wide range of "off the books" ventures ranging from organized criminal gangs and back alley car repair businesses to hustlers, street musicians, artists, and a homeless person who is not simply sleeping behind a building but actually providing a service as a night watchman. He notes that those involved see such activity not as illicit behavior but as work or as a business.

Not surprisingly, many informal sector businesses are started by those with few other opportunities. Unable to find work, they are "pushed" into entrepreneurship by their circumstances rather than being "pulled" by recognition of an attractive opportunity (Block et al., 2015). Yet, regardless of the motivation to launch them, these businesses provide a living to many families. They typically do not require much in the way of resources, rely on the ongoing abilities of the entrepreneur to bootstrap and stretch resources, and can prove to be quite resilient in overcoming obstacles, dealing with setbacks, and surviving the ups and downs of the marketplace.

While not paying taxes or having to comply with regulations may seem attractive, there are significant drawbacks to operating as an informal business. First and foremost, as they are operating illegally, they are subject to discovery and then being closed down and/or fined. This likelihood increases if they achieve any sort of success and hence become more visible. Success thus becomes a motivator to formalize the business. Clients who know the business is unregistered may well expect to pay less than they otherwise would for the goods or services. Informal sector businesses are also ineligible to bid on government contracts, receive permits and licenses, obtain business bank accounts, qualify for bank loans and business credit cards, and apply for many grants.

As observers have come to recognize the potential of these "under the radar" businesses, a philosophy of encouraging them rather than forcing them to shut down or formalize has, to differing degrees, emerged in a number of countries (Bromley, 2013; Potts, 2008). Specifically, they provide jobs for a large section of the population who would otherwise be unemployed, and contribute to the well-being of local communities suffering from significant social and economic disparities (Debrah, 2007). Further, the sector represents a kind of incubator, producing many ventures that eventually do formalize. While many are commodity businesses, they sometimes uncover new market niches and introduce novel product or service ideas that other firms can learn from.

Support for these kinds of businesses has also given rise to the microcredit revolution that is sweeping the globe (Bhatt et al., 1999; Brown, 2010). It came to prominence based on the highly successful work of Nobel Prize winner Muhammad Yunus and the Grameen Bank in Bangladesh. The Grameen Bank self-supports a diverse mix of poor people by means of very small loans on easy, extended terms without requiring collateral. Their trademark methodology of group lending allows someone to start a business without having to engage in expensive moneylender programs. Group lending uses the trust of fellow members as collateral, and the members receive loans as long as all members make current payments. Subsequently, microenterprise development organizations have emerged not only throughout the developing world, but also in such developed economies such as the United States, Canada, the European Union, South Korea, Japan and Australia (Servon, 2006).

CONCLUSIONS

In this chapter, we have examined the nature of the most prominent category of entrepreneurial venture, the survival business. These are the easiest ventures to start, and compared to the other venture categories, involve the lowest risk while generating the smallest returns. Of the four venture types, the survivalist is arguably the least entrepreneurial, and yet, in some ways, these individuals demonstrate highly entrepreneurial behavior. They are not inventing disruptive innovations, transforming markets or employing large numbers of people. Yet, despite their vulnerable nature, they can prove to be highly resilient in the face of adverse circumstances. They are able to make the most out of relatively little, and can be quite creative at bootstrapping, bartering, sharing and leveraging resources.

By and large, survivalists receive little support from society. There are few training or mentoring programs available to them, and they often do not qualify for tax incentives, supplier diversity initiatives or other forms of small business support. They are generally unable to access traditional debt or equity sources of funding, but can benefit from the increased (but still relatively small) number of local microcredit programs that are being established. In short, they are largely excluded from the entrepreneurial ecosystems in their communities, where the focus tends to be on fostering growth businesses.

Without survival ventures, millions of entrepreneurs would go without a livelihood or source of income. The make-up artist, manuscript editor, cleaning company, street vendor, or logo designer who seeks jobs through an online bidding platform each fills a small but relevant niche in the marketplace. While many are sole operators, others employ family members and lower-skilled workers. Some, like the Uber driver, make high growth companies possible. And importantly, these ventures provide a vehicle for self-development as the entrepreneur learns how to serve customers, manage money, organize operations and market themselves.

REFERENCES

Abraham, R. (2012). Doing business at the base of the pyramid: The reality of emerging markets. *The Journal of Field Actions: Field Actions Science Reports, Special Issue 4: Fighting Poverty, Between Market and Gift.*

Banerjee, A.V. and Duflo, E. (2007). The economic lives of the poor. *Journal of Economic Perspectives, 21*(1), 141–167.

Bhatt, N., Painter, G., and Tang, S.Y. (1999). Can microcredit work in the United States? *Harvard Business Review, 77*, 26–27.

Block, J.H., Kohn, K., Miller, D., and Ullrich, K. (2015). Necessity entrepreneurship and competitive strategy. *Small Business Economics, 44*(1), 37–54.

Bromley, R. (ed.) (2013). *The Urban Informal Sector: Critical Perspectives on Employment and Housing Policies.* Amsterdam: Elsevier.

Brown, G. (2010). When small is big: Microcredit and economic development. *Technology Innovation Management Review*, November. Accessed October 2018 at http://timreview.ca/article/392.

Debrah, Y.A. (2007). Promoting the informal sector as a source of gainful employment in developing countries: Insights from Ghana. *The International Journal of Human Resource Management, 18*(6), 1063–1084.

Internal Revenue Service (2018). *SOI Tax Stats: Nonfarm Sole Proprietorship Statistics.* Accessed November 5, 2018 at https://www.irs.gov/statistics/soi-tax-stats-nonfarm-sole-proprietorship-statistics.

Mani, A., Mullainathan, S., Shafir, E., and Zhao, J. (2013). Poverty impedes cognitive function. *Science, 341*(6149), 976–980.

Morris, M.H., Pitt, L.F., and Berthon, P. (1996). Entrepreneurial activity in the Third World informal sector: The view from Khayelitsha. *International Journal of Entrepreneurial Behavior & Research, 2*(1), 59–76.

Morris, M.H., Santos, S., and Neumeyer, X. (2018). *Poverty and Entrepreneurship in Developed Economies.* Cheltenham, UK and Northampton, MA, USA: Edward Elgar Publishing.

Potts, D. (2008). The urban informal sector in sub-Saharan Africa: From bad to good (and back again?). *Development Southern Africa, 25*(2), 151–167.

Servon, L. (2006). Microenterprise development in the United States: Current challenges and new directions. *Economic Development Quarterly*, *20*(4), 351–367.

Shah, A.K., Mullainathan, S., and Shafir, E. (2012). Some consequences of having too little. *Science*, *338*(6107), 682–685.

Tirado, L. (2015). *Hand to Mouth: Living in Bootstrap America*. New York: Penguin.

Venkatesh, S.A. (2006). *Off the Books: The Underground Economy of the Urban Poor*. Cambridge, MA: Harvard University Press.

4. Lifestyle ventures: seeking stability

INTRODUCTION

One of the most common forms of start-ups is the lifestyle venture. It is the locally owned and operated bar, hardware store, day care center, hair salon, machining shop or copy business. More than a survival business, which exists on a hand-to-mouth basis just covering costs, the lifestyle venture can be relatively profitable. It affords the entrepreneur a decent living, and so supports a lifestyle for them and their families. Sometimes referred to as "mom and pop operations," they are small in size, independent, usually full-time operations with employees, often family-owned, with limited capacity.

The lifestyle entrepreneur seeks incremental increases in sales and profits, but without meaningful expansion of the scope of operations or increases in the employee base. Thus, any growth occurs within a fairly fixed set of parameters (i.e., space, inventory, staffing, operating hours, marketing). He or she may add new products or services, increase the physical space in which the business operates, move the business to a better location, and sometimes will open a second or even third location. But the business tends to remain small and local. There is no quest for 10 to 20 locations, or to expand the market being served to multiple cities or a large region.

Entrepreneurs frequently establish these types of businesses around their specific skills, interests or knowledge base. They tend to be motivated by a desire for independence, to be their own boss, and to contribute to their communities. The business provides a source of income substitution (including benefits) to the owner, replacing what they would get working for someone else. It employs small numbers of people on a full- and part-time basis, and is completely dependent on the entrepreneur, or owner-operator, not only to run things but also to provide labor within the business. Additionally, a lifestyle business tends to be embedded in the community in a number of important ways.

In this chapter, we explore the nature and importance of these ventures, identifying the specific characteristics that make them a unique category. We examine how they emerge, and how they come to define the lifestyle of the entrepreneur. Some of the more significant strategic and operational challenges confronted by lifestyle entrepreneurs are investigated, and the relative efficiency and role played by technology in these ventures are reviewed. Based on their characteristics and the challenges they face, implications are drawn for ways lifestyle ventures can be sustainable.

THE IMPORTANCE OF LIFESTYLE VENTURES IN THE ECONOMY

Precise numbers are difficult to obtain, as collected statistics do not distinguish lifestyle ventures from other types of small businesses. However, it is possible to get a sense of the critical role these ventures play in the economy. Here we use data from the United States, but there are similar overall patterns across the 34 countries that make up the Organisation for Economic Co-operation and Development (Global Entrepreneurs Report, 2018; OECD, 2017; see also Kelley et al., 2016).

One way to distinguish lifestyle ventures from survival ventures is employees (Marks, 2018). Most survival businesses do not have (or do not report having) any employees, while lifestyle ventures typically (but not always) do. There are about 30 million small businesses in the United States and about one-fourth of these have employees (BNP Paribas Global Entrepreneurs Report, 2016; Office of Advocacy, 2018). This puts the number at about 7.8 million ventures, from which we then need to remove growth-oriented ventures, which are estimated at between 15 and 20 percent of the total (Davidsson, 1991; Phillips and Kirchhoff, 1989). Approached in this manner, there about 6.24 million lifestyle businesses. Of these, almost all have fewer than 50 employees, and the large majority are termed 'microenterprises' because they have fewer than ten employees.

In focusing on employment, it is important to keep in mind how much it varies by industry. A good-sized restaurant can easily employee more than 50 people across all shifts, a machine shop or a local law firm may employ as few as 12, and a technology-based firm with significant revenue might have only five employees. A key differentiator is the labor intensity versus capital intensity versus technology intensity of the company's operations.

In assessing the impact of these ventures, they are more a source of stability in the economy and less a source of dynamism. Small firms make up 99.7 percent of employing firms, with lifestyle ventures accounting for over 40 percent of all jobs in the economy at a given point in time (Du and O'Connor, 2018; Fairlie, 2015). The typical business employs just under six people. Their owners can make a decent living, earning an average salary (excluding any bonuses and profit sharing) of about $60,000 (Payscale, 2018). This suggests these businesses help build the middle class. They serve localized customer demand and can fill market niches that are less attractive to larger regional and national competitors. Further, they maintain and improve upon the facilities in which they operate (and often the immediate surroundings) and contribute to the circular flow of money that remains in the local economy (and any associated multiplier effect) and to the tax base. These ventures are also an important part of the fabric of the communities in which they are based. The entrepreneur will hire from nearby, sponsor community events, volunteer in support of local causes and join civic organizations. When these various factors are considered together, it becomes clear that lifestyle ventures are a stabilizing force in cities and towns across the globe.

At the same time, these ventures are a smaller contributor to economic dynamism. While they add jobs, these are a relatively small proportion of net new employment, with many more jobs created by managed growth and aggressive growth ventures (see Chapters 5 and 6). And although they do sometimes introduce products, services and business processes that are new to the market, they are not a major source of innovation or patents. Similarly, they contribute to the entry and exit rates of new ventures, and so to a reallocation of economic resources, but their effect here is more one of quantity than quality. In any given year, sizeable numbers of lifestyle ventures are launched (over 400,000) and similar numbers fail or otherwise withdraw from the market. However, because they start small and remain small, tend to utilize resources that are more simple and functional (see Chapter 7), have physical capital but remain more labor intensive, and contribute less in the way of intellectual property, the impact of their entry or exit is much less significant than is the case for growth ventures.

UNDERLYING CHARACTERISTICS OF LIFESTYLE VENTURES

What do a wedding dress shop, bed and breakfast establishment, local accounting firm and small online retailer have in common, other than the limited size of their operations, which defines them as lifestyle businesses? Figure 4.1 illustrates some of their shared characteristics. To begin with, each business is centered on the owner, who actively

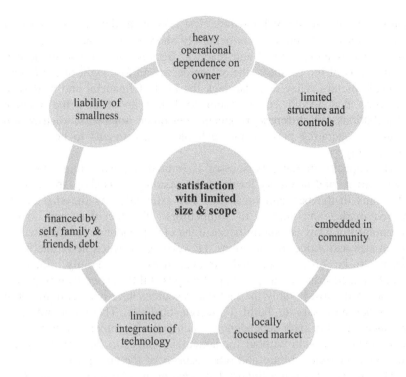

Figure 4.1   Common characteristics of lifestyle ventures

participates in all aspects of the business (e.g., hiring, firing, supervising, administration, payroll, production or service delivery, marketing, supplier issues, customer problems and so on). Decision-making is centralized, while operations are more personalized and informal. For the founder of a successful lifestyle venture, especially in the early years of the business, the hours are long and the payment to themselves is relatively low. Hence, they may work harder and earn less than they would being employed by someone else. The trade-off in terms of independence, decision-making autonomy, involvement of family members, a sense of self-worth and accomplishment, and a belief that one is contributing to the community is well worth it to many of these individuals.

These entrepreneurs can find they are so busy working *in* the business that they do not have as much time to work *on* the business (see Gerber, 2001). So while there is planning and budgeting activity, the emphasis tends to be more on daily operations, month-to-month performance and seasonal fluctuations (e.g., tax season for the accounting firm, peak tourist season for the bed and breakfast). As such, the time horizons of each of these entrepreneurs is generally shorter term, and the management style is more tactical and reactive. Because they are so enmeshed in all facets of the business, the entrepreneur can lose sight of the bigger strategic picture. They can also lack the kind of financial and analytical expertise that would enable them to better understand the relative contributions of different products, customer segments, distribution channels, operating periods and technology investments to bottom-line profitability.

The capacity of these businesses is limited internally (e.g., by store size, staffing and inventory levels of the wedding dress shop, the number of rooms in the bed and breakfast) and externally (by the size of the served market and number of competitors). The fact that they do not meaningfully grow is usually because the entrepreneur is satisfied with a given size and scope of operations. However, even when he or she has a desire to be bigger, personal circumstances (e.g., family, financial, health-related issues) can pre-empt this possibility. Other factors play a role as well, most notably the fact that resources have been committed in a manner necessary to build a lifestyle business. These commitments produce a kind of path dependency which make it problematic to achieve significant expansion without fundamental changes to the resource pool, management style, culture and other aspects of the enterprise.

The end result, from a financial standpoint, is a business that needs to (a) cover costs, (b) remain competitive, and (c) sustain a particular level of income/savings. This means the entrepreneur is focused on finding ways to incrementally increase annual revenues, and implement efficiencies that will reduce costs. Remaining competitive also means that some amount of money must be put back into the business to periodically add or update products or services, expand inventory levels, improve customer service, replace equipment and maintain facilities, and keep pace with technology. While they do not seek significant expansion, these entrepreneurs will sometimes expand their physical space or capacity (e.g., adding an extension to the bed and breakfast), or open a second or third location (e.g., of the wedding dress store). Funding these efforts usually involves some combination of personal investment, retained earnings and debt financing.

The riskiness of these ventures varies, and can best be understood by considering two dimensions of risk: the probability of loss and the magnitude of loss. Failure rates for start-up businesses over the first five years average just over 50 percent, with significant differences across industries (US Bureau of Labor Statistics, 2016). This would indicate reasonably high risk. However, should the venture fail, the actual amount of potential loss, after whatever assets can be sold and debts or obligations negotiated, is frequently not substantial, at least in relative terms. This is especially the case today, when many things can be leased, contracted for or outsourced instead of purchased or owned. Perhaps more significant are the psychic or emotional costs of failure. In making financial commitments, the lifestyle entrepreneur will often attempt to minimize the potential downside loss as opposed to maximizing the upside potential of the venture.

Lifestyle businesses are not dominant in their fields, and usually do not engage in many new or innovative practices. This does not mean innovation is completely absent from these ventures, as some do come up with ideas for product or service improvements or modifications, novel marketing approaches, and creative approaches to accomplishing tasks (process innovations). But for most of them, innovation activity, if present at all, is infrequent and incremental in nature. Also, they generally do not invest all that much in technology. Instead, fairly basic technologies (point of sale systems, cloud computing, accounting and payroll software, mobile business applications, customer relationship software) may be employed to enhance operations.

In addition to these shared characteristics, a number of myths and misconceptions have been popularized regarding these types of ventures. Box 4.1 provides some examples. Two of the more prominent myths concern extremely high failure rates, which we have noted are actually much lower than many believe, and efficiency. It is assumed by many that lifestyle ventures are not efficient, in that they are frequently labor-dependent businesses, with basic physical capital and limited technology incorporated into operations. Further, the small scale on which the business is run, coupled with resource constraints, means they struggle to realize any economies in purchasing or production. They suffer from the so-called liability of smallness, which suggests they have limited bargaining power with suppliers and other external stakeholders (Aldrich and Auster, 1986). Further, in their early days, they are making lots of mistakes and trying to figure out how to do a number of things. These factors can be offset, to some degree, by the fact that these entrepreneurs run relatively lean operations that rely on bootstrapping rather than big budgets. They are creative in leveraging the resources of others (e.g., borrowing, re-purposing, sharing and bartering for resources), in stretching resources and using non-conventional resources to accomplish tasks.

BOX 4.1   COMMON MYTHS ABOUT LIFESTYLE VENTURES

Throughout the years, many myths have arisen about lifestyle ventures which can produce inappropriate stereotypes. A few of the most notable myths (and an explanation to dispel each of them) include the following:

Myth 1: *Most Lifestyle Ventures Fail*

The common folklore is that nine out of ten of these new ventures will fail. The facts do not support such a contention. In fact, there is evidence that close to 50 percent of these start-ups were still surviving five years later. Additionally, 28 percent voluntarily closed down, and only 18 percent actually "failed" in the sense of leaving behind outstanding liabilities (US Bureau of Labor Statistics, 2018).

Myth 2: *Lifestyle Venture Founders Do Not Plan*

Although lifestyle entrepreneurs frequently base their ventures around previous experiences and personal interests, this does not mean they do not plan. Indeed, they are often very methodical people who plan their moves carefully. Not only are they more likely than in years past to start with a formal business plan, but also ongoing financial and operational planning is commonplace.

Myth 3: *Lifestyle Ventures Are Inherently Inefficient*

Lifestyle ventures are thought to be highly inefficient because they tend to be more labor than capital intensive, make purchases in small quantities, and do not incorporate some of the latest technologies into operations. However, they are often very lean operations that are able to leverage and stretch resources and use resources creatively, keeping costs under control.

Myth 4: *Lack of Finance Is the Key Issue Determining Venture Failure or Success*

Ventures need capital to survive, and many business failures occur because of a lack of adequate financing. However, money is not the only bulwark against failure. Failure is an indicator of other problems, including managerial incompetence, lack of financial understanding, ill-advised investments, product quality problems, and poor inventory management. Many successful entrepreneurs have overcome a lack of money through bootstrapping and leveraging.

Myth 5: *Lifestyle Ventures Are Unstructured and Chaotic*

There is a tendency to think of lifestyle entrepreneurs as people who shoot from the hip and ask questions later. They are assumed by some to be disorganized and unstructured. The reality is that lifestyle entrepreneurs are heavily involved in all facets of their ventures, and they usually have a number of balls in the air at the same time. As a result, they are typically well-organized individuals who tend to have a system designed to keep things straight and maintain priorities.

Myth 6: *Successful Lifestyle Ventures Are All about Luck*

Being in "the right place at the right time" is always an advantage – but "luck happens when preparation meets opportunity" is an equally appropriate adage. Prepared lifestyle entrepreneurs who seize the opportunity when it arises often seem "lucky." What appears to be luck is actually preparation, determination, desire, knowledge and innovativeness.

Myths such as these tend to undermine our appreciation for the critical role played by lifestyle ventures in the economy. By understanding their true nature, we can better appreciate their needs and the challenges they face, and better support their sustainability.

WHAT DO LIFESTYLE ENTREPRENEURS LOOK LIKE?

We can identify some general patterns in the demographic make-up of small firms with employees (Office of Advocacy, 2018), the large majority of which are lifestyle ventures. In the United States, just over half of the entrepreneurs are 50 years or older, with one-third between 35–49 years old, and 16 percent under 35 years of age. While 55 percent are owned by men, 36 percent are women-owned, and 9 percent are jointly owned by men and women. With regard to race, Whites own 72 percent of these firms, Hispanics own 13.5 percent, Blacks own 6.3 percent, and Asians own 6.2 percent. The percentages of lifestyle ventures run by women and minorities are far higher than for managed and aggressive growth ventures. In terms of educational backgrounds, 39 percent have a bachelor's degree or higher, 33 percent have some college education, and 28 percent have a high school education.

Experian (2019) reports that the average amount of debt carried by lifestyle entrepreneurs is just under $200,000, while their average household income is $91,600, or about $20,000 higher than the average consumer. Most lifestyle entrepreneurs operate from their own premises, with about 23 percent being home-based, including a number of internet-based companies. People who are franchisees constitute 5 percent of these ventures. While this data is for the United States, patterns are similar in other developed economies (OECD, 2017).

The founder of a lifestyle business is motivated by a mix of factors, with the quest to become wealthy not featuring as a major consideration (Carsrud and Brannback, 2011; Kuratko, 2020). Most of these entrepreneurs seek to make a decent living, while also being driven by a desire to:

- build something of their own
- fill a need
- be independent and not have to work for someone else
- have control over decision-making
- create a lifestyle around the business
- create jobs and develop people, and/or
- contribute to the welfare of their communities.

They seek to do so while avoiding the pressures of higher growth ventures (Kuratko et al., 1997). Some want to build a nest egg for their children, and hope to pass the business on to a family member. However, they frequently find little interest among their heirs in taking over the firm (Stavrou, 1999). A serious problem with many of these businesses is the lack of any exit plan or strategy, especially in countries where the population of business owners is aging (Morris, 2006). The most common exit approaches include sale of the business, liquidation of assets and simply ceasing operations.

A SEARCH FOR STABILITY AND COMFORT

In Chapter 1, we discussed entrepreneurship as a personal journey. When the typical lifestyle venture is started, the entrepreneur has a business concept in mind and may prepare a business plan. He or she makes a wide range of decisions regarding facilities, staffing, equipment purchases, operating hours, the product and service mix, target markets, price points, marketing approaches, customer service and other operational matters. Many of these decisions are best guesses. They are often flawed if not completely incorrect. They can be based on incorrect assumptions, outdated information or data that does not apply to the entrepreneur's situation.

Sometimes it is obvious when a decision is wrong. More commonly, though, the poor decisions that lie at the root of weak business performance are less apparent. It can take considerable trial and error as the entrepreneur makes adjustments to or changes various decisions, learns from the results, and then further adjusts the same or other decision variables. The implication is that an effective business model can take time to emerge. Consider the lifestyle entrepreneur who launches a hair salon. It is only with time that he or she discovers the right number of stylist chairs or stations, number of staff, booking schedule, mix of styling services, and inventory of hair care and other products. Similarly, many other insights only become apparent after trial and error, such as discovering the best layout of the facility, the better suppliers to rely upon, and the most effective marketing channels and messages.

Some of these entrepreneurs are unwilling or unable to experiment, or fail to learn from trial and error. Others never uncover a winning combination of decision variables. The result may be failure, or a business that continues to struggle over time. But for the ventures that achieve some level of success, a viable business model eventually emerges.

What distinguishes lifestyle ventures more than any other factor is how they deal with this successful business model, once it is uncovered. The entrepreneur must decide whether to simply maintain what is clearly working or pursue meaningful growth. In lifestyle businesses, the choice is maintenance and stability. In effect, a formula now exists, and a maintenance approach involves adhering to this formula, and making the kinds of occasional improvements that enable the business to remain competitive. Sales and profits might remain relatively stable or increase incrementally, but the entrepreneur has brought the business to a size and scope with which he or she is comfortable (Holland and Shepherd, 2013).

KEY OPERATIONAL CHALLENGES

The lifestyle venture confronts a number of critical operational challenges (see also Box 4.2). Chief among these is the confluence of four adverse factors: high levels of competition, the liability of smallness, struggles in differentiating the business, and the time demands placed on the entrepreneur.

The large majority of these ventures are in industries with relatively low entry barriers, which can result in multiple local competitors together with large national chains and big online players. A small toy store or picture framing shop is competing with other local small businesses (including a gift shop that sells some toys or art store that does framing), as well as with large box stores, national chains and a host of online providers including Amazon and Etsy. The intensity of competition creates pressure to keep prices down unless the entrepreneur is able to find a source of sustainable differentiation (e.g., unique product offerings, customization, highly personalized service or focusing on the needs of a narrow customer niche). However, achieving differentiation that cannot easily be imitated generally costs money. At the same time, the liability of smallness that was discussed earlier keeps unit costs relatively high compared to those of larger competitors. Meanwhile, because the entrepreneur is deeply enmeshed with all facets of the venture (and in the community), and is a source of labor within the business, there are onerous demands placed on his or her time. Freeing up time to think and act strategically, negotiate effectively from a position of weakness, and successfully differentiate the business can be an especially vexing challenge.

BOX 4.2   MAJOR CHALLENGES CONFRONTING LIFESTYLE VENTURES

Lifestyle ventures are not simply "little big businesses." They face a number of challenges that make them unique (Kuratko and Hornsby, 2018). Six of the more common issues include:

Smaller size: The distinction of smallness finds the lifestyle venture with less bargaining power in dealing with suppliers, large customers and financiers, and makes it more difficult to handle large orders and achieve economies in production. It can also be difficult to attract talent to a lifestyle venture.

The one-person-band syndrome: The business is the entrepreneur and the entrepreneur is the business, so the natural tendency is to do everything. This can be overwhelming and eventually dysfunctional. Yet the entrepreneur will often resist hiring additional people and delegating responsibilities.

Shorter-term orientation: Because the entrepreneur becomes so immersed in every facet of the business, he or she can have little time for planning and analysis, and may not recognize emerging threats or opportunities until it is too late. It also becomes more difficult for the entrepreneur to keep abreast of new trends, best practices and emerging technologies.

Differentiation: Lifestyle businesses generally operate in industries with low entry barriers and face considerable competitive pressure. They source from the same suppliers and lack much in the way of intellectual property. As a result, it can be difficult to differentiate the business from those of competitors.

Vulnerability: Lifestyle ventures, including the most profitable among them, are quite vulnerable when adverse developments occur. A serious illness on the part of the entrepreneur, a bad investment decision, loss of a few key customers, entry to the market of a large competitor, a downswing in the local economy or a period of financial mismanagement can easily put the firm out of business.

> *Community obligations:* The visibility of the business and the fact that most of its customers tend to be local create strong pressure for the entrepreneur to be highly engaged in the community. The entrepreneur frequently devotes considerable time, money and products or services to local causes, activities and events.
>
> The impact of these challenges is ongoing, even as the business ages. Over time the entrepreneur can find ways to enhance the firm's bargaining position, plan better, create more differentiation or lessen vulnerability, but improvements in most of these areas often prove difficult to sustain for very long.

Two additional problem areas that represent significant operational risks in these ventures concern fixed costs and inventory management. Effective lifestyle business owners will seek to minimize fixed cost commitments, but certain of these expenses (rent, insurance, employee benefits, travel, interest payments) can be unavoidable. If sales volumes and margins are too low, it becomes impossible to cover these fixed costs, making the business financially vulnerable. With inventory, the challenge lies in determining what to buy, when and in what quantities. It can take years for the entrepreneur to master the ability to maintain the right levels of inventory of the right mix of items, especially absent sophisticated software management systems, and when buying in less than optimal order size quantities. As a result, the firm's scarce cash flow can be tied up in inventory that will never sell.

THE ILLUSION OF WORK-LIFE BALANCE

An interesting question surrounding these ventures concerns whether the entrepreneur's lifestyle defines the business or the business dictates the entrepreneur's lifestyle. These types of ventures allow for both possibilities. Hence, a person who owns and manages a bed and breakfast establishment, a small law firm or a day care center might limit the numbers of guests or clients or children that they will accommodate, or the days and hours that they operate. In this way, the entrepreneur is designing the business in a manner that allows for a particular lifestyle. Greater work-life balance might be possible. This, of course, assumes that enough revenue can still be generated to support the entrepreneur and maintain the business, which can be problematic in a highly competitive marketplace.

Alternatively, consider the person who is running a restaurant, retail store, local fitness club or small farm. Here, the hands-on nature of the business, employee supervision requirements, typical work schedules or workload demands, and need to address peaks and valleys of daily and weekly customer traffic make significant cutbacks in time devoted to the enterprise harder to implement and sustain. In short, it becomes difficult for the entrepreneur to extract himself or herself from the business for any period of time.

On balance, it is our conclusion that the business is more likely to dictate the entrepreneur's lifestyle than the other way around. Although the entrepreneur may wish to avoid the stress that comes with managing a larger and faster growing enterprise, the lifestyle venture can still be extremely time consuming and emotionally draining. This sometimes remains the case even after a sustainable business model has been uncovered.

A NOTE ON FRANCHISEES AS LIFESTYLE VENTURES

The proportion of lifestyle ventures that are franchises (about 12 percent) represent an interesting departure from a number of the characteristics and challenges we have discussed in this chapter. While the general trend is toward franchisees who establish enough locations to be considered managed growth ventures, the majority of franchisees have only one or two locations (Daley, 2015). According to the International Franchise Association, there are approximately 780,000 of these establishments in the United States and they are responsible for over 8.8 million jobs, with an estimated economic output of $889 billion (Haller and Weisbord, 2016).

Franchisees seek even more stability and predictability than other lifestyle entrepreneurs. A franchise certainly can fail, particularly based on poor location or incompetent execution of the franchise agreement. However, because they are based on a proven business formula, which is usually augmented by ongoing marketing, training, research and other forms of support from the franchisor, their likelihood of success is much higher that most lifestyle ventures. Difficulties related to differentiation, smallness and a long learning curve for the entrepreneur are overcome by membership in the larger franchise organization. The trade-off comes in terms of the upside profit potential of the franchise. The need to share a percentage of revenues with the franchisor coupled with territorial restrictions that limit volume and a lack of flexibility in how things are done can lead the franchisee to realize smaller net profits than many independent lifestyle entrepreneurs.

CONCLUSIONS

In this chapter we have examined entrepreneurs who create businesses that provide for lifestyle needs, and who experience the autonomy of venture ownership without the pressure of high growth and major investment. The owners prefer a more stable and less aggressive approach to running an enterprise, even if the business itself can be quite demanding. These ventures operate within narrow sets of parameters, and, in spite of significant competitive, size-related and economic obstacles, many of them make decent profits. In essence, the lifestyle entrepreneur fills a void or gap in the marketplace that many of the growth-seeking ventures simply ignore.

Yet, these ventures represent an important component of any economy. Although 80 percent of them have fewer than 20 employees, they account for more than 40 percent of total employment. They contribute to the tax base and add value to their local communities in a variety of ways. Lifestyle entrepreneurs are not a source of major innovation, but they do produce many incremental improvements to products and services and develop creative new business practices. And, in spite of limited resources, they are resilient in the face of economic downswings.

The resilience of these firms is tied to the fact that they can be nimble and adaptable, even if the entrepreneur is slow to initially recognize threats. Although they operate at a resource and efficiency disadvantage compared to larger and faster-growth enterprises, lifestyle entrepreneurs tend to be adept at bootstrapping, stretching resources and leveraging the resources of others. While technology represents a major threat, it can also serve as a critical vehicle for their survival. In the final analysis, these ventures are a stabilizing force that enables a middle-class existence for the entrepreneur and provides value to millions of customers.

REFERENCES

Aldrich, H.E. and Auster, E.R. (1986). Even dwarfs started small: Liabilities of age and size and their strategic implications. In B.M. Staw and L.L. Cummings (eds), *Research in Organizational Behavior*, Vol. 8. Greenwich, CT: JAI Press, pp. 165–198.

BNP Paribas Global Entrepreneurs Report (2016). Accessed April 15, 2019 at https://group.bnpparibas/en/news/bnp-paribas-global-entrepreneurs-report-2016.

Carsrud, A. and Brannback, M. (2011). Entrepreneurial motivations: What do we still need to know? *Journal of Small Business Management*, 49(1), 9–26.

Daley, J. (2015). Why multi-unit franchise ownership is now the norm. *Entrepreneur*, June. Irvine, CA: Entrepreneur Media Inc.

Davidsson, P. (1991). Continued entrepreneurship: Ability, need, and opportunity as determinants of small firm growth. *Journal of Business Venturing*, *6*(6), 405–429.

Du, K. and O'Connor, A. (2018). Entrepreneurship and advancing national level economic efficiency. *Small Business Economics*, *50*(1), 91–111.

Experian (2019). *The Face of Small Business*. Costa Mesa, CA: Experian Information Solutions.

Fairlie, R.W. (2015). *Kauffman Index of Entrepreneurial Activity, 1966–2014*. Kansas City, MO: Ewing Marion Kauffman Foundation.

Gerber, M.E. (2001). *The E-Myth Revisited: Why Most Businesses Don't Work and What to Do about It*. New York: Harper Collins.

Global Entrepreneurs Report: The Positive Search for Impact (2018). Accessed at https://group.bnpparibas/en/news/2018-global-entrepreneur-report-search-positive-impact.

Haller, M. and Weisbord, J. (2016). IFA: Franchise businesses to continue growth trend in 2016, outpacing economy-wide pace. IFA, Forrás, January. Accessed September 6, 2019 at http://emarket.franchise.org/FranchiseOutlookJan2016.pdf.

Holland, D.V. and Shepherd, D.A. (2013). Deciding to persist: Adversity, values, and entrepreneurs' decision policies, *Entrepreneurship Theory and Practice*, *37*(2), 331–358.

Kelley, D.J., Ali, A., Brush, C., Corbett, A.C., Kim, P., and Majbouri, M. (2016). *Global Entrepreneurship Monitor United States Report 2016*. Wellesley, MA: Babson College.

Kuratko, D.F. (2020). *Entrepreneurship: Theory, Process, Practice*, 11th edn. Mason, OH: Cengage Publishers.

Kuratko, D.F. and Hornsby, J.S. (2018). *New Venture Management*, 2nd edn. New York: Routledge, pp. 57–64.

Kuratko, D.F., Hornsby, J.S., and Naffziger, D.W. (1997). An examination of owner's goals in sustaining entrepreneurship. *Journal of Small Business Management*, *35*(1), 24–33.

Marks, G. (2018). The US Census Bureau says there are 32m small businesses – they're wrong. *Guardian*, September 3. Accessed May 1, 2019 at https://www.theguardian.com/business/2018/sep/23/how-many-small-businesses-us-census-bureau-wrong.

Morris, M.H. (2006). Implications of business transfer patterns in a developed economy. White Paper, Dutch Ministry of Economic Affairs, *Entrepreneurship in the Netherlands*, 8th edn, ed. J. Snijders.

OECD (2017). *Entrepreneurship at a Glance 2017*, Paris: OECD Publishing. https://doi.org/10.1787/entrepreneur_aag-2017-en.

Office of Advocacy (2018). *Small Business Profile*. Washington, DC: US Small Business Administration.

Payscale (2018). *Average Small Business Owner/Operator Salary*. Accessed March 13, 2019 at https://www.payscale.com/research/US/Job=Small_Business_Owner_%2F_Operator/Salary.

Phillips, B.D. and Kirchhoff, B.A. (1989). Formation, growth and survival; Small firm dynamics in the US economy. *Small Business Economics, 1*(1), 65–74.

Stavrou, E.T. (1999). Succession in family businesses: Exploring the effects of demographic factors on offspring intentions to join and take over the business. *Journal of Small Business Management, 37*(3), 43.

US Bureau of Labor Statistics (2016). *Business Employment Dynamics*. Washington, DC: US Department of Labor. Accessed May 22, 2019 at https://www.bls.gov/bdm/entrepreneurship/entrepreneurship.htm.

US Bureau of Labor Statistics (2018). *Business Employment Dynamics*. Washington, DC: US Department of Labor.

5. Managed growth ventures: learning to fly

INTRODUCTION

Some entrepreneurs are not content with a business that generates enough profit to get by or support a comfortable lifestyle. They seek sustained growth and ongoing expansion of the business, but they also strive to achieve this growth in a deliberate and controlled manner. We refer to these businesses as managed growth ventures, and they constitute between 15 and 20 percent of start-ups (Davidsson, 1989, 1991; Phillips and Kirchhoff, 1989).

Importantly, with this type of venture, the entrepreneur is not simply trying to increase revenue from current operations, or improve profits by reducing costs, which is common in many lifestyle ventures. Rather, the objective is to expand the nature and scope of the business. Managed growth can be accomplished in a number of ways. It could involve steadily adding new locations, expanding one's current territory or market reach, entering new markets, creating new products or revenue drivers, developing entirely new lines of business, or acquiring another firm. Frequently, it involves some combination of these approaches.

In this chapter we explore the nature of these types of ventures, including what they have in common as well as elements that contribute to their diversity. We consider the core requirements for managed growth, and then examine the underlying characteristics of these types of ventures. Attention is devoted to the unique role played by innovation and risk in these firms. The different paths to achieving managed growth are assessed. Finally, some of the more common mistakes made by companies seeking this type of growth, and how these can be avoided, are investigated.

FOUR EXAMPLES

Consider some examples of managed growth firms. First, a successful real estate agent working for a big national firm decides to strike out on her own and create an independent agency. Beginning with a single office in a mid-sized city in Ohio, and focusing primarily on residential housing units, our entrepreneur establishes a solid beachhead in a highly competitive marketplace over the first 15 months of operations. Based on her unique approach to selecting and hiring agents combined with aggressive marketing and strong leadership skills, the company achieves impressive growth. Over the ensuing six years, she is able to open 10 additional offices throughout the metropolitan area, while adding an arm of the business that concentrates on commercial properties. Building on this foundation, by the end of 15 years the business has opened branch offices in three other cities located within the same region of the country, added divisions for property management and title insurance, and acquired a small construction and home improvement company. Most recently, our entrepreneur has, with three partners, obtained a charter and launched a community bank that specializes in real estate lending.

Our second example concerns two college students who start a bar near the campus they attend in Oklahoma. They name the business Eskimo Joe's to reflect that they sell the coldest beer in town. They steadily grow the business, and one of the founders eventually buys out the other. To combat loss of patrons when the college drinking age is raised, food is introduced, including some distinct menu items that help build the reputation of the business, and this becomes a big contributor to profits. The facility is incrementally expanded and eventually covers an entire city block. Experiencing growing demand for merchandise with the distinct Eskimo Joe's logo of a smiling Eskimo boy and his dog, a Joe's Clothes business is added at the main restaurant location as well as in mall locations and pop-up stores in other parts of the state and online. Sister restaurants are added that include Mexico Joe's and Italian Joe's (Joseppi's). The volume of branded merchandise grows to the point that a promotional products division is launched to produce such merchandise for themselves and other companies. Although the business clearly could have been franchised, with hundreds of locations added across the country, the company opted instead for steady, managed growth.

As a third example, consider Custom Manufacturing & Engineering (CME), a woman-owned business based in Tampa, Florida. Started by former employees of Lockheed Martin, the founders were attempting to build upon their technical expertise and experience in contracting with the US military. As a managed growth company, CME has a history of steady expansion on three critical fronts: the capabilities of the business, the mix of products and services offered, and the kinds of customers and industries served. The product mix has incrementally grown to encompass everything from cable assemblies and wire harnesses to portable solar energy generators, mobile chargers, power distribution systems and remote sensors. CME started by developing products for other businesses, but also has created its own branded product lines. Company capabilities have expanded over time to include product design, engineering, lean manufacturing, prototyping, fabrication, assembly, testing, encapsulation, potting, calibration, refurbishing and repairing. The markets served today include aerospace, defense, military, commercial, automotive, transportation, power and energy customers. Consistent growth led the company to relocate from a 30,000 square feet facility to one that included 49,000 square feet, and this has subsequently been expanded to 100,000 square feet.

Our final example involves Dean (Dino) Cortopassi, the son of Italian immigrants, who grew up on his father's farm and started his own farming operation while still in high school. He goes on to build a very successful business producing tomatoes, cherries, olives, kidney beans and other agricultural products. Over time, he recognized the limited strategic leverage held by the farmer as a price taker. This led him to expand vertically into food processing. He builds what eventually becomes the world's largest fresh-pack tomato cannery. His innovative spirit then leads to the branding of a commodity, tomatoes. Under this branding strategy, the company becomes a leading supplier of a line of high quality tomato sauces, purees and pastes to upscale Italian restaurants and pizzerias across the country.

These four companies could not be more different in terms of the products, markets and resources around which they built their success. Yet, each has succeeded based on a managed growth approach. Each was developed in a manner consistent with its core capabilities, but also based on organizational learning, innovation, adaptability and entrepreneurial drive.

THE REQUIREMENTS FOR GROWTH

For a venture to sustain growth, there are three basic requirements: growth potential, a desire for growth, and the ability to manage growth (Sexton and Bowman-Upton, 1991). The first of these requirements is concerned with the nature of the business itself and its market, while the other two have more to do with the people involved in running the venture.

Potential for Growth

Some ventures cannot achieve meaningful growth regardless of who is running them or the amount of resources invested in the business. There are severe limits on growth potential, and these are traceable to factors related to the industry and market in which the company operates. A nail salon offering manicures and pedicures, a business that paints homes, or one that provides personal counseling services all represent cases in point. Each of these operates in an industry with low entry barriers, with lots of competitors, and where it is difficult for any company to differentiate itself on a sustainable basis. If one business tries something new that works, the others are easily able to copy the improvement. Thus, it becomes difficult to build a unique brand. They are also not industries that lend themselves to the development of new technological possibilities that could dramatically lower costs or create new sources of customer value. Their labor intensity combined with other production constraints limit the kind of volumes the businesses can handle. These volumes are further limited by characteristics of the market in which the ventures must compete. These tend to be well-established, mature markets where overall growth is limited. Sales volumes are spread across a large number of competing firms, each with a relatively small piece of the pie. Small volumes limit the ability of the entrepreneur to achieve economies in procurement or production. The end result of these factors tends to be relatively low profit potential, which makes it difficult for the entrepreneur to reinvest in the company and its expansion.

Desire for Growth

At the heart of any managed growth business is a desire on the part of the entrepreneur to create something bigger. Although there are those who stumble upon growth that they were not seeking, and figure out how to manage this growth, the more typical case finds the entrepreneur striving for growth as an integral part of what they set out to accomplish. At the same time, a large number of entrepreneurs do not desire meaningful growth, and will avoid growth opportunities if they arise (Gray, 2002). These types of individuals are quite happy with a lifestyle or even a survival venture. Consider the person who launches a bed and breakfast establishment and enjoys making a success of the business, while having no desire to own five or ten additional bed and breakfast locations. This lack of desire for growth can be traced to any number of causes. Some entrepreneurs seek a balance between the demands of the business and the requirements of their personal and family lives. They may also tend to associate growth with more stress. Others perceive growth as risky, especially if it could threaten what has been achieved in building a successful business. Still others may question their skills or capacity for running something that is too large or overwhelming. Or, as might be the case with our proprietor of the bed and breakfast, the founder finds the business to be fulfilling as it is, enjoying what they do, and proud of what they deliver to their customers.

Ability to Manage Growth

Even if attractive growth opportunities are present, and the entrepreneur has a desire to grow, the business may still fail to achieve meaningful growth. Although sometimes due to unpredictable and uncontrollable developments, a more fundamental cause concerns the limitations of the entrepreneur and his or her team. Attitudes, skills and capabilities required to facilitate and manage growth differ from those required to start a business.

As companies grow in size and scope, even when in a controlled fashion, the managerial requirements become more complex. Complexity is added as the array of products and services sold, market segments served, transactions processed, inventory acquired, logistics coordinated, locations supported and employees managed are steadily increasing. There is much more to control, and more opportunity for error. A supportive infrastructure must be put in place to address these requirements. This infrastructure includes formal systems, processes, structures and controls. It is often necessary to add managers with professional expertise to oversee key functional areas of the business.

From an attitudinal perspective, the entrepreneur can fail to appreciate the need to change how the business is run or the need to learn new ways of doing things. He or she can resist bringing in the kinds of talent needed to implement professional management practices and incorporating new technologies. Additionally, comfort with running the business in a more informal and personal manner can find the entrepreneur failing to adopt the kinds of formal systems and structures on which sustained growth depends.

Beyond this, in the early stages of a new venture the entrepreneur is often forced to be involved in all facets of the business, frequently handling everything from procurement and production to sales, shipping and customer service. One possible outcome of this need for a hands-on approach is that, over time, the entrepreneur becomes a micromanager, and is unwilling to engage in the kind of delegation of authority and responsibility required to successfully operate a larger and more complex enterprise.

Growth is especially dependent upon the entrepreneur's ability to think and act strategically, first, in determining both the direction and timing of business expansion, and second, in coordinating all the interacting parts of the enhanced business. He or she must also be adept at financial planning, setting priorities when allocating resources, and managing cash flows. Here, the ability to balance the needs of existing operations against the requirements of new products, markets, locations and other growth opportunities becomes important. Further, skills related to human resource management and the creation of systems and routines are critical. Other skills and capabilities become relevant depending on the type of business involved.

Desire for Growth and Ability to Manage Growth	Low	Medium	High
High	Lifestyle Ventures	**Managed Growth Ventures**	Aggressive Growth Ventures
Low	Survival Ventures Lifestyle Ventures	Lifestyle Ventures	**Managed Growth Ventures**

Potential for Growth Based on
Industry and Market Factors

Source: Modified and adapted from Sexton and Bowman-Upton (1991).

Figure 5.1 Determinants of growth and venture types

Figure 5.1 illustrates how these three factors interact to define types of ventures. Here, we have placed the personal factors (desire for and ability to manage growth) on the vertical axis and industry/market factors (growth potential of the business) on the horizontal axis. Unlike survival and lifestyle ventures, which tend to have shortcomings on at least two, if not all three, of these factors (i.e., both are classified as low in Figure 5.1), the successful managed growth business seeks controlled growth, demonstrates the capacity to manage this growth, and is able to uncover growth prospects which are moderate in scope. In addition, when the venture has very high growth potential and reasonably capable management, but these prospects are not realized because of a lower desire for rapid growth, a managed growth venture can also result. Let us consider in more depth the underlying nature of this type of venture.

ANATOMY OF A MANAGED GROWTH VENTURE

What makes these ventures unique is their ability to sustain growth despite the fact that they (a) frequently operate in highly competitive markets (like most lifestyle ventures), and (b) are usually not built around technological breakthroughs that are scalable (as with many aggressive growth ventures). They operate in a kind of middle ground, where success is based on strong performance in local and regional markets, or in a somewhat narrowly defined niche within a broader market, rather than by rapidly scaling on a national or international basis. They are adept at building a brand or strong market identity, and at proactively marketing their products and services. They adapt their business models and operations as new opportunities emerge.

Key characteristics of managed growth ventures are summarized in Table 5.1. The diversity among these ventures suggests some characteristics are fairly universal, while others are shared by many, but not all, of these firms. This tendency can be demonstrated by considering the ventures described at the beginning of this chapter. Common to all four ventures was a desire for growth and sense of alertness to new opportunities. However, the extent to which growth followed a specific plan, or capitalized more on opportunities as they emerged, varied across these firms, with a greater tendency toward the latter. They are inclined toward a medium-term planning horizon. Whether or not they have a formal growth plan, once a growth opportunity is identified and committed to, they have tended to implement these new directions in a planned manner.

In all four cases, growth efforts have built upon and been consistent with the core capabilities of the firm, although the direction for growth has included horizontal movement (e.g., all four businesses as they expanded in existing markets), vertical movement (e.g., the farming/food processing and custom engineering firms as they expanded up or down the value chain), concentric diversification (the restaurant, real estate and custom engineering businesses as they moved into new business areas complementary to the core business) and acquisition (e.g., the farming/food processing venture as it bought out other firms). Each emphasized the development of management capacity (i.e., enhanced managerial

Table 5.1   Key characteristics of managed growth firms

Usually Present	Frequently Present	Occasionally Present
• controlled growth • opportunity alertness • strong cash flow pressures • strategic adaptation • process technologies • professional managers • formal management systems, processes and controls • product differentiation • new products, new markets and/or new locations • local/regional market focus or operation in narrow niche in national or global markets • strong brand and/or market identity	• extensive competition • process innovation • adaptable growth plan • limited intellectual property • family ownership • some economies from size • medium-term planning horizon • internal consistency among growth elements/directions for growth • proactive marketing and/or sales efforts • debt financing	• major product innovation • equity financing • succession plan • horizontal diversification • vertical diversification • concentric diversification • strategic partnerships/alliances • growth by acquisition • franchising on a limited regional basis

Note: Managed growth firms demonstrate a number of common features, yet also tend to be quite diverse. As a result, we can distinguish characteristics that virtually all of them have in common within most or in a sizeable number of these ventures.

skills, building a strong team, adding professional managers) coupled with development of organizational capacity (creating structures, systems, processes, routines). Each incorporated technologies into operations (e.g., in such areas as production, financial management, logistics and customer support) which have led to greater efficiencies and enhanced capacities in terms of the volumes of business they can handle, particularly compared to lifestyle or survival ventures. In addition, all four faced serious cash flow pressures related to supporting existing operations while at the same time fueling growth.

Three of our examples involve family ownership, a common tendency among managed growth businesses, although many of them employ other ownership and management structures. While equity financing from outside investors is occasionally involved, or a partner is taken on who brings capital to the business, managed growth is more often achieved through founder financing, family and friends, money reinvested from earnings and debt financing. A surprising number of managed growth firms do not pursue any outside financing, and evidence suggests having outside capital does not produce higher growth rates (Dunkelberg and Cooper, 1982). But when outside money is involved, it is most often in the form of debt rather than equity. Debt comes primarily in the form of commercial bank loans, including lines of credit, as well as through capital leases and supplier credit. A challenge with equity funding for these types of ventures concerns how the investor will receive returns. As the firm is not going to go public, and there may be no plans to sell the venture in the foreseeable future, an equity investor must either be satisfied with dividend payments or some commitment by the founder to buy back their shares at a premium at some future point in time.

Each of these firms developed its own intellectual property (IP), but they vary in terms of the manner and extent to which it is legally protected (e.g., patents, copyrights, trademarks, trade secrets) or the extent to which it provides them with competitive advantage. Hence, our custom engineering and farming/food processing ventures arguably get more advantage from IP than does our real estate firm. As these firms expanded, all of them developed process innovations, or significant improvements in the ways in which business tasks are accomplished.

One might also ask why these entrepreneurs opt for growth. Davidsson (1989) provides evidence that growth willingness tends to be associated with higher achievement motivation on the part of the entrepreneur, expected financial returns, and a sense that growth will provide more independence (reduce external dependencies). In terms of growth deterrents, the most significant were fear of reduced employee well-being and loss of supervisory control. Once firms reached a size of 5–9 employees, it was found that deterring forces overrode the motivating incentives for growth in the large majority of cases.

Finally, we know little about the descriptors of the entrepreneurs behind managed growth companies. They tend to be more educated and have more business-related experience prior to starting their ventures (Dobbs and Hamilton, 2007; Storey, 1994). Dunkelberg and Cooper (1982) found that for entrepreneurs whose current business was much the same as the business where he or she formerly worked as an employee, there was more growth. Beyond this, they appear to be relatively diverse in terms of age and ethnicity, although women and African Americans are under-represented (Cooper et al., 1989; Morris et al., 2006). Overall, there do not appear to be any dominant characteristics of the entrepreneur that explain successful achievement of managed growth (Smallbone and Wyer, 2000).

DIFFERENT PATTERNS OF GROWTH

There has been surprisingly little research on the underlying patterns in the ways managed growth firms tend to emerge. Part of the challenge here is the lack of longitudinal research on small firms of different types, as well as disagreement regarding which indicators of growth should be employed. Does one focus on sales, profits, employees or locations, and is the emphasis on relative growth (i.e., percentage increases), absolute growth (i.e., actual increases), or a weighted average of relative and absolute growth rates (e.g., the Birch Index)? Further, growth rates vary considerably simply based on one's industry (Coad, 2007; Dunkelberg and Cooper, 1982).

Coad (2007) concludes that growth occurs in an inherently erratic manner, but is tied to the evolving productivity levels and learning processes in these organizations. Garnsey (1998) further suggests it is linked to the firm's ability to routinize operations and develop problem-solving repertoires that enable demanding situations to appear more routine. Others (e.g., Churchill and Lewis, 1983; Griener, 1972) propose particular growth stages through which firms move, but these staged models are criticized as being too simple, overly deterministic, and for failing to allow for the continuous process of change in emerging organizations.

Although it would seem managed growth can occur in innumerable ways, let us consider some basic patterns. The most obvious pattern would be *steady, consistent growth*. Here, the business experiences ongoing increases in its revenues and employee base on a quarter by quarter basis virtually from the start of the business, usually as it expands its market reach, marketing efforts and/or mix of (usually related) products/services being sold. A second model would entail *staged growth*, where business expansion follows a kind of step function. So, the pattern finds performance fairly stable for a number of quarters, and then some action is taken (a new opportunity is pursued) that jumps performance outcomes to a new level. A major new line of business or new product category might be introduced, or an entirely new market may be entered. Performance then remains relatively stable at this new level, until the firm decides to pursue its next new opportunity. This pattern can also result from a planned schedule of adding new locations or franchisees over time. Yet another pattern would involve *sporadic growth*. The business now experiences little growth for a fairly extended period, with bursts of expanded activity at irregular intervals. The entrepreneur is able to capitalize on (generally unexpected) market developments, such as the exit of a key competitor, a regulatory change, major new customers entering the market or a natural disaster.

Other possibilities exist, including combinations of the three patterns. These patterns vary in the extent to which the catalysts for growth are more internal (e.g., motives, goals and strategies of the leadership team and available resources within the firm) or external (e.g., changes in the customer, competitor, supplier, technological, regulatory and social environments). They have important managerial implications, as the growth pattern will affect the amount of planning required, cash flow needs and sources, the kinds of organizational systems and controls necessary to support growth, and when these systems and controls are introduced. As such, while growth can be difficult to predict, it is important that it be anticipated.

Another question concerns whether growth is dependent on how big or small the venture is when first launched. Cooper et al. (1989) provide evidence that initial firm size does matter in some regards. They found that those starting firms that are initially larger were more likely to have the backgrounds (education, management experience, goals that were more managerial in nature) necessary to assemble the kinds of resources needed for sustained growth, and also to have partners. These entrepreneurs were more apt to start ventures related to previous jobs they held, and get advice from professional advisors. Yet, firms that are initially larger were more likely to encounter serious problems in their early years compared to smaller counterparts. At the same time, they were less likely to fail. Surprisingly, the subsequent tendency to grow did not differ between firms that started larger and those launched on a more modest basis.

ENTREPRENEURIAL ORIENTATION

Entrepreneurship is involved any time a venture is launched but, as they develop, organizations will differ in their entrepreneurial orientation (EO), or how entrepreneurial they are. A firm's entrepreneurial orientation refers to the combined amounts of innovativeness, risk-taking and proactiveness that are evidenced in how the business is managed (Covin and Wales, 2012). While survival and lifestyle firms tend to have relatively low entrepreneurial orientations, EO plays a key role as the managed growth firm looks for new markets, products and ways of conducting business.

Innovation is sometimes the driver in these firms, as with the custom engineering example at the start of the chapter, but more often it plays a more supportive role. Dobbs and Hamilton (2007) suggest it may be a correlate rather than cause of growth. Further, innovation in these firms is frequently directed at processes, or ways of doing things, rather than products. For instance, with the food processing firm discussed earlier, innovativeness and proactiveness were fundamental to the manufacturing and marketing processes they implemented. Risk-taking is reflected in the growth moves of all four of the firms, but the planned and controlled nature of this growth suggest intermediate levels of risk. On balance, levels of EO in managed growth firms tend to be in the moderate range (Coad, 2007).

A significant challenge for these firms is the ability to maintain their entrepreneurial orientations as they get larger. The addition of structure, controls and management systems can create inertia within an organization. Once instituted, these elements tend to expand and reinforce one another. They can eventually serve to slow the organization down, cause management to miss opportunities, and make it more difficult to experiment, change or try new things.

COMMON MISTAKES MADE WHEN SEEKING MANAGED GROWTH

For those entrepreneurs who seek growth, a number of considerations can keep the venture from actually growing, and will sometimes lead to business failure. Chief among these are the following errant assumptions, misjudgments and shortcomings.

Failure to Stick to the Knitting

The four company examples we started with in this chapter suggest successful managed growth firms usually build around a core competency or focus. The directions for growth may involve product and/or market development, expansion in horizontal or vertical directions, and even concentric diversification, but the firm is pursuing opportunities that are consistent with its strengths. Hence, they select opportunities that require new learning but that also build upon what the venture already does, the capabilities it already has, and the resources it has developed.

Stated differently, they avoid opportunities that may be quite attractive in terms of potential returns, but that involve a number of critical elements (human capital, technologies, cost structures and potential shared costs, customers, supply chains, distribution channels and so forth) that are unrelated, or far removed, from the knowledge, resources, skills and capabilities with which they are familiar and around which they have built their success.

Not Understanding Cash Flow

While not as intense as with aggressive growth ventures, cash flow pressures can be significant when trying to facilitate managed growth. This is because the venture must spend money faster than it is making money. The pressures here are three-fold. First, there are start-up costs related to the establishment of a new location, development of new products, creation of a new line of business, or entry into a new market. Second, when pursuing the new opportunity, it may take a while before breakeven is reached, meaning cash flow from new operations is negative during this time period. Third, the organization can incur ongoing costs in adapting its existing systems (e.g., accounting, control, communications, human resource management and logistical systems) to support the new business opportunity. As cash flow is needed to support both the existing and the new business, the entrepreneur is often engaged in a kind of balancing act. Taking too much money from existing areas of the business to support new areas can lead to alienated customers and eventual loss of revenue, which further exacerbates cash shortages. Meanwhile, not initially investing enough in the new business opportunity (and the resources needed to support the new opportunity are almost always greater than anticipated) can result in it failing or a need for even greater investment in order to keep the new area of business afloat. Having a sufficient safety margin in terms of cash often means incurring debt financing, yet the costs of servicing the interest and principal on the debt can further contribute to cash flow pressures over time.

Insufficient or Ineffective Delegation

As we have noted, growth requires that the entrepreneur delegate key roles and responsibilities to other employees. In a sense, he or she must give up control over particular activities in order to gain control over a larger and more diverse enterprise. Involved here are the willingness as well as the ability to delegate, and many entrepreneurs have shortcomings in one or both areas. Both can be difficult, as it means allowing someone else to accomplish a task that the entrepreneur may be able to better perform. It involves trust, as the entrepreneur must be willing to allow the person to fail, which is often costly and compromises other areas of the business. Finally, successful delegation can require the entrepreneur to develop a different leadership style than the one employed in successfully launching the business. Modifying one's approach to supervising and motivating employees can be especially problematic for many business owners.

Over-reliance on Family Members, Friends and Existing Employees

Growth brings with it more complex demands in potentially every facet of the business. Companies often outgrow the capabilities of the people who were there at the beginning, while the entrepreneur is slow to recognize or appreciate the implications of these shortcomings. The appropriate response in most instances is to bring in managers having appropriate professional experience. Yet, these kinds of managers can be expensive and they bring change to the organization. All too often, the entrepreneur will instead place family members, friends and employees who started with the firm in its early days into key managerial positions. Such assignments are either based on biased interpretations of the abilities of these individuals or the hope that they will grow into the job (Liu et al., 2015). Nepotism and loyalty to friends and current employees might have benefits, but they often undermine the ability of the firm to sustain growth (Morris et al., 1997; Vinton, 1998).

Avoidance of Infrastructure Development

The environment in the early days of most start-up firms can be characterized as unstructured, informal and fairly personal – while growth requires much more in the way of structure, formal processes, operational planning and professional management practices (Allen, 2006). We can label this mix of mechanisms as the company infrastructure. Consider a business with 20 customer transactions a day versus one that processes 300 transactions a day; or envision one with two locations compared to one with 22 locations; or picture an enterprise that serves one local market and customer group and contrast it with one serving 14 cities, a large region of the country, or a mix of consumer, business and government customers. In all these situations, it would be virtually impossible to get all the work done while controlling costs, maintaining quality and satisfying customers unless the entrepreneur invests in the development of company infrastructure.

The nature of this infrastructure differs depending on the type of business and industry in question, but some common areas for development might include:

- Deployment of more sophisticated accounting systems and processes.
- Establishment of formal budgets for marketing, operations, staffing, travel, spending on technology, and other key business areas.
- Adoption of technology to enable better management and control of growing volumes and types of inventory, a larger and more diverse supplier pool, and more complicated logistics.
- Design of formalized processes for recruiting, hiring and evaluating employees.
- Creation of databases that capture detailed information on clients (and what they buy), prospective customers, sales and margins by product/service category, suppliers and their performance, customer complaints, quality control problems, customer acquisition costs, order fulfillment costs, employee performance, and a host of other operational variables.
- Formulation of approval processes for purchases, travel and other key expenditures.
- Design of systems for efficient management of billing, invoicing, payroll, and tax collection and payment.
- Implementation of training and development systems for employees.
- Formalization of rules and processes governing internal and external communications.
- Enhancements to the firm's abilities to track market trends, competitors' actions, technological developments and regulatory requirements.

For most managed growth companies, these kinds of developments tend to occur in response to problems and needs that come up as growth occurs. Yet, there are entrepreneurs that resist building this infrastructure, or do so too slowly. The result can be not simply a lack of growth, but the actual demise of the business as problems begin to multiply (e.g., rising costs, inconsistent quality, poorly served customers, overwhelmed employees, cash shortages).

Why do entrepreneurs fail to appreciate the need to build the requisite infrastructure? Many do not understand what is needed, or lack the knowledge and experience in how to address infrastructure needs. Some resist change, believing that what worked in launching the business and getting it stabilized will also work when trying to grow the business. They may also like the informality and personal nature of things at present, and think that building infrastructure will only lead to bureaucracy and unnecessary overhead (and in fact too much infrastructure can have this effect). Yet another cause is the amount of expenditure necessary to develop the infrastructure. The sample list of items above demonstrates not only that significant change must occur over time, but also that significant investment may be necessary. Money tends to be tight in small firms, and the entrepreneur may tend to prioritize making and selling products or services over developing the organization. The return on investment in infrastructure can prove harder to measure, which is another reason to put such spending off.

Inadequate Competencies Related to Alertness, Adaptation and Ambidexterity

The path to growth often emerges as an entrepreneur pursues a venture. He or she becomes aware of new opportunities and their potential fit with the company as a function of being in business, serving customers, working with technologies and managing operations. As a result, growth occurs based on the entrepreneurial alertness of the entrepreneur (Tang et al., 2012), and the ability to determine which opportunities represent a good fit with the business, its capabilities and its resources.

Once they are selected, acting on growth opportunities requires adaptation. The entrepreneur may need to adapt the existing business model, management style, employee skill sets, marketing approaches, financial structure, distribution channels, methods of production, and much more. Entrepreneurs vary, however, in their willingness and ability to adapt (Schindehutte and Morris, 2001). Adaptation means modifying, adjusting and changing fundamental aspects of the business, sometimes in ways that are not self-apparent ahead of time. The implication is that the entrepreneur must experiment, learn quickly, adjust, experiment further, learn more, make additional adjustments and so on until the capabilities of the organization are aligned with requirements of the growth opportunity.

Adapting to the new opportunity does not mean the existing operations of the business can be ignored. There is a need to balance allocation of resources (i.e., effort, money, time) in maintaining performance in the traditional areas of business operations against the requirements of new areas of focus. The term 'ambidexterity' is used to describe the organization's balancing skills (Volery et al., 2015). A variety of elements contribute to becoming more ambidextrous, including management's abilities at compartmentalizing, multitasking, playing multiple roles, establishing and adjusting priorities on a timely basis, finding synergies between aspects of existing and new operations, and handling greater complexity. It is also facilitated by some of the considerations discussed above, most notably the development of infrastructure, professionalization of the management team and management of cash flows.

CONCLUSIONS

A managed growth venture is a unique kind of entity that combines stability with ongoing pursuit of opportunity, innovation with efficiency, and expansion with control. It lies between the local focus of the lifestyle venture and the global scalability of the aggressive growth venture, simultaneously competing with both types of firms.

Entrepreneurs who create these organizations are generally not content with the status quo. They differ in how much they want to grow, and may get to an optimal size and scale beyond which they believe things are not controllable, or otherwise become problematic (i.e., having to incur the various costs of coordinating an increasingly large and more bureaucratic organization). But they build impressive organizations, create a considerable number of jobs, and provide superior value to local and regional (and some national and global) customers.

The growth achieved by these ventures sometimes happens by accident, but it is more often an informed and intentional process, even if influenced by unpredictable and unexpected developments (Penrose, 1959). If we consider the four managed growth businesses introduced at the start of the chapter, their success is arguably tied to being able to think and act strategically. This means moving beyond an exclusive focus on operational management and tactical moves found in many lifestyle ventures. The entrepreneurs must develop an ability to balance existing operations against the recognition and pursuit of new opportunities. Advantage must be achieved and maintained against smaller local competitors while aggressive moves of larger national players must be anticipated and countered. Innovation plays a role, but it tends to be continuous as opposed to disruptive innovation (Coad, 2007).

In the end, building a business with 20 locations is not the same as having a single location that is simply replicated 19 times. Managed growth involves complexity and requires managerial sophistication. While growth is dynamic and difficult to control, these entrepreneurs are able to affect a kind of bounded expansion of their enterprises, and to sustain this over time.

REFERENCES

Allen, K.R. (2006). *Growing and Managing a Small Business: An Entrepreneurial Perspective.* Boston, MA: Houghton Mifflin Harcourt.

Churchill, N.C. and Lewis, V.L. (1983). The five stages of small business growth. *Harvard Business Review,* May–June, 30–50.

Coad, A. (2007). Firm growth: A survey. Max Planck Institute of Economics, Papers on Economics and Evolution No. 0703, Jena, Germany.

Cooper, A.C., Woo, C.Y., and Dunkelberg, W.C. (1989). Entrepreneurship and the initial size of firms. *Journal of Business Venturing,* 4(5), 317–332.

Covin, J.G. and Wales, W.J. (2012). The measurement of entrepreneurial orientation. *Entrepreneurship Theory and Practice,* 36(4), 677–702.

Davidsson, P. (1989). Entrepreneurship – and after? A study of growth willingness in small firms. *Journal of Business Venturing,* 4(3), 211–226.

Davidsson, P. (1991). Continued entrepreneurship: Ability, need, and opportunity as determinants of small firm growth. *Journal of Business Venturing,* 6(6), 405–429.

Dobbs, M. and Hamilton, R.T. (2007). Small business growth: Recent evidence and new directions. *International Journal of Entrepreneurial Behavior & Research,* 13(5), 296–322.

Dunkelberg, W.C. and Cooper, A.C. (1982). Patterns of small business growth. In *Academy of Management Proceedings,* No. 1. Briarcliff Manor, NY: Academy of Management, pp. 409–413.

Garnsey, E. (1998). A theory of the early growth of the firm. *Industrial and Corporate Change,* 7(3), 523–556.

Gray, C. (2002). Entrepreneurship, resistance to change and growth in small firms. *Journal of Small Business and Enterprise Development,* 9(1), 61–72.

Greiner, L. (1972), Evolution and revolution as organizations grow. *Harvard Business Review,* 50(4), 37–46.

Liu, C., Eubanks, D.L., and Chater, N. (2015). The weakness of strong ties: Sampling bias, social ties, and nepotism in family business succession. *The Leadership Quarterly,* 26(3), 419–435.

Morris, M.H., Williams, R.O., Allen, J.A., and Avila, R.A. (1997). Correlates of success in family business transitions. *Journal of Business Venturing,* 12(5), 385–401.

Morris, M.H., Miyasaki, N.N., Watters, C.E., and Coombes, S.M. (2006). The dilemma of growth: Understanding venture size choices of women entrepreneurs. *Journal of Small Business Management,* 44(2), 221–244.

Penrose, E.T. (1959). *The Theory of the Growth of the Firm.* New York: John Wiley.

Phillips, B.D. and Kirchhoff, B.A. (1989). Formation, growth and survival; small firm dynamics in the US economy. *Small Business Economics,* 1(1), 65–74.

Schindehutte, M. and Morris, M.H. (2001). Understanding strategic adaptation in small firms. *International Journal of Entrepreneurial Behavior & Research,* 7(3), 84–107.

Sexton, D.L. and Bowman-Upton, N.B. (1991). *Entrepreneurship: Creativity and Growth*. New York: Macmillan.

Smallbone, D. and Wyer, P. (2000). Growth and development in the small firm. In S. Carter and D. James-Evans (eds), *Enterprise and Small Business*. Harlow: Prentice-Hall, pp. 391–400.

Storey, D.J. (1994). *Understanding the Small Business Sector*. London: Routledge.

Tang, J., Kacmar, K.M.M., and Busenitz, L. (2012). Entrepreneurial alertness in the pursuit of new opportunities. *Journal of Business Venturing*, 27(1), 77–94.

Vinton, K.L. (1998). Nepotism: An interdisciplinary model. *Family Business Review*, 11(4), 297–303.

Volery, T., Mueller, S., and von Siemens, B. (2015). Entrepreneur ambidexterity: A study of entrepreneur behaviours and competencies in growth-oriented small and medium-sized enterprises. *International Small Business Journal*, 33(2), 109–129.

6. Aggressive growth ventures: changing the world

INTRODUCTION

Much of the attention given to entrepreneurship in the popular media concerns ventures that experience explosive growth. These are often disruptive businesses that change markets, industries, societies, and sometimes, the world. Although far fewer in number, they create a disproportionate number of patents, jobs and wealth in society, and can enhance the global competitiveness of a nation. We shall refer to them as "aggressive growth" ventures. Examples include household names like Amazon, Dell Computer, Facebook and Uber. They include a wide range of technology companies (e.g., bio-tech, pharmaceutical, medical technology, nano-technology, robotics, artificial intelligence), but also companies in more traditional industries (e.g., beverages, logistics, civil engineering, mining). Further, many franchise operations (e.g., food, fitness, cell phone repair, personal care) have achieved aggressive growth.

Aggressive growth ventures can generate huge returns to founders and investors, but also represent significant risk. They are often trying to create a market that does not exist, or significantly change how people address a particular need. They require extraordinary amounts of resources to fuel growth, which leads them to rely heavily on large equity investments from outside parties. As a result, the founder(s) must generally be willing to give up a substantial amount of ownership. They are faced with the dilemma of having either a large majority share of a multi-million dollar company or a relatively small share of a multi-billion dollar company.

While aggressive growth may seem desirable, the challenges that come with rapidly scaling an enterprise can be overwhelming if those involved are not prepared. These are especially volatile ventures, with high stress levels, and tremendous demands placed on the founding team and early stage employees. The problems encountered increase in complexity as growth is initially realized and then accelerates. New capabilities must be developed on a real-time basis. Company infrastructure struggles to keep pace as what was a 40-person operation quickly becomes a company with 400 and then 4000 employees. As a result, the entrepreneur's "desire for growth" can be much greater than the actual ability to "manage growth" (see Chapter 5).

In this chapter we take an in-depth look at these aggressive growth ventures. Attention is devoted to the significant positive as well as potentially adverse impacts they have on an economy. Unique characteristics of these enterprises are reviewed, with implications drawn for managerial capacity and other critical needs and requirements. We examine the role played by different forms of innovation in facilitating growth. A distinction is drawn between ventures that are more technology-driven versus market-driven, and what this means for how growth is achieved. Finally, we explore the nature of exit strategies and how they affect a variety of considerations within these ventures.

GAZELLES, UNICORNS AND DECACORNS

Aggressive growth ventures represent a very small percentage of the total population of entrepreneurial firms (Morelix and Russell-Fritch, 2017). If we consider all firms started over a ten-year period, less than 1 percent achieve aggressive growth. And if we consider all firms that have employees in the United States, it is estimated that there are 79.1 aggressive growth firms for every 100,000 companies. Further, as aggressive growth is difficult to maintain indefinitely, almost two-thirds of high growth firms are ten years old or younger.

Yet, high growth ventures have a disproportionate impact on the economy. David Birch (1987) called these firms *gazelles*, an animal known for its speed. A gazelle, by his definition, is a business establishment with at least 20 percent sales growth every year (for five years), starting with a base of at least $100,000. Birch and colleagues (1995) demonstrated that gazelles accounted for virtually all the net new employment growth between 1990 and 1994 in the United States. Henrekson and Johansson (2010) found they generated practically as many new jobs (10.7 million) as the entire US economy (11.1 million) over a multi-year period. The "average" company among this 1 percent generates an astounding 88 net new jobs annually, compared to the 2–3 net new jobs generated by the average firm in the economy as a whole (Stangler, 2010).

The impact is also significant when focusing on revenue growth. Shane (2009) reports that aggressive growth firms that receive venture capital investments account for roughly 10 percent of all business sales in the United States. Separately, the World Economic Forum (WEF) analysed four major databases that captured faster growing firms in 13 countries and found a number of consistent patterns (Foster et al., 2011; Henrekson and Johansson, 2010; Markman and Gartner, 2002). Two key findings include: (a) the top 1 percent of the firms accounted for just over 20 percent of revenue growth (approximating a 1/20 rule); and (b) the top 10 percent of the companies accounted for just over 55 percent of the revenue growth.

The explosive growth they achieve is reflected in the valuations placed on these companies. In the early 2000s, the idea of a tech start-up that had yet to go public (pre-IPO) having a $1 billion market valuation was a fantasy. For example, neither Google nor Amazon (or any other original dotcom venture) were ever worth $1 billion as private companies. However, this has changed as disruptive innovations are driving the creation of numerous billion-dollar start-ups. The term *unicorn* was introduced as a label for such ventures. Smartphones, inexpensive sensors and cloud computing are examples of new technologies that have enabled new internet-connected services to be introduced into traditionally non-tech industries. For example, Uber has disrupted the taxi industry while Airbnb has had a similar impact on the hotel industry.

As of 2018, there were more than 153 ventures that had been valued at $1 billion or more by venture capitalists, and this trend can only be expected to increase. As they continue to grow, many start-ups are surpassing the $1 billion level and achieving the $10 billion level. These firms, including Facebook, Uber and Airbnb, are now referred to as *decacorns* (Black, 2018).

Equity financing plays a big part in this kind of growth. Unicorns in the United States alone raised over $19 billion in 2018 across 62 financings. Moreover, this vast sum comes on the heels of three straight years in which venture capital raised by unicorns eclipsed $17 billion. Although some of this is to fuel organic growth of these unicorns, much of it helps pay for their acquisition of other rapidly growing start-ups (e.g., Facebook acquiring messaging WhatsApp for $19 billion and Oculus for $2 billion; Google acquiring smart thermostat maker Nest for $3.2 billion; Apple acquiring headphone maker Beats for $3 billion; Microsoft acquiring the Swedish gaming company responsible for *Minecraft* for $2.5 billion). Acquisition of high growth start-ups allows these companies to gain access to new innovations and markets while providing an exit strategy for new innovative start-ups (Kuratko, 2020).

Not only do these aggressive growth entrepreneurial firms have an enormous economic impact, they are the chief source of dynamism within the economy. They develop disruptive innovations that create new sources of value and productivity growth. They change market structures and industry norms. They reallocate societal resources from less to more efficient uses. Importantly, the new sources of value they introduce and the markets they create often serve as catalysts for the launch of many other new firms.

CHARACTERISTICS OF AGGRESSIVE GROWTH VENTURES

As with our other three venture types, there is considerable diversity among aggressive growth ventures. Their growth can be based on the development of highly innovative products/services, a new market category, rapid geographic or product line expansion, acquisitions of other businesses, or some combination of these. Yet, they have a number of characteristics in common that make them unique as a category. Chief among these are the following:

- higher risks and greater potential returns than other venture types
- rapid scaling of the enterprise
- extraordinary resource requirements needed to fuel growth
- the ability to maintain a strong entrepreneurial orientation
- volatile and less predictable external environments
- demanding work conditions that can be both rewarding and highly stressful
- struggles to develop the internal company infrastructure rapidly enough to support ever-expanding operations
- constantly evolving sets of influences (e.g., existing and new employees, board members, marketplace demands, changing technology, internal control systems) that serve to define the company culture.

Most entrepreneurs do not have the personal characteristics, motivations, skill sets and/or access to types of resources necessary to build this type of venture, which helps explain why so few of them tend to emerge.

Although sometimes launched by a solo entrepreneur, these ventures are more frequently started by a team of founders. Women and minorities tend to be under-represented (Morris et al., 2006). The founders usually take a lower (or no) salary in the early years, but receive equity shares and see their returns when the company dramatically increases in value. The business is guided by a shared vision among the key stakeholders. However, achieving aggressive growth is not always the original intention of the founders. As the business is being developed, there is usually less concern with profit generation and more focus on building the value of the firm. And though there are exceptions, most aggressive growth ventures involve outside equity investors who often hold a sizeable ownership stake. These outside investors, and particularly venture capital firms, can sometimes undermine the enterprise by prioritizing revenue growth targets over development of a sustainable company.

The growth demonstrated by these ventures is often described as a "hockey stick" pattern, where revenue initially increases at a fairly moderate, linear pace and there is then an inflection point where growth takes off at an exponential rate. Figure 6.1 provides an illustration. This pattern is generally applied to sales, but can also describe growth in numbers of customers, website hits, business valuation and other performance indicators. The hockey stick pattern suggests there is an initial period where the business is launched and considerable trial and error takes place, but eventually a viable business model starts to emerge, and as the company refines it and builds out a platform, sales rapidly accelerate. However, the specific pattern varies among aggressive growth ventures both in terms of how long the initial period of more modest growth lasts (when the inflection point occurs) and for how long they can sustain exponential growth. With Netflix the take-off started in its third year, but for Amazon it was a slower ramp up with sales really accelerating after eight years. While companies like Amazon and Google have found ways to sustain accelerated growth, others such as Go Pro (cameras) have seen a leveling or decline in sales after a few years of rapid growth. Moreover, high revenue growth does not necessarily mean profitability, as it can take five or more years before any profits are realized, and these can remain modest for some time.

Although commonly assumed to be technology companies, this is not the case. A majority of aggressive growth firms are not high-tech, and they actually can be found in a wide array of industries, with a heavier concentration in services (Henrekson and Johansson, 2010). In a study involving eight countries, only about one-third were high-tech companies (OECD, 1998). Separately, Hathaway (2018) examined 5000 growth companies in the United States, and found 29 percent were from high-tech industries. He found they were more concentrated in larger metro markets, but could often be based in mid-sized cities. Further, they tend to be found in areas with a higher share of workers with college degrees, a larger percentage of people employed in high-tech industries, a population with a bigger share of the population of prime entre-preneurship age (35–44 years old), and a higher rate of business formation.

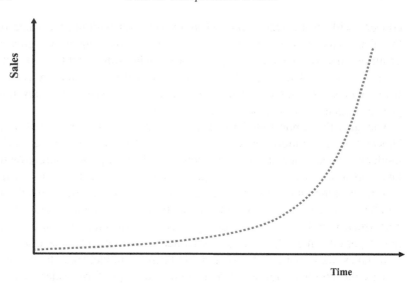

Figure 6.1   Hockey stick growth pattern

Finally, these ventures are distinguished by the types of exit strategies they pursue. While there are some aggressive growth ventures where the founders remain with and build the company over many decades, such as Dell Computer, more often they are acquired by larger firms or become publicly traded companies. Because most of them require equity investments from angel investors, venture capitalists and private equity firms, these investors expect significant returns. As a result, they place pressures on the organization to meet the kinds of performance targets that will make it attractive to acquiring companies and those who underwrite initial public offerings.

INNOVATION, TECHNOLOGY AND THE AGGRESSIVE GROWTH VENTURE

Aggressive growth ventures demonstrate a strong entrepreneurial orientation, meaning they tend be more innovative, risk-taking and proactive in the way they approach running the business.

They are doing something new and potentially disruptive. Yet, newness can take different forms. Many aggressive growth companies are based on a new and novel product or service. Others are able to adapt an existing product or service or extend an offering into an area where it is not presently available. The first of these approaches is often referred to as *new-new*; the second as *new-old* (Kuratko et al., 2017; Thiel, 2014).

A useful framework in this regard examines different dimensions of newness (Kuratko et al., 2017). Presented in Figure 6.2, technology newness is distinguished from market newness. At issue is whether entrepreneurs exploit opportunities by leveraging incremental or more discontinuous (or radical) technological advances and are involved in incremental or more radical market disruption. Ventures can be classified based on where they fall on the combinations of these two dimensions.

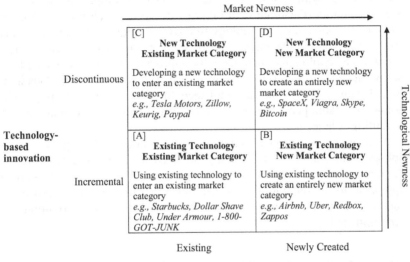

Source: Adapted from Kuratko et al. (2017).

Figure 6.2 Entrepreneurial newness framework

At one extreme, entrepreneurs can exploit a discontinuous new technology to provide a product or service intended to significantly disrupt the market through the creation of a new product-market space. This would embrace the highest level of innovation "newness" relative to other alternatives. Consider the first company to market a surgical tool for use in laser eye surgery. Because the company is exploiting a radical technology, they are dealing with high levels of technological uncertainty, and need to help the market understand, accept and embrace a major technological advance (see Quadrant D in Figure 6.2).

At the other extreme, entrepreneurs who create an organization to exploit or incrementally improve an existing technology and seek to operate within an established market category confront the lowest levels of innovation "newness" relative to other alternatives (see Quadrant A in Figure 6.2). Examples might be Starbucks or 1-800-GOT-Junk. Coffee shops and junk removal have been around for a long time. But both companies brought innovative business models and a proactive approach to the market and achieved significant growth.

Between these two extremes can be found entrepreneurs who create and exploit a significant technological advance to compete in an existing market category (Quadrant C in Figure 6.2). Tesla developed new battery and electric powertrain technology to create a unique position within the established automobile market. Also between the two extremes, a new venture may exploit and incrementally improve on an existing technology but participate in the establishment of a new market category (Quadrant B in Figure 6.2). Airbnb accomplished this by adapting existing technology to enable people to share their private residences as an alternative to renting a hotel room.

With aggressive growth ventures that are not developing new technologies, innovation is still usually involved in their success. However, the innovativeness is found in the design of the business model, a novel approach to production or service delivery, how the firm prices or captures revenue, or the ways in which marketing or distribution are accomplished.

FAILING TO CROSS THE CHASM

Some aggressive growth ventures are able to initially penetrate the market, and generate moderate sales, but never achieve take-off, or exponential growth in sales. One of the reasons for this failure concerns the inability to transition from customers who are so-called innovators or early adopters to the mainstream marketplace. This transition has been termed "crossing the chasm" by Geoffrey Moore (1999) in his classic book.

Particularly where a firm has developed major technological advances or innovations that create new markets, it is typical to encounter market resistance. Customers are unfamiliar with the product category and resist buying for a host of reasons. Not only might they not understand the product or service, how it works, or exactly what it does, but trying something truly novel entails risk. The customer can have strong loyalties to something that currently exists, even if inferior to the new innovation.

They can also perceive the costs (both financial and psychological) of switching to something new and different to be quite high. The firm is effectively leading customers rather than following them.

As illustrated in Figure 6.3, new innovations take time to diffuse into the marketplace. Rogers (1964) was the first to demonstrate that the rate at which customers adopt something new demonstrates a fairly normal distribution. As a result, he organizes customers into categories based on how early or late they tend to buy an innovative new product. So, innovators and early adopters are the first to try the new item, with the early majority, late majority and laggards waiting increasing amounts of time before each group enters the market. Each group represents a certain percentage of the overall market for the innovation.

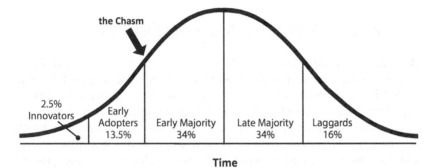

Source: Adapted from Rogers, E. M (1964). *Diffusion of Innovation*, New York: The Free Press and Moore, G. A. (1999). *Crossing the Chasm*, New York: HarperBusiness.

Figure 6.3   Innovation diffusion curve and the chasm

The initial customers who try something new are more willing to take risks and will try the innovation because they have a unique need or requirement. As it has just been developed, the product itself may still have problems or shortcomings (think of the first cellular telephone), but it introduces some new capability or possibility that is especially valued by these first customers. So what matters to these early customers is the functional capability, or what the innovation actually does (a minimum feature set). What Moore (1999) recognized was a fundamental difference between those first to buy (innovators and early adopters) and the other three categories of users, which we can think of as the mainstream market. The latter are more conservative and unwilling to put up with any bugs or initial design shortcomings. They assume the functional capability is there and has been refined, and care more about aesthetics (e.g., nice appearance, stylish design, easy to use) as well as branding, packaging, customer service, price deals and special promotions (a whole feature set).

Moore's chasm is the gap that exists between these two groups. Firms seeking aggressive growth can fail to cross this chasm and penetrate the mainstream market, often because they are led by individuals with strong technological backgrounds who fail to appreciate or develop the necessary marketing capabilities. They can be more concerned with continually advancing the technology and adding new technical features and options, while ignoring or having a disdain toward things like branding and packaging. Although they may see these marketing elements as superficial or secondary, the mainstream market places a high priority on them, and so sales do not take off.

TECHNOLOGY PUSH VERSUS MARKET PULL

A related issue affecting the ability to achieve aggressive growth is the extent to which the firm is more pushed by technological possibilities or pulled by an understanding of market needs and requirements. This is especially critical in high-tech firms, which are often started by founders with strong technical backgrounds. Not surprisingly, a strong technical orientation will pervade the culture that emerges in the company. This can sometimes lead to a belief that great technology is the primary requirement for marketplace success. An adaptation of a statement most commonly attributed to philosopher Ralph Waldo Emerson says that "if you build a better mousetrap the world will beat a path to your door." Technology-push companies often fail because they adhere to this belief, creating products that are better mousetraps that nobody (or at least not enough customers) wants (Calantone and Cooper, 1979).

The opposite of a technology-push orientation is a venture that is pulled by what customers in the market are asking for. Unfortunately, a market-pull orientation relies on customers to know and be able to express their needs. Not only is this not always the case, but customers typically cannot envision bold new product innovations that would change their lives. As a result, an overly strong customer focus can lead to more incremental innovation where new features or options are added to existing products. The company misses opportunities for breakthrough innovation.

The ability to achieve a proper blend of these two orientations, where the company is able to match technological possibilities to marketplace needs and expectations, is the key to sustaining exponential growth over multiple years.

Our discussion of crossing the chasm suggests the market is always evolving, indicating high growth ventures ultimately succeed based not on how far they can push the technology. Rather, they are able to produce bold new innovations that are customer-centric, with ongoing adaptation of their value propositions and marketing approaches.

MANAGERIAL CONSIDERATIONS IN AGGRESSIVE GROWTH VENTURES

Scaling for a high growth venture involves a tenuous balance. On the one hand, the founder(s) are trying to create the kinds of internal systems, structures and controls that will enable rapid growth. The firm finds itself in a race between addressing external demands (from an expanding customer base, suppliers, distributors, regulators, financiers and others) and building internal capacity. On the other hand, they are attempting to maintain a strong entrepreneurial orientation throughout the organization, ensuring the firm remains creative, flexible and adaptable.

Balance implies that the systems and controls that must be put in place to achieve control allow for discretion in people's jobs and permit experimentation in finding solutions to the complex demands of growth. Importantly, they do not come at the expense of employee trust. Further, delegation becomes even more critical than in the managed growth firm, as the strategic challenges facing senior management are increasing in volume, complexity and the speed at which they appear and must be addressed. As the venture starts to grow, the distinction between authority and responsibility becomes more apparent. Authority always can be delegated, but it is also important to create a sense of worker responsibility. Achieving this sense of responsibility and personal ownership in a high stress, chaotic work environment where roles are often fuzzy is a unique managerial test. It requires enlightened leadership with a clear vision and the ability to get employees to believe they are an important part of something bigger than themselves.

Implementing effective human resource management practices becomes a central priority. Proper attention to such issues as recruitment and selection of quality workers, job design, technology in the workplace, performance appraisals, employee compensation (often including a financial stake in the firm) and staff morale is vital, particularly in what is usually a high intensity workplace. The demands placed on workers, and the potential for turmoil, mistakes and burnout, suggest the need to attend to the psychological side of the work environment. The feeling of importance, a sense that the work is meaningful, and a belief that the individual is contributing to the venture's growth can be even more important to employees than salary and working conditions.

The firm is also trying to balance exploration and exploitation. Exploration involves the ongoing recognition and pursuit of new opportunities, development of new technological advances, and creation of new lines of business. Exploitation is concerned with capitalizing upon the opportunities the firm has already pursued, ensuring markets are fully penetrated and the value being created is fully translated into profits. Each requires different kinds of resources and capabilities. High growth ventures tend to be more heavily focused on exploration than exploitation (Colombelli et al., 2013). This can be the firm's eventual undoing, as exploitation is critical for establishing strong and sustainable positions within markets and generating the kinds of returns necessary to continually fuel growth.

All of this suggests that changes must occur in the managerial style of the entrepreneur as the company moves from the start-up phase to take-off. Among all the transitions that take place within the organization, Hofer and Charan (1984, p. 2) note, "probably the most difficult to achieve and perhaps most important for organizational development is that of moving from a one-person, entrepreneurially managed firm to one run by a functionally organized, professional management team." The entrepreneurial skills that were key to getting the venture launched must give way to managerial skills, and many entrepreneurs are unable to make this transition (Bradley et al., 2011).

Steve Jobs of Apple is a good example of an entrepreneur and innovator who had to learn to be a manager. Gallo (2011) shares insights from the lessons learned by Jobs in building a company that was both innovative and profitable. Some of these include:

- *Help people find what they love in their work.* If people do what they love, motivation and performance are never questioned.
- *Put a dent in the universe.* Inspire your workforce to develop a sense of meaning in their performance as it relates to what the firm is trying to accomplish. Develop a sense of purpose in everyone's job.
- *Sell dreams not products.* Everyone wants to work at something significant in this world. Create a dream that is bigger than the entire workforce.
- *Say no to 1000 things.* Remain focused on the simplicity of what can be done. Avoid the temptation to "add on" constantly and keep everyone aimed on the few areas of excellence.

- *Master the message.* Communicate with your employees continuously. Use stories and examples to make them understand the true message you intend for the atmosphere of the venture.

The entrepreneur is able to envision the firm as a larger entity, and anticipate the associated needs for financial resources, people, skills and capabilities, management systems, structures, controls, and more. In the final analysis, while aggressive growth is hard to predict or control, it must be planned for and adroitly managed.

THE DARKER SIDE OF AGGRESSIVE GROWTH

Rapid growth brings with it a host of potential ethical and moral problems. Companies can find themselves over-working employees and making them choose between the company and meeting personal needs and family responsibilities. Extreme cash flow needs can find them making promises to customers that they may not be able to fulfill, paying bribes, and failing to meet financial obligations to suppliers, employees and others. Pressures to meet performance targets can lead firms to take shortcuts that serve to damage the environment, compromise customer and/or employee safety, misuse investor money, and mislead outside parties with inaccurate financial reports.

Recent years have witnessed numerous scandals involving aggressive growth ventures. For example, Lending Club was charged with lying to consumers by promising loans with no hidden fees, when in reality the company deducted hundreds to thousands of dollars in hidden fees from loans. After raising what was, at the time, the largest US tech IPO of $1 billion in 2014, Lending Club's stock price fell dramatically (Griffith, 2016). More recently, Facebook exposed 87 million users' data to improper use by Cambridge Analytica (Harris and Alter, 2018). An even more revealing case involved Theranos, a Silicon Valley pharmaceutical start-up.

Founded in 2003 by Stanford University drop-out Elizabeth Holmes, the company claimed to have invented groundbreaking technology that could run a full range of laboratory tests on just a few drops of blood (Carreyou, 2018). Holmes attracted over $900 million from high-profile investors. By 2014 and after six rounds of funding, Theranos achieved a valuation of over $9 billion (Wattles and Kelley, 2018). Holmes publicly promoted the revolutionary miniLab technology used to complete blood tests on single pricks of blood. In reality, Theranos never used the miniLab for patient testing in its clinical laboratory. Further, the company opened 40 wellness testing centers in Walgreens pharmacies, falsely claiming patient blood tests involved their technology and machine. This resulted in 7.5 million voidable blood test results. In 2015, questions began to arise about the inaccuracy of Theranos' tests, which led to a major investigation. Within two years, the company valuation was lowered to $800 million and Holmes's net worth dropped from $4.5 billion to $0. After facing lawsuits from investors, failing multiple regulatory laboratory inspections, seeing their former partner Walgreens lay off associated staff, and facing criminal charges, Theranos closed their doors. Holmes scaled Theranos quickly to revolutionize blood testing technology and potentially change the world. Instead, she created a whirlwind of scandal by "blitzscaling" the company and allowing her motivated blindness to fog her judgment.

Blitzscaling is an approach to very rapidly expanding a company that entails taking significant risks and incurring shorter-term inefficiencies. The company is making an all-in bet, so it either wins big or loses big (Sullivan, 2016). Key problems are ignored as everything is focused on achieving growth. Ventures such as PayPal, Google, eBay, Facebook, LinkedIn, Twitter and Uber have all utilized blitzscaling to quickly scale their businesses. However, in doing so, they take on far more risk than would be the case with a normal, rational process of scaling. And they incur organizational inefficiencies by quickly bringing on hundreds of new hires while attempting to maintain a quality workforce.

This kind of all-out approach to moving a company to the next order of magnitude in size and scale requires, and very quickly depletes, immense financial resources. If the company does not get to the targeted level of scale, it can fail to attract the additional resources that could then allow it to move to the next level. They may attempt to "fake it until they can make it" in terms of developing a product that delivers as promised. As a result, there can be huge pressures to cut ethical corners and engage in fraudulent behaviors while ramping up, as was the case with Theranos. Not compromising in the face of such pressures requires that the company has strong character, adheres to core values, and devotes attention to the development of an ethical culture.

CONCLUSIONS

While they represent the smallest proportion of entrepreneurial ventures, aggressive growth firms have the most dramatic impact. As a major source of product, service and process innovation, when they succeed, they can revolutionize industries, create new markets and bring greater efficiencies to the value chain. They create most of the new jobs and enhance the competitiveness of economies. Yet, they are the high risk ventures, in some instances generating remarkable returns to founders and investors, and in other cases producing spectacular failures.

These ventures are unique not simply in their quest to rapidly scale, but in the strategic challenges they confront. While they require significant investment, often in multiple stages, their most important resources tend to be more intellectual than physical or financial. What are initially simple must quickly become complex organizations. This means that strong entrepreneurial capabilities must be complemented by professional management skills, and basic business structures must be replaced by sophisticated systems and controls. While this kind of growth can be exhilarating, it also produces work environments that are extremely demanding, stressful and wrought with conflict.

For those involved, the creation of an aggressive growth venture is a very chaotic journey. As we have seen in this chapter, navigating this journey is all about balance. The entrepreneur must learn to strike a balance between exploration and exploitation, between meeting immediate requirements and achieving the longer-term vision, between building systems and controls (internal infrastructure) and maintaining an entrepreneurial orientation, and between technology-push and market-pull considerations. Doing so under the extreme pressures involved in scaling an enterprise makes it essential that these efforts are guided by core values and a strong sense of ethical behavior.

REFERENCES

Birch, D.G. (1987). *Job Creation in America: How Our Smallest Companies Put the Most People To Work*. Urbana, IL: University of Illinois at Urbana-Champaign's Academy for Entrepreneurial Leadership Historical Research Reference in Entrepreneurship.

Birch, D.L., Haggerty, A., and Parsons, W. (1995). *Who's Creating Jobs?* Boston, MA: Cognetics Inc.

Black, G.J. (2018). Unicorn Report. PitchBook Data, PitchBook.com

Bradley, S.W., Wiklund, J., and Shepherd, D.A. (2011). Swinging a double-edged sword: The effect of slack on entrepreneurial management and growth, *Journal of Business Venturing, 26*(6), 537–554.

Calantone, R.J. and Cooper, R.G. (1979). A discriminant model for identifying scenarios of industrial new product failure. *Journal of the Academy of Marketing Science, 7*(3), 163–183.

Carreyou, J. (2018). Blood-testing firm Theranos to dissolve. *Wall Street Journal*. Accessed May 7, 2019 at https://www.wsj.com/articles/blood-testing-firm-theranos-to-dissolve-1536115130.

Colombelli, A., Krafft, J., and Quatraro, F. (2013). High-growth firms and technological knowledge: Do gazelles follow exploration or exploitation strategies? *Industrial and Corporate Change*, *23*(1), 261–291.

Foster, G., Davila, A., Haemmig, M., He, X., and Jia, N. (2011). *Global entrepreneurship and the Successful Growth Strategies of Early-stage Companies: A World Economic Forum Report*. New York: World Economic Forum USA Inc.

Gallo, C. (2011). *The Innovation Secrets of Steve Jobs*. New York: McGraw-Hill.

Griffith, E. (2016). The ugly unethical underside of Silicon Valley. *Fortune*. Accessed March 22, 2019 at http://fortune.com/silicon-valley-startups-fraud-venture-capital/.

Harris, J. and Alter, A. (2018). Insight outlook California dreaming corporate culture Silicon Valley. *Accenture*. Accessed March 22, 2019 at https://www.accenture.com/us-en/insight-outlook-california-dreaming-corporate-culture-silicon-valley#.

Hathaway, I. (2018). High-growth firms and cities in the US: An analysis of the Inc. 5000. February 5. Washington, DC: Brookings Institution.

Henrekson, M. and Johansson, D. (2010). Gazelles as job creators: A survey and interpretation of the evidence. *Small Business Economics*, *35*(2), 227–244.

Hofer, C.W. and Charan, R. (1984). The transition to professional management: Mission impossible? *American Journal of Small Business*, *9*(1), 1–11.

Kuratko, D.F. (2020). *Entrepreneurship: Theory, Process, Practice*, 11th edn. Mason, OH: Cengage Publishers.

Kuratko, D.F., Fisher, G., Bloodgood, J., and Hornsby, J. (2017). The paradox of new venture legitimation within an entrepreneurial ecosystem. *Small Business Economics*, *49*(1), 119–140.

Markman, G.D. and Gartner, W.B. (2002). Is extraordinary growth profitable? A study of *Inc. 500* high-growth companies. *Entrepreneurship Theory and Practice*, *27*(1), 65–75.

Moore, G.A. (1999). *Crossing the Chasm*. New York: HarperBusiness.

Morelix, A. and Russell-Fritch, J. (2017). *Kauffman Index 2017: Growth Entrepreneurship National Trends*. Kansas City: Kauffman Foundation.

Morris, M.H., Miyasaki, N.N., Watters, C.R., and Coombes, S.M. (2006). The dilemma of growth: Understanding venture size choices of women entrepreneurs. *Journal of Small Business Management*, *44*(2), 221–244.

OECD (1998). *Fostering Entrepreneurship*. Paris: OECD Publications.

Rogers, E.M. (1964). *Diffusion of Innovation*. New York: Free Press.

Shane, S. (2009). Why encouraging more people to become entrepreneurs is bad public policy. *Small Business Economics*, *33*(2), 141–149.

Stangler, D. (2010). *High-growth Firms and the Future of the American Economy*. Kansas City: Ewing Marion Kauffman Foundation.

Sullivan, T. (2016). Blitzscaling. *Harvard Business Review*, *94*(4), 15.

Thiel, P. (2014). *Zero to One: Notes on Startups, or How to Build the Future*. New York: Crown Business.

Wattles, J. and Kelley, H. (2018). The rise and fall of Elizabeth Holmes. *CNN Business*. Accessed May 7, 2019 at https://money.cnn.com/2018/06/16/technology/theranos-elizabeth-holmes timeline/index.html.

7. A resource-based perspective on venture types[1]

INTRODUCTION

How can we explain and/or predict the emergence of our four venture types? One way to look at each type is from the vantage point of resources – the types of resources each has, and the manner in which these resources are deployed. Brush and Chaganti (1998) suggest resources in small firms can play a greater role than strategy in explaining how they perform. Resources determine what the entrepreneur is able to create, and what the venture is able to become. They provide the means for experimentation, risk-taking, and development of proactive approaches that enable growth. As such, one of the most significant challenges confronting entrepreneurial ventures is the determination of how resources can best be used to achieve sustainability.

A prominent theory in the business literature argues that resources have particular properties that, when present, can provide competitive advantage (Barney et al., 2001; Wernerfelt, 1984). Termed the resource-based view (RBV), the focus is on the need for firms to assemble resources that have these critical properties. Just as important is how management puts these resources to work, and specifically how they are accumulated, bundled and leveraged by the firm (Sirmon et al., 2007). As we shall see, both the types of resources available and how they are managed will tend to differ significantly across our four types of ventures.

In this chapter we explore the relationships between how resources are configured and managed, the type of venture that is created, and performance outcomes. For the four different venture types we investigate the configuration of the resource portfolio, the properties of these resource configurations, and the bundling and leveraging processes involved when managing resources. Implications are drawn for how each type of venture tends to evolve. We also examine the central role of resources in explaining why the venture created by the entrepreneur often differs from what was intended, and why ventures struggle to transition from one type to another.

101

RESOURCE TYPES AND THEIR PROPERTIES

Resources can be defined as "anything which could be thought of as a strength or weakness of a given firm" (Wernerfelt, 1984, p. 172). They include physical capital (plant and equipment, geographic location, vehicles, raw materials), financial capital (revenues, debt, equity and retained earnings), human capital (training, experience, intelligence, skills), social capital (networks, relationships, shared values, mutual trust) and organizational capital (culture, planning procedures, controlling and coordinating systems) (Barney and Clark, 2007). They can be tangible (e.g., a truck or 3-D printer) or intangible (e.g., intellectual property). Amit and Schoemaker (1993, p. 35) go a step further in distinguishing resources from capabilities, explaining that "resources are stocks of available factors that are owned or controlled by the organization, and capabilities are an organization's capacity to deploy resources."

The resource-based view of the firm (RBV) focuses on the importance of resources and their implications for sustainable competitive advantage and firm performance (Wernerfelt, 1984). Using resource-based logic, a firm has a sustained competitive advantage when it is creating more economic value than other firms in the same industry, and when other firms are incapable of duplicating the benefits of this strategy (Barney and Clark, 2007). The path to achieving an advantage begins by first having resources that are more *heterogeneous*, or that differ (or can be made different) from those of competitors, and more *immobile*, or not readily transferable to competing firms (Barney, 1991). Building upon this foundation, a resource can potentially contribute to *sustainable* competitive advantage based on four additional properties: *valuable (V)*, meaning that it enables the firm to improve its market position vis-à-vis competitors; *rare (R)*, suggesting it is in short supply and not commonly found among actual and potential future competitors; *imperfectly imitable and non-substitutable (I)*, meaning that it is difficult for competitors to copy the resource or substitute an equivalent; and *exploitable by the organization (O)*, meaning there must be organizational processes that allow the firm to adequately capitalize on the resource in achieving sustainable advantage (Barney and Clark, 2007).

Beyond these VRIO properties, we must also consider how resources are managed. Sirmon et al. (2007) proposed a three-stage model for managing resources strategically: (a) structuring the resource portfolio; (b) bundling resources; and (c) leveraging capabilities. Structuring the portfolio refers to the complete collection of all the tangible and intangible resources that are controlled or owned by the firm. Bundling resources involves the firm organizing them in such a way that they can contribute to the recognition and exploitation of opportunities and consequently lead to development of competitive advantages. Finally, after structuring and bundling resources, it is important to examine how the capabilities formed by bundling resources can be leveraged within the firm and externally (Ireland et al., 2003).

RESOURCES AND VENTURE TYPES

Resources represent a unique lens that can help us better understand the functioning of the four types of ventures created by entrepreneurs. Survival, lifestyle, managed growth and aggressive growth ventures are shaped by the resources and resource management capabilities that their founders are able to develop, which in turn will determine the venture's competitive advantage and strategy (Grant, 1991). In essence, resources serve to define the nature of the venture type and its outcomes. This is not only based on the initial mix of resources, but also the range of resources available to the firm once a given business model has taken root.

There is a reciprocal effect between the resources available and the type of venture created, such that the resources the entrepreneur knows of and can access determine what sort of venture is created, while the type of venture created in turn limits the kind of resources that are available. On the one hand, the resource portfolio is limited by the circumstances and background of the entrepreneur, impacting the type of venture that results. This is especially the case for intangible resources (Brush et al., 2001). On the other hand, characteristics of the venture, such as its proprietary knowledge, employee base, product mix, profit margins and growth potential, delimit the kinds of resources the venture is able to attract. Further, the interplay among venture type, resources and the entrepreneur's agency, goals and aspired outcomes will influence venture development over time.

To further understand these relationships, let us now consider four different factors as they apply to each of the venture types: (a) the configuration of the firm's resource portfolio; (b) the VRIO attributes of the resource configuration; (c) the bundling processes involved with resources; and (d) the leveraging processes applied to resources.

The Resource Portfolio of Entrepreneurial Ventures

The configuration of a venture's resource portfolio includes the acquisition, accumulation and elimination of resources. Each venture type will have a unique resource portfolio, which in turn defines its business model and operational capabilities, and affects the evolution of the venture and its performance over time. To describe the configuration of these resource portfolios, we sort resources (both tangible and intangible) into the five categories mentioned earlier: physical capital, financial capital, human capital, organizational capital and social capital. Table 7.1 characterizes resource portfolios for the four types of ventures.

Survival ventures
These ventures often have no physical location, sometimes operating from the entrepreneur's home, a stall or public market. They are characterized by lack of employees, little to no use of technology, absence of machinery, and limited access to supplies and raw materials. Financial resources include limited personal savings and any generated revenues which are intended principally for the owner's subsistence. Feedback primarily comes from the local marketplace, while the entrepreneur has little in the way of professional development opportunities. The organizational resources of survival ventures are characterized by daily planning, defining day-to-day procedures, and simple control and coordination systems. The social resources of survival ventures are tied to the small personal network of the entrepreneur, suggesting little social capital.

Lifestyle ventures
These ventures typically operate from their own premises, usually limited to one or two locations in the same geographic area. They have access to basic technology and raw materials, and own or lease basic equipment, machinery and furnishings. They are able to attract some debt financing based on personal guarantees, while building a small amount of equity in the business over time. Human resources in lifestyle ventures are organized in a simple horizontal structure, requiring medium to high labor intensity, some technical know-how and job-related skills. In addition to market feedback, the venture creates basic internal controls with an emphasis on cost savings and efficiency. Social resources of lifestyle ventures center on extended families together with local business and personal networks. They have limited social capital, and a few local inter-firm relationships, with some linkages established with similar businesses in the same geographic area.

Table 7.1 Characterizing the resource portfolios of venture types

		Survival Venture	Lifestyle Venture	Managed Growth Venture	Aggressive Growth Venture
Tangible assets					
Physical technology, the firm's plant and equipment, geographic location, access to raw materials, machinery	Physical resources	Single geographic location or home-based No technology Limited access to raw materials Absence of equipment	One or two locations Simple technology Uneconomical procurement Basic, functional equipment and machinery	Steady expansion of facilities Moderately sophisticated technology & equipment Quality materials in economic quantities	High tech State of art facilities Sophisticated machinery Knowledge-based equipment Considerable outsourcing
Revenues, debt, equity and retained earnings	Financial resources	Minimal revenues – just enough to generate subsistence No business bank credit No retained earnings	Stable revenues Some bank loans, credit Low retained earnings Owner(s) control equity	Growing revenues Some outside equity Bank loan availability Moderate retained earnings	Exponential revenue growth High outside equity Large capital gains Ample debt facilities available High retained earnings

Table 7.1 (continued)

		Survival Venture	Lifestyle Venture	Managed Growth Venture	Aggressive Growth Venture
Intangible assets					
Training, experience, judgment, intelligence, relationships between managers and workers, technical know-how	Human resources	Few if any employees Informal structure High labor intensity Lack of technical know-how Exchange based relationships Lack of feedback	Simple HR structure Medium labor intensity Lower technical know-how Basic employee training Supervisory relationship Personal relationship with employees	Professional HR structure Lower labor intensity Higher technical know-how Moderate training levels Focus on individual and team development	Online HR platform Lowest labor intensity Highest technical know-how Strong innovation capacity Individual and team development Continuous training/improvement Participatory management
Firm's culture, planning procedures, controlling and coordinating systems, reputation inside and outside the firm, brand names, in house technology knowledge, efficient procedures	Organizational resources	Day-to-day planning Day-to-day procedures Informal controls and hands-on coordination by entrepreneur Personal reputation Little documentation	Maintenance planning Standardized operating procedures Simple controls Simple process technology Culture built on stability and consistency Local reputation	Strategic planning Building infrastructure to support steady growth Professional control & coordination systems Regional reputation Strong company culture Strong regional brand	Planning for scalability Expanding infrastructure for rapid growth Rapid learning Innovation-driven Proactive and creativity-based culture Strong national/global brand
Relationships among individuals within the organization (internal); and between those within the firm and external parties	Social resources	Personal social network Lack of social capital Centers on family, friends, past customers	Local social network Limited social capital Few local inter-firm relations Social ties with local client base, suppliers, involvement in community activities	Solid regional social network Considerable social capital Solid intra-firm relations Moderate level of local and regional inter-firm relations	Scalable social network Strong and rich sources of social capital Strong intra-firm relations Extensive global inter-firm relations
Summary characteristics of the configuration of resources		**Formative simple & formative utilitarian**	**Robust simple & robust utilitarian**	**Formative complex & formative instrumental**	**Robust complex & robust instrumental**

Managed growth ventures

These ventures are characterized by multiple locations or operations that expand across one or more larger regions. They have a growing pool of physical resources that can enable a steady expansion of facilities and employees, moderately sophisticated technology and equipment, and an expanding infrastructure to support steady growth. The entrepreneur may be able to attract some external equity investment together with commercial debt, and healthy retained earnings are regularly used to support growth and expansion. Human resources demonstrate flexibility as they are organized around a functional and centralized structure, with lower labor intensity and higher technical know-how and expert knowledge. In addition to engaging in sound financial and strategic planning, the organization builds effective internal systems and processes, including control measures that ensure both efficiency and effectiveness by providing feedback across a range of performance-related variables. The organization is able to leverage relationships with a diverse network of individuals and organizations, both private and public. A rich pool of social capital is regularly enhanced as the organization interacts with local and regional companies, creates jobs, contributes to local economic development, and reinvests in its local community.

Aggressive growth ventures

These ventures are characterized by extensive knowledge-based assets including patents, strong innovation capacity and incorporation of leading-edge technologies. While less concerned with owning physical assets, they are able to access a wide variety of physical and other resources through outsourcing, leveraging and strategic alliances. As such, they have access to extensive equipment and facilities. Based on an innovative, rapid growth business model, these ventures demonstrate high potential for large equity investments from angels, venture capitalists and institutional investors, and also can attract significant debt capital. The organization has an evolving organic structure that develops according to product and market needs. Workers typically demonstrate high technical know-how, sophisticated knowledge and strong innovation capacity. There is low labor intensity due to automatization. Process innovation is ongoing as the organization continually develops new systems and controls to address needs associated with the rapidly expanding scale and scope of operations. Aggressive growth ventures have a scalable social network, with a strong and rich pool of social capital, and strong global inter- and intra-firm relations.

Taken a step further, the resource development pathway proposed by Brush et al. (2001) allows us to capture the resources of each venture type along two axes: complexity and productive application. In terms of complexity, each resource type ranges on a scale from simple to complex, where simple resources are characterized as tangible, discrete and property-based; and complex resources are intangible, systemic and knowledge-based. In terms of their application to productive processes, resources range on a scale from utilitarian to instrumental. Utilitarian resources refer to direct applications of productive processes or combinations used to develop other resources, while instrumental resources provide access to other resources.

These two dimensions can be further distinguished based on whether they are formative or robust. Formative refers to very rudimentary resources necessary to accomplish the basic work or functions of the enterprise, while robust resources have more power or capability in terms of the number and/or types of tasks they can accomplish, and are consistent with the notion of resource versatility (Nason and Wiklund, 2018). Combining the simple versus complex and utilitarian versus instrumental axes with the formative/robust distinction, we can distinguish the four types of entrepreneurial ventures (Figure 7.1).

Specifically, based on the kinds of resources each type of venture tends to have, we suggest:

- Survival ventures will be predominately characterized by simple and utilitarian-formative resources, as they primarily have tangible, rudimentary resources used in providing basic goods and services.
- Lifestyle ventures can be described in terms of simple and utilitarian-robust resources, as they employ predominantly tangible and discrete resources which can be more formative or more robust: for example, a hot plate used by a small restaurant (a simple resource) can be more rudimentary (only allowing for a few hotdogs to be prepared at a time, and not allowing for changes in the temperature of the cooking process); while a roller grill for hotdogs (the same type of simple resource) can be more robust (as it permits cooking 85 hotdogs at a time, allows for different temperatures if needed, and is more efficient from an energy standpoint).
- Managed growth ventures will have complex and instrumental-formative resources, as this type of venture has more in the way of intangible and knowledge-based resources which are potentially able to generate additional resources.

- Aggressive growth ventures are organized around complex and instrumental-robust resources, as their key resources are intangible, systematic, and utilized as a platform to engender other resources in a timely and productive way. Complex and instrumental resources can be more formative or robust. For example, an innovation planning system (a complex resource) can be fairly rudimentary (targeting a specific department of the organization, having strict guidelines, and employing specific predefined problem-solving scenarios); or it can be more robust (where it can be applied to all departments of the organization, encourages trial and error, provides feedback and encourages discussion, and targets the multiple aspects and domains of venture).

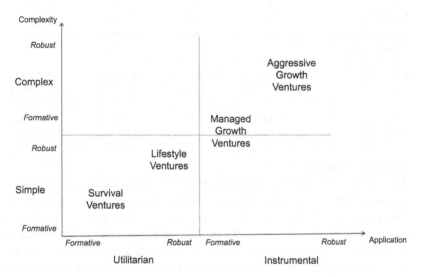

Figure 7.1   Characterizing the resource portfolios of different venture types

VRIO and the Four Types of Ventures

Going a step further, we can characterize the resources of each venture type based first on how heterogeneous and immobile they are, and then on their VRIO properties. Table 7.2 provides a summary.

Table 7.2   VRIO framework applied to resource portfolios of venture types

	Survival Venture	Lifestyle Venture	Managed Growth Venture	Aggressive Growth Venture
Firm resource heterogeneity	No	————————————————→		Yes
Firm resource immobility	No			Yes
Valuable?	No	Yes	Yes	Yes
Rare?	No	No	Yes	Yes
Inimitable?	No	No	Yes	Yes
Exploited by the organization?	No	No	No	Yes
Competitive implication	Competitive disadvantage	Competitive parity	Temporary competitive advantage	Sustained competitive advantage
Economic performance	Below normal	Normal	Above normal	Far above normal

Survival ventures

The resource portfolio is mostly comprised of homogeneous resources, meaning that its resources are equivalent to those of other similar firms. The resources of survival ventures are easily moved across competitors, and thus are mobile in the short run. The simple and utilitarian-formative resources of these businesses exhibit very limited value and rareness, are easily imitable and the organization may be constrained in how well it can exploit these resources. Consequently, the resources configuration portfolio of survival ventures constitutes a competitive disadvantage for the firm, resulting in poor economic performance.

Lifestyle ventures

The resource portfolio reflects a relatively small degree of heterogeneity. Most of the resources are fairly easy to replicate and implement by competitors, and so they tend to be mobile. Lifestyle ventures seek to develop sufficient resource capability to permit maintenance of the business. For instance, with a local restaurant, resources are characterized by the potential ability to provide marginal value (e.g., their family cooking style) that enables them to remain competitive (finding ways to conserve on costs or nominally improve revenues) but gives them no real sustainable advantage (Barney and Arikan, 2001). Commonly operating in highly competitive environments, their resources have a modicum of rareness, and this generally can be imitated or substituted for, while the organization is constrained in its abilities to exploit its fairly fixed pool of resources in new or different ways. The result is competitive parity of lifestyle ventures, often producing steady but modest economic performance.

Managed growth ventures

The resource portfolio consists of a rich combination of homogeneous and potentially heterogeneous resources, and both mobile and immobile resources. For instance, a chain of emergency medical clinics with 35 locations across a region may have a number of physical, human, financial and social resources that are fairly generic and readily available to competitors, while also developing unique operating systems, technical skills sets and financial capacity that cannot be easily traded in markets and are more difficult to accumulate and imitate by competitors. Managed growth firms are able to develop portfolios that include resources that are valuable, rare and inimitable, which contribute to the competitive advantage of the firm within local and regional markets. The inimitability of the resources is the distinctive attribute of the managed growth firm's resource portfolio, meaning the firm has critical resources that are costly for local rivals to imitate or substitute. At the same time, the venture may be vulnerable to entry into its markets by larger outside players who can imitate key advantages. The organization is not exploiting the full competitive potential of its resource portfolio and capabilities, and its organizational processes, procedures and policies are constraining potential competitive advantage. This resource configuration pattern contributes to above average economic performance and steady growth.

Aggressive growth ventures

The resource portfolio is characterized as being completely heterogeneous and immobile, reflecting the uniqueness and specificity of those resources. There are clear barriers limiting the abilities of other firms to acquire or internally develop similar resources. These knowledge-based resources are not mobile, transferable or tradable across firms. The aggressive growth resource portfolio allows for the exploitation of its valuable, rare and costly to imitate resources. To the extent that the four attributes of resources are realized by the aggressive growth firm, this type of venture has significant potential to create a sustainable competitive advantage and above normal economic performance. Sustainable competitive advantage is defined as the point when the firm "is creating more economic value than the marginal firm in its industry and when other firms are unable to duplicate the benefits of this strategy" (Barney and Clark, 2007, p. 52).

Bundling Processes of Entrepreneurial Ventures

The resource portfolio of a given venture type is the basis for developing the firm's unique capabilities. Capabilities require the organization of resources in such a way that they can contribute to the recognition of opportunities, serve as an essential vehicle for creating value, lead to the development of competitive advantages, and result in superior performance. This is the purpose of resource bundling (Ireland et al., 2003).

Bundling comprises three different processes: stabilizing, enriching and pioneering (Sirmon et al., 2007). Stabilizing is typical for firms competing in environments with low uncertainty, and involves maintaining current capabilities, or making minor incremental improvements such as updating specific areas of knowledge and skills, to maintain an existing competitive advantage. Enriching is associated with firms that want to acquire new advantages using capability extension, and aims to expand and improve an existing capability as a meaningful improvement based on adding a new specific knowledge or skill set. Finally, pioneering is defined as the integration of new and unique resources that, via exploratory learning and experimentation, can stimulate the creation of novel and unique capabilities. Pioneering adds a new disruptive resource to the firm's configuration portfolio, contributes to value creation, is mostly manifested in firms operating in high uncertainty and dynamic environments, and aims to gain and maintain a sustainable competitive advantage over time (Sirmon et al., 2007). We can see different patterns in terms of the use of these three resource bundling processes based on the type of venture in question (Figure 7.2).

Survival ventures

Capabilities tend to center on the core task or work of the entrepreneur (e.g., plumbing, painting, making simple craft products). Many basic business capabilities (e.g., bookkeeping, marketing) may be non-existent or severely under-developed, reflecting a lack of resources and inefficiency. These realities undermine the ability to add value for customers, with the focus instead on providing a subsistence income for the owner. Absent any real competitive advantage, little to no bundling occurs.

Lifestyle ventures

The characteristics and resource portfolios of lifestyle firms are reflective of ventures operating in an environment with lower uncertainty, with maintenance and stability objectives, competing in a fairly stable market, where slight updates of certain critical resources are sufficient for the venture to continue operating. For example, this type of venture may require minimal training to learn how to operate a new software system or meet a new regulatory requirement from the local government. Thus, the stabilizing bundling processes are typical for lifestyle ventures.

Managed growth ventures

Their characteristics and resource portfolios have specific capabilities that require updating and extension across time. Achieving steady growth, wealth creation, and ongoing differentiation of products or services requires some expansion of current capabilities, and goes beyond mere updating of skills. These firms will add new products and services, enter new markets, and integrate new technologies into their operations. Thus, managed growth ventures primarily adopt enriching bundling resource processes.

Aggressive growth ventures

These ventures operate in highly uncertain and extremely dynamic environments. There is a need for significant and continuous improvement, ongoing learning, and the organization is regularly involved in exploration processes. It is of utmost importance that firm capabilities which are quite valuable, rare, imperfectly imitable, and non-substitutable receive ongoing enhancements. The focus on scalability and fast growth requires the intensive integration of new resources to the configuration portfolio, and extensive experimentation and learning to continually develop novel capabilities. Thus, aggressive growth ventures typically will use the pioneering bundling resource strategy.

Overall, meaningful differences in approaches to resource bundling among the venture types have important implications for their resource management processes. Despite the fact that different resource bundling processes are relevant for each venture type, the most efficient process of bundling capabilities is one that can lead to leveraging and consequently to the exploitation of opportunities and development of competitive advantages.

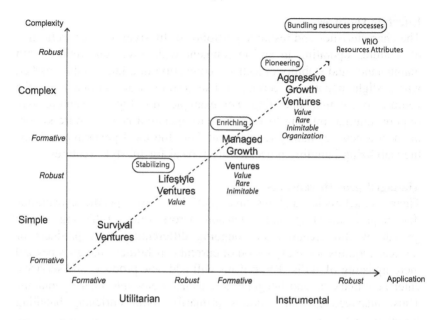

Figure 7.2   The resource portfolio, resource attributes and bundling processes for entrepreneurial ventures

Leveraging Processes of Entrepreneurial Firms

Subsequent to the bundling stage, firms have to leverage their bundled capabilities, or try to use them to create customer value and owner wealth (Ireland et al., 2003). Leveraging is concerned with matching internal capabilities to external market conditions. Leveraging processes include three serial and complementary stages: mobilizing, coordinating and deploying. Mobilizing entails the identification of capabilities needed to support capability configurations that create value and wealth; coordinating refers to the integration of the mobilized capabilities into effective capability configurations; and deploying comprises the actual use of the capability configurations to make the leveraging strategy work. Both coordinating and deploying are part of the implementation of a leveraging strategy (Sirmon et al., 2007).

There are three main leveraging strategies: resource advantage, market opportunity and entrepreneurial opportunity (Sirmon et al., 2007). The resource advantage strategy aims to leverage existing capability configurations in order to generate a distinctive competence. For example, a managed growth venture can mobilize a specific capability configuration in marketing by hiring specialized talent to gain an advantage in a niche market. The resource advantage strategy aims to narrow the gap and establish a fit between the competencies of the firm and the target market in order to gain a competitive advantage. The market opportunity strategy seeks to capitalize on new opportunities for which the firm already has capabilities, but these capabilities must be reconfigured. For example, a managed growth venture might identify an opportunity in an adjacent market, and seeks to reconfigure its logistics capabilities to address this opening. The capability configuration may first require bundling resources in order to create the configuration required to exploit the new opportunity. The entrepreneurial opportunity strategy entails developing capability con-figurations to create new opportunities, such as new product/services that can be exploited in new markets. This type of leveraging strategy usually requires a configuration of innovation-related capabilities. Hence, an aggressive growth venture in the healthcare sector can mobilize and coordinate its R&D and marketing capabilities to create a breakthrough pharmaceutical product addressing a need within an unserved market.

Researchers generally argue for a contingency perspective, suggesting firms might use all of these strategies at different points in their evolution and depending on external conditions (e.g., Sirmon et al., 2007). Yet, we believe the pattern in leveraging processes will vary across the four types of ventures (Figure 7.3).

With survival ventures, there may well be a dearth of strategy. Their severely limited resource pool and lack of bundling processes find them operating in a more reactive mode, where no formal strategies are formulated. Lifestyle ventures, with their focus on the status quo and maintenance of a working business model, will emphasize resource advantage strategies. While their resources may have limited value, they strive to capitalize on resource configurations that give them a better fit with local market needs, enabling them to remain competitive. Alter-natively, with their focus on resource advantage, they struggle to respond to any sort of disruptive change in their markets. Managed growth firms will similarly employ resource advantage strategies to remain competitive and create value in existing markets. However, they will also capitalize on new and emerging opportunities that are typically related to the products/services and markets where they currently operate. They will periodically employ market opportunity strategies that support their planned or controlled growth aspirations. With aggressive growth ven-tures, as the environmental context moderates the relation between leveraging strategies and their outcomes over time, they are incentivized to adopt all three leveraging strategies. Yet, stakeholder expectations and resource investments (most notably a configuration of R&D, engineering, marketing and financial capabilities) find the firm pressured to adopt entrepreneurial strategies that result in the creation of new products and markets.

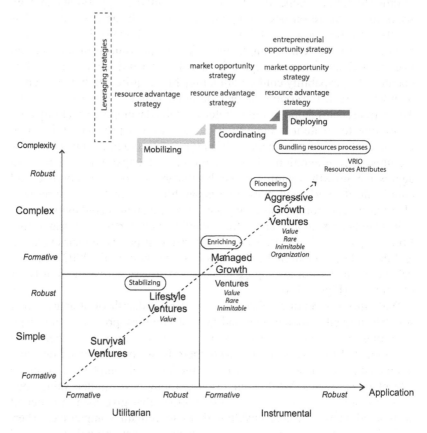

Figure 7.3   The resource portfolio, resource attributes, bundling processes and leveraging processes for entrepreneurial ventures

RESOURCE DYNAMICS, MAINTAINING ADVANTAGE AND THE STABILITY OF TYPES

From an RBV perspective, every decision within an organization is a resource decision, with potential implications for the properties of the firm's resource portfolio at a point in time. Yet the VRIO properties change as (a) particular resources age, depreciate, are discarded or lost; (b) new resources are acquired; (c) resources are unbundled or re-bundled in new ways; (d) leveraging strategies are modified or new ones introduced; and (e) external developments occur, particularly when strategic industry factors (e.g., new competitor entry, economic downturn, new industry regulation, natural disaster) impact the firm. The ability to adjust, adapt and innovate as conditions change becomes the key to maintaining and enhancing VRIO properties over time.

Let us consider how these dynamics can differ across the four venture types. In a survival venture, with simple and utilitarian-formative resources, the dynamics principally result in allocating efforts to maintain existing resources as long as possible, and saving to replace these resources as they become depleted or lost, while struggling to acquire any new types of resources. Lack of valuable, rare or inimitable resources, with little ability to bundle or pursue effective leveraging strategies, finds the firm marginalized on an ongoing basis. It is unable to meaningfully differentiate itself, forced to compete on a price basis, able to generate enough returns to pay bills but unable to get ahead, and extremely vulnerable to external developments.

With lifestyle ventures, the deployment of simple and utilitarian-robust resources enables the firm to create value in local market niches and generate relatively small but steady rents. Lack of rare or inimitable resources finds firms tending to imitate the moves of one another. The rents generated afford a lifestyle for the entrepreneur and his or her family. Stability resource bundling and resource advantage leveraging strategies are deployed as these rents are also used to periodically enhance facilities and equipment and introduce new products or services for purposes of maintaining the current market position. Where, despite low barriers, fewer competitors are present, the venture can sustain itself for long periods of time.

The complex and instrumental-formative resources of the managed growth venture produce valuable, rare and inimitable properties. However, limits on the organization's potential for exploitation constrain its growth horizon. The result is steady growth over time as the organization opens new locations, expands its geographic scope, and goes after new markets. Here, new resources are continually added, requiring enriching bundling processes that extend current capabilities. Meanwhile, leveraging strategies provide the firm with a superior market fit and hence advantage over competing firms, but also enable exploitation of new opportunities by reconfiguring existing capabilities. The abilities to continuously leverage intangible resources while enhancing efficiencies in key administrative functions are critical for sustained performance in local and regional markets.

For aggressive growth ventures, complex and instrumental-robust resources result in major product and process innovation that is often disruptive in the marketplace. Resource strategies initially emphasize experimentation as the firm strives to identify optimal methods of creating and capturing value from their innovation(s). Sustaining advantage requires that resources be significantly reconfigured as the firm initially reaches early adopters but then seeks to penetrate mainstream markets (Moore, 2006). They must be deployed in ways that enable rapid scaling and continued advancement of the underlying technology, both of which require considerable ongoing investment. Timing is vital, as these innovations can be introduced before the market is ready for them, and bundling and resourcing efforts are unable to accelerate market readiness.

In considering these dynamics, the question arises as to whether ventures tend to evolve from one type to another (e.g., from lifestyle to managed growth). Resources are fundamental in establishing the venture at the outset, and their characteristics and attributes define the venture type, while simultaneously constituting an endemic constraint on the ongoing development of the venture, and delimiting the resource horizon of which the entrepreneur becomes aware and is able to exploit. Resource acceleration, or the rate at which entrepreneurs grow their resource base (Morris et al., 2010), is lowest within survival ventures and highest for aggressive growth ventures. Survival and lifestyle ventures have, a priori, a more constrained resource portfolio than managed and aggressive growth ventures, and thus the probability of expanding their resource base over time is also reduced when compared to high growth ventures. Thus, quality and quantity of the resource portfolio of a venture impact, at launch and over time, the pace and level of evolution of that venture.

As such, resource portfolios, their VRIO characteristics, and approaches to resource bundling and leveraging largely ensure that the venture types remain relatively discrete and independent forms. That is, a survival venture most typically remains a survival venture, it is rare that a lifestyle venture becomes a managed growth venture, and few managed growth ventures ever evolve to the point where they achieve aggressive growth (Webb et al., 2013). Conceptually, the distance to be traveled in moving from one type of venture to another gets greater as we move from survival to lifestyle, managed growth and then aggressive growth. Alternatively, while one can imagine a circumstance where a lifestyle venture declines to the point that it is really more of a survival venture, in general we believe a given venture thrives or fails as a particular type.

Consistent with this argument, as we shall see in Chapter 8, each type of venture tends to form a unique organizational identity.

This is not to say that firms cannot transition from one type to another, only that it is more the exception than the rule. For instance, the disciplined survival entrepreneur who manages sustained savings over a long period of time, experiences an unexpected windfall gain, or benefits from some other fortuitous environmental development, may be able to acquire or develop resources that are valuable. The entrepreneur may learn to exploit this resource, adopt stabilizing bundling processes, and maintain a working business model which emphasizes resource advantage strategies.

DIFFERENCES IN PERFORMANCE OUTCOMES

Based on our discussion up to this point, the respective resource configurations and resource management capabilities of the four venture types suggest that the performance potential increases as one moves from survival to lifestyle to managed growth and then aggressive growth. This potential is not realized by all firms within a given category, as some fail to recognize and/or access the appropriate resource bundle, or they do not develop the capabilities necessary to capitalize on VRIO attributes (Morrow et al., 2007). Even among high growth ventures, then, growth may not translate into above average rents or sustainable advantage. Hence, there will be wide performance fluctuations not only across the four venture types, but within each of these venture categories.

This also suggests that survival and lifestyle ventures will be at a competitive disadvantage relative to managed growth and aggressive growth ventures. Yet, when one type (e.g., a lifestyle venture such as a local taxi company) finds itself competing with another type (e.g., an aggressive growth venture such as Uber or Lyft), it is possible for the former to survive in spite of its relative disadvantage. In this example, the lifestyle venture will likely fail if it seeks to compete directly with, or on the same terms as, the aggressive growth venture. Rather, the lifestyle firm must focus on its available resources and how they can be bundled and leveraged to capitalize on narrow niches that the aggressive growth firm finds less attractive (or a weaker fit with its business model), or that represent momentary or shorter-term opportunities.

While they do not achieve the superior rents associated with sustainable competitive advantage, survival and lifestyle firms can generate income and survive indefinitely. Their abilities to do so are tied to differences in goals, what they personally require from the venture, kinds of assets that are key to their operations, and lower cash flow and financial resource requirements, as they are not investing in growth and intangible assets for future competitiveness. They compete in local markets, operating in small market niches where they may be able to achieve a momentary advantage (e.g., due to location, timing or lack of direct competition). Again, the ventures that outperform others within their same category over time are able to do so based on their abilities to pursue appropriate resources and realize the potential of the resources they are able to marshal.

CONCLUSION

The chapter provides a theoretical frame for better understanding the four venture types. We emphasize how different aspects of resources define the type of venture that will emerge from the entrepreneurial process, and how the venture contributes to economic development. It establishes the central functions of the entrepreneur as assembler, configurer, bundler and leverager of resources. Each venture type is defined by its resource portfolio and the associated properties of these resources, as well as how they are bundled and leveraged by the organization. Ultimately, resources and how they are managed determine what the venture can become and what it is not capable of becoming.

NOTE

1. Elements of this chapter were contributed by Susana Santos, Assistant Professor of Entrepreneurship, Rowan University, Glassboro, New Jersey.

REFERENCES

Amit, R. and Schoemaker, P.J. (1993). Strategic assets and organizational rent. *Strategic Management Journal, 14*(1), 33–46.
Barney, J.B. (1991). Firm resources and sustained competitive advantage. *Journal of Management, 17*, 99–120.
Barney, J.B. and Arikan, A. (2001). The resource-based view: Origins and implications. In M.A. Hitt, R. Freeman, and J. Harrison (eds), *Handbook of Strategic Management*. Oxford: Blackwell Publishers, pp. 124–185.
Barney, J.B. and Clark, D. (2007). *Resource-based Theory: Creating and Sustaining Competitive Advantage*. New York: Oxford University Press.
Barney, J.B., Wright, M., and Ketchen, D.J. (2001). The resource-based view of the firm: Ten years after 1991. *Journal of Management, 27*(6), 625–641.

Brush, C. and Chaganti, R. (1998). Business without glamour? An analysis of resources of performance by size and age in small service and retail firms. *Journal of Business Venturing*, *14*, 233–257.

Brush, C., Greene, P., Hart, M., and Haller, H. (2001). From initial idea to unique advantage: The entrepreneurial challenge of constructing a resource base. *Academy of Management Executive*, *15*(1), 64–80.

Grant, R. (1991). The resource-based theory of competitive advantage: Implications for strategy formulation. *California Management Review*, *33*(3), 114–135.

Ireland, R.D., Hitt, M.A., and Sirmon, D. (2003). A model of strategic entrepreneurship: The construct and its dimensions. *Journal of Management*, *29*(6), 963–989.

Moore, G.A. (2006). *Crossing the Chasm*. New York: Collins Business.

Morris, M.H., Kuratko, D.F., Allen, J., Ireland, R.D., and Schindehutte, M. (2010). Resource acceleration: Extending resource-based theory in entrepreneurial ventures. *Journal of Applied Management and Entrepreneurship*, *15*(2), 4–25.

Morrow, J., Sirmon, D., Hitt, M., and Holcomb, T. (2007). Creating value in the face of declining performance: Firm strategies and organizational recovery. *Strategic Management Journal*, *28*, 271–283.

Nason, R.S. and Wiklund, J. (2018). An assessment of resource-based theorizing on firm growth and suggestions for the future. *Journal of Management*, *44*(1), 32–60.

Schoemaker, P. (1990). Strategy, complexity and economic rent. *Management Science*, *36*, 1178–1192.

Sirmon, D., Hitt, M., and Ireland, R.D. (2007). Managing firm resources in dynamic environments to create value. *Academy of Management Review*, *32*(1), 273–292.

Webb, J., Morris, M.H., and Pillay, R. (2013). Microenterprise growth at the base of the pyramid: A resource-based perspective. *Journal of Developmental Entrepreneurship*, *18*(4), 743–758.

Wernerfelt, B. (1984). A resource-based view of the firm. *Strategic Management Journal*, *5*(2), 171–180.

8. How ventures develop unique identities

INTRODUCTION

People tend to develop identities that reflect how they see themselves at a fundamental or core level, such as being a hard worker, patriotic citizen or loving mother (Stryker, 1987; Stryker and Serpe, 1994). Identities also emerge at the organizational level. Based on their interactions over time, the people that make up an organization come to develop a set of beliefs regarding what is central, distinctive and enduring about a business (Albert and Whetten, 1985). Hence, those within an organization may see the business as one that cares about its employees, is conservative with resources, or is closely connected to the community.

These identities can serve to distinguish individuals or organizations from one another. They can also serve to establish commonalities among those having shared identities. Further, when a salient identity is activated, it can motivate behavior (Callero, 1985; Carter, 2013; Stryker and Serpe, 1994). In the case of an entrepreneur, identity is activated when he or she perceives meaning in a social situation that matches the meaning of the identity. Identities can also serve as a control mechanism, as there is a tendency to seek situations where there is congruence between identity meanings and how the individual or organization appears to others (Burke, 1991) and to attempt to have the enactment of the identity verified by others (Carter, 2013).

In this chapter we explore the role played by identity in our four venture types. Attention is first devoted to the entrepreneurial identity of the founder, and how this might influence the tendency to develop a survival, lifestyle, managed growth or aggressive growth venture. We also consider the likelihood that this is a two-way relationship, with outcomes from each venture type serving to affect the founder's identity. We then move to the concept of organizational identity. It is argued that a number of the underlying characteristics that define the venture types are key determinants of the kind of organizational identity that emerges. We conclude that firms of a given type will tend to develop a shared identity. In addition, because these identities become central to the existence of each type, and yet are sufficiently distinct from one another, we examine how they become an obstacle to the venture evolving into a different type. Finally, the importance of identity in establishing and maintaining the legitimacy of each type of venture is examined.

IDENTITY AND THE ENTREPRENEUR

An identity refers to the stable qualities, beliefs, personality, appearances and/or expressions that define a person, group or organization. It provides a sense of uniqueness and continuity, effectively positioning an entity relative to others (Carter, 2013; Whetten, 2006). It is established and reinforced over time as positive and negative events are experienced, choices are made, various others are interacted with, and things are accomplished.

Our interest is the identity of the founder of a new venture, and the identity that emerges for the venture itself. These two are likely inter-related, especially in the early stages of a business. As Schein (1974) notes, the person and his or her identity are strong determinants of the venture that is being created. Hence, in their work on accidental entrepreneurs, Shah and Tripsas (2007) demonstrate how self-identity affects subsequent firm strategies and growth trajectories. However, Schein also suggests that what is created can influence the founder's identity (see also Stryker, 1987). This likelihood is consistent with Downing's (2005) social narrative work in which he described the co-emergence of individual and collective identities in entrepreneurial ventures.

For entrepreneurs, like everyone else, there are multiple components of their self-identities. Examples could include a salient identity as a mother or father, religious person, amateur musician, member of a particular ethnic group or military veteran. One's profession (e.g., teacher, police officer, nurse, accountant) is often a factor in identity formation. In this regard, multiple aspects of the entrepreneur's role would seem to be salient influences on self-identity, including a strong degree of individualism and self-reliance, high levels of uncertainty and engagement levels, major stress, and the potential for personal and business failure. Moreover, different meanings might be associated with entrepreneurial behavior based on organizational outcomes over time, such as seeing oneself as a job creator, innovator, builder, contributor to the community, winner in the competitive marketplace and/or successful risk-taker (Down and Reveley, 2004; Morris et al., 2006; Murnieks et al., 2012).

Hoang and Gimeno (2005) distinguish four dimensions of entrepreneurial identity: identity attributes (i.e., personal traits associated with the role, such as being a risk-taker), identity content (i.e., the tasks of the entrepreneur, such as opportunity discovery or organization building), how the individual regards the role of the entrepreneur (i.e., positive or negative assessments) and identity centrality (i.e., the importance of an entrepreneurial identity relative to other identities constituting the individual's self-concept) (Hoang and Gimeno, 2005). These dimensions are interacting as individuals experience the venture and engage in social interactions, resulting in updates to and refinements of their entrepreneurial identity.

It would seem that the type of venture created by the entrepreneur might also influence self-identity (Figure 8.1). As entrepreneurial identity emerges, it tends to affect information processing, learning and behavioral choices. The kinds of events and experiences being processed by the individual, and how they are processed, and the learning they produce vary significantly depending on venture context (Morris et al., 2012). Both the volatility of novel and disruptive events and the frequency or pace at which they are encountered are likely to be greater in an aggressive growth venture compared to a lifestyle venture. As a result, particular attributes and content associated with entrepreneurial identity, such as the levels of ambiguity, uncertainty and stress experienced, or the extent to which significant risks are being taken or new opportunities are pursued, may be more present in the high growth context (see Vesala et al., 2007).

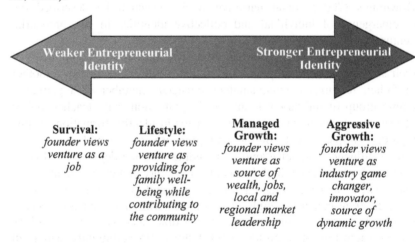

Survival:	Lifestyle:	Managed Growth:	Aggressive Growth:
founder views venture as a job	*founder views venture as providing for family well-being while contributing to the community*	*founder views venture as source of wealth, jobs, local and regional market leadership*	*founder views venture as industry game changer, innovator, source of dynamic growth*

Figure 8.1   Entrepreneurial identity and the four types of ventures

Entrepreneurial identity is also linked to entrepreneurial motivation and goal setting (Carland et al., 1984). The strength and stability of the entrepreneurial identity will determine the strength and stability of the motivational pull toward identity-congruent action and goal setting (Carsrud and Brännback, 2011; Oyserman, 2009). For example, a "survival" entrepreneur will have different motives and will formulate different performance goals than a founder of an aggressive growth venture. His or her entrepreneurial identity state can therefore reinforce his or her general (e.g., need for achievement, locus of control, vision, passion and so on) as well as task-specific (e.g., goal setting and self-efficacy) motivation (Baum et al., 2001; Locke and Lathan, 2002; Shane et al., 2003). Further, experiences and outcomes vary by venture type as the business emerges, and these have an impact on entrepreneurial identity formation. As Carsrud and Brännback (2011) have noted, entrepreneurial identity and motivation are not clearly organized, stable or integrated hierarchical systems, but often vary based on the interaction of personal and contextual factors and the nature of the entrepreneurial experience.

For instance, positive and negative outcomes (e.g., successfully opening a second location or launching a new product in a managed growth firm, or failure to generate enough cash flow to support one's family in a survival venture), and the associated impact on the entrepreneur's affective state, could lead to changes in role regard and the centrality placed on the entrepreneurial identity relative to other self-identities held by the individual (Baron, 2008).

Initial support for these arguments is provided in the empirical work of Morris and colleagues (2018). They provide evidence of differences in the strength of overall entrepreneurial identity based on the type of venture created by the entrepreneur. Specifically, they found founders of all four types of ventures appear to have an entrepreneurial identity. However, the tendency to self-identify as an entrepreneur is weakest among those founding survival ventures, followed by lifestyle ventures. Both managed growth and high growth venture founders demonstrated the strongest entrepreneurial identities, with no significant difference between these two categories.

ORGANIZATIONAL IDENTITY

The organization being created is also taking on an identity. Organizational identity refers to the collective understanding among an organization's members of the features presumed to be central and relatively permanent, and that distinguish the organization from other organizations (Albert and Whetten, 1985). Martin et al. (2011) suggest it is a combined construal of the history, culture, structure, status, reputation and related characteristics of the organization. It gives meaning to the experience of work and is formed from the interactions among those involved with the organization (Glynn, 2000). While related to them, organizational identity is distinct from image, company climate and brand identity (Corley et al., 2006).

The importance of organizational identity is tied first to its role as a defining and stabilizing mechanism for those working within the venture (Fisher et al., 2017). In addition, identity is instrumental in establishing the legitimacy of a business entity in the eyes of external stakeholders, which enables the entrepreneur to gain access to new opportunities and resources (Lounsbury and Glynn, 2001). Navis and Glynn (2010, 2011) demonstrate patterns in the dynamics of legitimacy and identity in ventures involved in creating a new market category. Webb et al. (2010) discuss the role of social capital in crafting an enterprise identity among survival ventures in under-developed economies, enabling them to identify and exploit opportunities.

Identity also impacts the organization's ability to change, how decisions are made, and the handling of internal conflicts and communication (He and Brown, 2013). It tends to be associated with entity-level commitments, obligations and actions (Whetten, 2006). If we consider entrepreneurial venture types, any differences among them when it comes to levels and types of commitment required, or obligations of the entrepreneur and employees, might be expected to produce differences in identity. With a survival venture, as the entrepreneur takes actions to eke out an existence, often with little to no resources and facing significant competition from which the firm is undifferentiated, one might expect an identity to emerge that centers around a continuous struggle to stay in business, being disadvantaged, or simplicity. Similarly, the strategy of a managed growth venture might be expected to reinforce the identity associated with steady, ongoing growth.

Morris et al. (2018) have empirically investigated differences in organizational identity among the four venture types. Their approach involved entrepreneurs evaluating their organizations using a set of 54 descriptive adjectives associated with new ventures in general. Entrepreneurs from each of the four venture types selected up to ten adjectives that described the identity of their businesses. They separately indicated the two adjectives that best described the venture's identity, and were also asked to add up to three adjectives not on the list but that described the venture's identity.

The identity descriptors emphasized by type of venture were as follows:

- Survival: local, friendly, day-to-day, people-centered, labor-intensive, small, simple, creative, struggling.
- Lifestyle: quality, independent, small, caring, people-centered, friendly, local, integrity, responsible.
- Managed growth: integrity, people-centered, friendly, community-focused, quality, value-creating, innovative, competitive, caring, strategic.
- Aggressive growth: innovative, technological, inventive, strategic, creative, small, quality, rapid growth, risk-taking, competitive.

A comprehensive picture of both the adjectives unique to each venture types, and those shared across types, can be found in Figure 8.2.

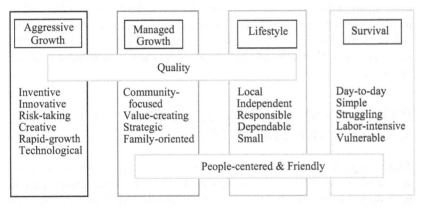

Source: Adapted from Morris et al. (2018).

Figure 8.2 Shared and unique identity descriptors for venture types

Separately, when asked to provide key identity attributes that were not in the inventory provided to them, the following were the most mentioned adjectives provided by venture type:

- Survival: difficult, demanding, persistent, flexible.
- Lifestyle: persistent, customer-driven, dependable, consistent.
- Managed growth: focused, nurturing, fun, service-oriented.
- Aggressive growth: disruptive, intense, nimble, hungry/driven, problem-solver.

The authors also applied cluster analysis to determine which attributes tended to cluster together across the entire sample of ventures. Here, they found four clusters. When the respondents from each type of venture were mapped onto these clusters, the results provided additional support for the uniqueness of organizational identity for different venture types.

Identity, or who we are as an organization, has many contributing elements. Some of these transcend the type of venture the organization happens to be. Hence, identity can be influenced by a range of other factors impacting the business, such as the nature of the customers being served, products being sold, neighborhood in which the business operates and characteristics of the founder (e.g., military veteran, member of an ethnic group, female-owned, disabled). But it is our contention that the underlying characteristics of each venture type, such as its vulnerability, inventiveness, community focus or smallness (see Chapter 2 for a detailed list of characteristics), have an overriding and ongoing impact on how those within the organization see the enterprise. Further, while identity can change over time, certain core elements tend to remain (Gioia et al., 2000), and these more permanent elements are tied to the survival, lifestyle, managed growth or aggressive growth nature of the business.

IDENTITY AND THE TENDENCY FOR VENTURES TO MAINTAIN THE STATUS QUO

There might be a logical tendency to view the four types of ventures discussed in this book as a continuum. Over time, then, ventures might be expected to transition from one type to another, such as from survival to lifestyle or from lifestyle to managed growth. In this view, each type is a different stage of development. But is this actually the case?

As noted in Chapter 7, we believe this tendency is more the exception than the rule, and that ventures rarely evolve from one type to another. Instead, our contention is that each venture type represents a discrete form, and that once the enterprise stabilizes around a business model that reflects a particular venture type, it tends to remain that type. Resources are assembled and allocated in a manner that supports the type of venture that emerges, and this process creates a path dependency. Once resources are configured in a particular way, it can be quite costly (and require new skills sets) to meaningfully change the configuration. As such, the resource configuration, managerial skills, management style, time horizons and other characteristics of the venture fundamentally conflict with those required to become a different type.

The distance between types may be greater as one moves from survival to lifestyle to managed growth to aggressive growth. For this reason, when a venture does evolve into a different type, the transition is easiest in going from survival to lifestyle, and most difficult in going from managed growth to aggressive growth.

An exception to the tendency for ventures to indefinitely remain the same type might be the aggressive growth venture. Aggressive growth is not usually sustainable over the longer term. At some point the organization becomes quite large and levels of structure and bureaucracy increase. However, even here, one might expect the venture to maintain characteristics of aggressive growth, such as a high entrepreneurial orientation, as we see with companies such as Google and Amazon as they mature and continue to grow. For these firms, the strategy often becomes one of acquiring emerging high growth firms that complement their core business in some way.

To the extent that the type of venture is associated with the identity that emerges for the organization, there are additional reasons to believe it is difficult for ventures to transition from one type to another. Gagliardi (1986) suggests that identity is so central to the ongoing functioning of an enterprise that organizations develop strategies that enable them to maintain their identities. This is particularly the case when the business is threatened or experiences disruptive turbulence in its external environment. He concludes that, in the face of such change, the organization will usually make changes in order to maintain what it has always been.

FIT BETWEEN PERSONAL AND ORGANIZATIONAL IDENTITIES

Ventures develop unique identities through the interaction of the individual entrepreneur and the venture itself. However, differences can arise between how entrepreneurs see themselves and how they see their ventures. In some instances these differences may not matter. But problems can arise when there is a poor fit between the entrepreneur's identity and the identity of the emergent venture.

Having a stronger entrepreneurial identity would seem to support the tendency to create a venture that demonstrates more innovation and growth. Yet, a number of factors will determine what sort of venture emerges and whether it succeeds. Hence, it is possible one could have strong entrepreneurial identity and yet create a managed growth or even a lifestyle venture. Conflict and frustration could develop, with the entrepreneur making risky decisions or unwise commitments that are inconsistent with the type of venture he or she is running. The result can be a muddled or unclear organizational identity, and poor company performance.

Similarly, someone who does not especially identify themselves as an entrepreneur, but has strong managerial skills and a great team, could create a high growth venture whose identity centers on inventiveness and technology advancement. Yet, it may be difficult to sustain this growth if the founder's identity centers on factors inconsistent with ongoing risk-taking, aggressive moves, exploration over exploitation, and disruptive change.

Another problem can arise when ventures are in one category for a period of years and then move to a different category. Consider a lifestyle venture that, based on changing circumstances, evolves into a managed growth firm. Again, while we believe this occurs more infrequently, when it does occur identity issues can impact eventual outcomes. This movement might reflect the fact that the founder has developed a stronger entrepreneurial identity. However, the organizational identity may still reflect the previous lifestyle nature of the venture. Organizational identity can be slow to change, suggesting it may not reflect the conditions and demands of the current venture. To the extent that organizational identity influences variables such as management style, strategy and culture (Gagliardi, 1986; He and Brown, 2013; Whetten, 2006), the subsequent performance of the venture may be undermined until the identity adjusts to reflect the new conditions in which the organization finds itself.

IDENTITY AND LEGITIMACY

When a venture is launched, it tends to suffer from the liabilities of newness and smallness (Aldrich and Auster, 1986; Stinchcombe, 1965). Lack of knowledge and experience in dealing with the many operational, financial, market-related and technological issues that surround the successful launch and growth of any business combined with limited volumes and a lack of bargaining power due to small size put the venture at a severe disadvantage. The organization is able to overcome these liabilities by establishing and maintaining legitimacy among external stakeholders (Navis and Glynn, 2011). These stakeholders have certain norms, beliefs, rules and procedures they use when assessing a venture, and complying with them is a prerequisite for attracting the variety of resources necessary for survival (Zimmerman and Zeitz, 2002). Compliance suggests the new venture is able to exceed a certain legitimacy threshold.

The kinds of resources required and the associated stakeholders differ for each of our four types of ventures, as discussed in Chapter 7. Accordingly, the requirements for legitimacy can also be expected to vary across the four types. Identity is one of the factors that contributes to legitimacy (Fisher et al., 2016). As it emerges, the venture's identity is conveyed to external stakeholders through identity claims. These are self-referential (tacit or explicit) claims that define the essence of the venture and signal its core attributes (Corley and Gioia, 2004). They help stakeholders make sense of, and define their role and purpose in relation to, the venture (Fisher et al., 2016).

The standards for legitimacy are likely to differ markedly for each of our venture types, and identity claims must reflect these differences. For example, with a survival venture, stakeholders may be more concerned that the business is legal, uses appropriate ingredients or materials, provides goods or services that are safe, and will still be around tomorrow. For a lifestyle business, the legitimacy threshold might be higher, tied now to the business having community connections, its understanding of local needs, and its willingness to stand behind its products. A managed growth business is likely to find that legitimacy is linked more to professionalism, efficiency, and superior product or service quality. Alternatively, the aggressive growth venture may need to convey its proactive nature, ability to continually innovate, technological capabilities, managerial capacity to scale an enterprise, and national or international market focus. If the venture's identity does not develop in ways that address these kinds of stakeholder expectations, its legitimacy will suffer, eventually resulting in the demise of the business.

Separately, as a venture develops over time, particularly with managed and aggressive growth ventures, legitimacy thresholds can be expected to change. Resource needs and requirements are evolving, leading the firm to reach out to new and different stakeholders. Expectations of the organization are changing, even among stakeholders that have interacted with the organization for some time. As a result, the organization's identity must evolve and adapt as well (Fisher et al., 2017). Yet, because identity in these emerging ventures is often connected to the identity of the founder, and it becomes imprinted in organizational routines and values, orchestrating appropriate changes can be quite challenging (Fisher et al., 2016). The implication is that, once it is established, legitimacy can be eroded when identity does not keep pace with external expectations.

CONCLUSIONS

Identity is a critical variable that distinguishes our four types of ventures. Decisions made when conceptualizing, launching and developing a new venture affect and are affected by the identities of the founder(s) and the organization that emerges. Moreover, self-identity and organizational identity interact with and impact one another.

At the founder level, our focus in this chapter has centered on the strength of one's identity as an entrepreneur. As a generalization, the strength of entrepreneurial identity should be greater as we move from the survival to lifestyle to managed growth and then aggressive growth ventures, or at least in moving from ventures that do not seek meaningful growth and expansion to those that do.

At the organizational level, we have approached identity as a collective sense among those who comprise the venture regarding "who we are" and "what we do." It defines the venture and shapes the venture's future direction. It is instrumental in establishing the legitimacy of the enterprise in dealings with external stakeholders. We propose that many of the characteristics that define each type of venture (as discussed in Chapter 2 and elaborated upon in Chapters 3 through 6) become embedded in their organizational identities. Additionally, fundamental differences in how the venture is experienced by the entrepreneur and employees of the business will influence the identity that emerges. The volume, velocity and volatility of novel events experienced by those within the venture is likely to vary significantly across our four venture types.

As a result, with survival ventures, identity may center on struggling, having a day-to-day existence, and being labor intensive and friendly. The identities of lifestyle ventures are likely built around smallness, being local and connected, integrity and dependability. Managed growth ventures would appear to have identities that emphasize being strategic, growing, a community focus and being people-centered. And aggressive growth ventures are more apt to develop identities that include innovation, invention, a technological orientation and disruption.

The organizational identity of an entrepreneurial venture is a complex construct that is not well understood. As such, richer insights are needed into the specific factors that drive the formation of identities for each venture type. In this chapter we have stressed the characteristics or properties that define the venture, but these characteristics can vary in importance. In addition, variables beyond venture type likely have an influence, such as industry category, market maturity, venture performance relative to similar firms, and elements of founder identity beyond the extent to which they see themselves as an entrepreneur.

An even greater challenge involves our understanding of the dynamics of these identities as the venture evolves. The more deeply established an identity becomes, the more difficult it is to modify. It becomes reinforcing and self-fulfilling. This is a principal reason why ventures of a given type do not tend to evolve into a different type over time. Yet, identities can change, especially in response to external contingencies, although it is unclear how much the underlying characteristics of each venture type place boundaries on the amount of change that can actually take place. Such change is especially important in managed growth and aggressive growth ventures, as growth tends to bring with it new stakeholders and differing stakeholder expectations.

REFERENCES

Albert, S. and Whetten, D.A. (1985). Organizational identity. *Research in Organizational Behavior*, 7, 263–295.

Aldrich, H.E. and Auster, E.R. (1986). Even dwarfs started small: Liabilities of age and size and their strategic implications. In B.M. Staw and L.L. Cummings (eds), *Research in Organizational Behavior*, Vol. 8. Greenwich, CT: JAI Press, pp. 165–198.

Baron, R.A. (2008). The role of affect in the entrepreneurial process. *Academy of Management Review*, 33(2), 328–340.

Baum, J.R., Locke, E.A., and Smith, K.G. (2001). A multidimensional model of venture growth. *Academy of Management Journal*, 44(2), 292–303.

Burke, P.J. (1991). Identity processes and social stress. *American Sociological Review*, 56(6), 836–849.

Callero, P.L. (1985). Role-identity salience. *Social Psychology Quarterly*, 48(3), 203–215.

Carland, J.W., Hoy. F., Boulton, W.R., and Carland, J.A.C. (1984). Differentiating entrepreneurs from small business owners. *Academy of Management Review*, 9(2), 354–359.

Carsrud, A. and Brännback, M. (2011). Entrepreneurial motivations: What do we still need to know? *Journal of Small Business Management*, 49(1), 9–26.

Carter, M.J. (2013). Advancing identity theory: Examining the relationship between activated identities and behavior in different social contexts. *Social Psychology Quarterly*, 76(3), 203–223.

Corley, K.G. and Gioia, D.A. (2004). Identity ambiguity and change in the wake of a corporate spin-off. *Administrative Science Quarterly*, 49(2), 173–208.

Corley, K.G., Harquail, C.V., Pratt, M.G., Glynn, M.A., Fiol, C.M., and Hatch, M.J. (2006). Guiding organizational identity through aged adolescence. *Journal of Management Inquiry*, 15(2), 85–99.

Down, S. and Reveley, J. (2004). Generational encounters and the social formation of entrepreneurial identity: "Young guns" and "old farts." *Organization, 11*(2), 233–250.

Downing, S. (2005). The social construction of entrepreneurship: Narrative and dramatic processes in the coproduction of organizations and identities. *Entrepreneurship Theory and Practice, 29*(2), 185–204.

Fisher, G., Kotha, S., and Lahiri, A. (2016). Changing with the times: An integrated view of identity, legitimacy and new venture lifecycles. *Academy of Management Review, 41*(3), 383–409.

Fisher, G., Kuratko, D.F., Bloodgood, J., and Hornsby, J.S. (2017). Legitimate to whom? Audience diversity and individual-level new venture legitimacy judgments. *Journal of Business Venturing, 32*(1), 52–71.

Gagliardi, P. (1986). The creation and change of organizational cultures: A conceptual framework. *Organization Studies, 7*(2), 117–134.

Gioia, D.A., Schultz, M., and Corley, K.G. (2000). Organizational identity, image, and adaptive instability. *Academy of Management Review, 25*(1), 63–81.

Glynn, M.A. (2000). When cymbals become symbols: Conflict over organizational identity within a symphony orchestra. *Organization Science, 11*(3), 285–298.

He, H. and Brown, A.D. (2013). Organizational identity and organizational identification. *Group & Organization Management, 38*(1), 3–35.

Hoang, H. and Gimeno, J. (2005). Entrepreneurial identity. In M.H. Morris and D.F. Kuratko (eds), *Wiley Encyclopedia of Management*, New York: John Wiley & Sons, pp. 103–109.

Locke, E.A. and Latham, G.P. (2002). Building a practically useful theory of goal setting and task motivation: A 35-year odyssey. *American Psychologist, 57*(9), 705.

Lounsbury, M. and Glynn, M.A. (2001). Cultural entrepreneurship: Stories, legitimacy, and the acquisition of resources. *Strategic Management Journal, 22*(6–7), 545–564.

Martin, K., Johnson, J., and French, J. (2011). Institutional pressure and ethics initiatives: The role of organizational identity. *Journal of the Academy of Marketing Science, 39*(5), 574–591.

Morris, M.H., Miyasaki, N.N., Watters, C.E., and Coombes, S.M. (2006). The dilemma of growth: Understanding venture size choices of women entrepreneurs. *Journal of Small Business Management, 44*(2), 221–244.

Morris, M.H., Pryor, C.G., and Schindehutte, M. (2012). *Entrepreneurship as Experience: How Events Create Ventures and Ventures Create Entrepreneurs.* Cheltenham, UK and Northampton, MA, USA: Edward Elgar Publishing.

Morris, M.H., Neumeyer, X., Jang, Y., and Kuratko, D.F. (2018). Distinguishing types of entrepreneurial ventures: An identity-based perspective. *Journal of Small Business Management, 56*(3), 453–474.

Murnieks, C., Mosakowski, E., and Cardon, M. (2012). Pathways of passion: Identity centrality, passion, and behavior among entrepreneurs. *Journal of Management, 40*(6), 1583–1606.

Navis, C. and Glynn, M.A. (2010). How new market categories emerge: Temporal dynamics of legitimacy, identity, and entrepreneurship in satellite radio, 1990–2005. *Administrative Science Quarterly*, *55*(3), 439–471.

Navis, C. and Glynn, M.A. (2011). Legitimate distinctiveness and the entrepreneurial identity: Influence on investor judgments of new venture plausibility. *Academy of Management Review*, *36*(3), 479–499.

Oyserman, D. (2009). Identity-based motivation and consumer behavior. *Journal of Consumer Psychology*, *19*(3), 276–279.

Schein, E.H. (1974). *Career Anchors and Career Paths. Industrial Liaison Program.* Cambridge, MA: Massachusetts Institute of Technology.

Shah, S.K. and Tripsas, M. (2007). The accidental entrepreneur: The emergent and collective process of user entrepreneurship. *Strategic Entrepreneurship Journal*, *1*(1–2), 123–140.

Shane, S., Locke, E.A., and Collins, C.J. (2003). Entrepreneurial motivation. *Human Resource Management Review*, *13*(2), 257–279.

Stinchcombe, A. (1965). Social structure and organizations. In J.G. March (ed.), *Handbook of Organizations.* Chicago, IL: Rand McNally, pp. 142–193.

Stryker, S. (1987). Identity theory: Developments and extensions. In K. Yardley and T. Honess (eds), *Self and Identity.* New York: Wiley, pp. 89–104.

Stryker, S. and Serpe, R.T. (1994). Identity salience and psychological centrality: Equivalent, overlapping, or complementary concepts? *Social Psychology Quarterly*, *57*(1), 16–35.

Vesala, K.M., Peura, J., and McElwee, G. (2007). The split entrepreneurial identity of the farmer. *Journal of Small Business and Enterprise Development*, *14*(1), 48–63.

Webb, J.W., Kistruck, G.M., Ireland, R.D., and Ketchen, Jr, D.J. (2010). The entrepreneurship process in base of the pyramid markets: The case of multinational enterprise/nongovernment organization alliances. *Entrepreneurship Theory and Practice*, *34*(3), 555–581.

Whetten, D.A. (2006). Albert and Whetten revisited: Strengthening the concept of organizational identity. *Journal of Management Inquiry*, *15*(3), 219–234.

Zimmerman, M. and Zeitz, G.J. (2002). Beyond survival: Achieving new venture growth by building legitimacy. *Academy of Management Review, 27*(3), 414–431.

9. The fit between type of venture and entrepreneur

INTRODUCTION

In considering the four types of ventures explored in this book, the question arises, "how do entrepreneurs decide what type of venture to create?" The answer is that they often do not decide, at least not before launching the business. Many entrepreneurs have an idea for a venture and do what is necessary to get it launched without necessarily thinking about whether it will be a survival, lifestyle, managed growth or aggressive growth venture. This is one reason why the insights from this book can be valuable to potential entrepreneurs.

At the same time, many of these individuals may have a sense of the scope or scale that they are hoping to achieve with a venture they are about to launch, and the kind of time and resource commitment they are willing to make. So, a person launching a bed and breakfast or a computer repair business may have a fairly clear picture of what they hope to create, envisioning a single location that employs a handful of people and generates a decent income for their family, or effectively a lifestyle venture. Similarly, someone with a technological breakthrough may see the potential to significantly change an industry and/or create a new market that is national or international in scope, effectively envisioning an aggressive growth venture.

Even where the entrepreneur has a mental picture of the enterprise they hope to create, they generally do not initially understand all the associated characteristics of the type of venture involved (see Chapters 3 through 6). These characteristics have implications for what it will take to succeed in the venture. Further, ventures tend to emerge in unintended ways based on the mistakes the entrepreneur makes, the obstacles and unexpected developments encountered as things unfold, and decisions made at critical points in time (see Chapter 1 and Lichtenstein et al., 2007). Even if the entrepreneur intended to create what is effectively a managed growth venture, what actually emerges may be a lifestyle venture.

For these reasons, it is important to consider the issue of fit between the type of venture being created and the nature of the individual who starts and runs the business. The personality, ambition, experiences, risk tolerance, values, time horizons, skills and other characteristics of the individual will influence how they build the business and what it becomes. In this chapter we attempt to examine how some of the unique attributes of entrepreneurs and the situations they confront impact the entrepreneur's decision process for a specific type of venture.

CHARACTERISTICS AND TRAITS OF ENTREPRENEURS

Entrepreneurship does not happen without entrepreneurs. The path each entrepreneur follows is idiosyncratic, determined by where they started, their motives, how they interpret and respond to ongoing developments, chance events, their goals and priorities and how they change with time, their willingness to take risks, and a host of other situational and personal factors. Further, among the population of entrepreneurs one will find a wide mix of ages, races, genders, religions, sexual orientations, income groups and educational backgrounds. As a result, it can be difficult to generalize about entrepreneurs or their ventures.

But are there certain characteristics that are more critical for entrepreneurial success, and might this vary based on our four types of ventures? A significant amount of research has attempted to address the question "who is the entrepreneur?" with scholars trying to identify various traits and characteristics associated with those who launch ventures. The findings have been mixed at best, with surprisingly little in the way of consistent results (Bird, 1989; Kuratko, 2020; Morris, 1998). It is generally believed that entrepreneurs tend to be optimistic, with a strong work ethic, and tolerant of ambiguity. They are also people who value their independence, and are resilient in the face of setbacks and failure. Let us further examine six of the more critical characteristics.

Achievement Motivation

Entrepreneurs are self-starters who are driven to excel against self-imposed standards, and to pursue challenging goals. This drive to achieve is well documented in the entrepreneurial literature, beginning with McClelland's (1961, 1986) pioneering work on motivation. Overcoming obstacles and accomplishing a goal is often a stronger motivator for these individuals than is money, title or power.

Perseverance

Total dedication to venture success can enable the entrepreneur to overcome obstacles and setbacks (Corbett and Katz, 2013). Sheer determination and an unwavering commitment to succeed often win out when facing odds that others might consider insurmountable. They can also compensate for personal shortcomings. The perseverance of the entrepreneur can be reflected in their willingness to mortgage a home, pay themselves very little, sacrifice family time, and endure a reduced standard of living for an extended period of time.

Calculated Risk-taking

Successful entrepreneurs are not gamblers – they are calculated risk-takers. They develop ventures in a calculated, carefully thought-out manner, where key risk factors are identified and approaches for mitigating or managing the risks are employed (Hvide and Panos, 2014; Xu and Ruef, 2004). They will find ways to minimize their downside exposure and avoid taking unnecessary risks. Where possible they will share the risks with others (e.g., through outsourcing, renting, selling on consignment, special terms with suppliers) or reduce the risks (e.g., by minimizing fixed costs, holding less inventory).

Opportunity Alertness

Entrepreneurs are opportunity-driven as opposed to resource-constrained. Limited resources do not hold them back from pursuing promising opportunities. More critically, they demonstrate strong alertness to opportunities. Entrepreneurial alertness is a person's ability to notice opportunities overlooked by others. When individuals are more alert, they demonstrate a better ability to uncover and clarify gaps and cues in the environment (Tang et al., 2012). Alertness is built upon a person's interpretation framework (reflective of their perceptual and cognitive processing skills and the mental schemas they rely upon), stock of knowledge, and everyday life experiences (Shepherd and DeTienne, 2005). Further, there is a greater tendency for opportunities to be recognized in areas of stronger interest, passion or vocation (Chen et al., 2009; Minniti, 2004).

Internal Locus of Control and Self-efficacy

There are those who bring a fairly deterministic outlook to life, believing external developments dictate their fate. They have an external locus of control. Entrepreneurs have an internal locus of control, believing they can affect change in whatever environments they find themselves. Events occur based on their own agency. Hence, they do not attribute outcomes to luck or fate, but instead see them as the result of their actions. This attribute is consistent with high achievement motivation and a desire to assume personal responsibility. It is associated with self-efficacy, or belief in one's ability to succeed in specific situations or accomplish a particular task, such as starting and growing a business (Bandura, 1997).

Passion

Passion for what one is doing is a fundamental component of the entrepreneurial mindset. It provides a coherent meaning to an emotional experience that centers on intense arousal and energy mobilization (Cardon et al., 2009). It is directed toward a person, object, concept or activity. It fuels the intensity felt when engaging in venture creation activities that are of deep interest, and the energy that enables entrepreneurs to achieve peak performance (Schindehutte et al., 2006).

One must be careful in concluding too much from these characteristics, as they are based on studies that differ in terms of who was sampled, how key descriptor variables were measured, and the quality of the underlying analysis. The sampling issue is our greatest concern, as the researchers behind such studies differed in terms of how they defined the entrepreneur. More specifically, they fail to distinguish among those who create survival, lifestyle, managed growth and aggressive growth ventures. We will return to this issue shortly.

SKILLS AND COMPETENCIES

Others have focused less on traits and more on the competencies and capabilities of the entrepreneur (Morris et al., 2013; Sánchez, 2013). A competency refers to the knowledge, skills, attitudes, values and behaviors that people need to successfully perform a particular activity or task, in this case launching and managing a successful enterprise (Rankin, 2004).

These competencies can be divided into two groups, managerial and entrepreneurial, as illustrated in Table 9.1. Managerial competencies involve skills that managers in any company must have, including someone trying to manage a start-up. So the entrepreneur must understand how to sell, how to manage cash flow, how to hire and supervise people, and how to ensure the quality of what is being provided to customers. But there are also skills unique to the entrepreneurial journey, where one is trying to create something from virtually nothing and make it sustainable. Examples include the abilities to assess opportunities, mitigate risks and leverage resources.

Table 9.1   Critical competencies involved in venture creation and growth

General Managerial Competencies	Specific Entrepreneurial Competencies
• Organizing	• Opportunity recognition
• Team building and staffing	• Opportunity assessment
• Communicating and social abilities	• Risk management/Mitigation
• Budgeting	• Conveying a compelling vision
• Delegation	• Tenacity/Perseverance
• Cash management	• Creative problem-solving/ Imaginativeness
• Controlling	• Resource leveraging
• Motivating	• Guerrilla skills
• Planning	• Value creation
• Directing and supervising	• Maintain focus yet adapt
• Operating (producing)	• Resilience
• Assessing	• Self-efficacy
• Selling	• Building and using networks
• Pricing	

The nature of the entrepreneurial journey reinforces why these entrepreneurial competencies are so vital. As a case in point, the emergent nature of venture creation finds the entrepreneur encountering novel events and unanticipated obstacles (Gartner, 1993). He or she is trying different approaches, making mistakes, and reacting to new opportunities that arise. These kinds of developments will reward skills at learning, adapting and innovating, while retaining an overall vision. Similarly, rarely does the entrepreneur have enough of the right kinds of resources, and so leveraging, networking and guerrilla skills become paramount.

Competencies are learnable. Yet, apart from any sort of classroom training, there is evidence to suggest that competencies associated with entrepreneurship are best mastered through experiential approaches to learning (Morris and Kaplan, 2014). Learning by doing can be accomplished through incubators, internships in entrepreneurial companies, pitch and business plan competitions, entrepreneurial mentoring programs, access to fablabs, makerspaces or other facilities where prototypes and products can be developed, working for entrepreneurs, and participating in business simulations, among other possibilities. These kinds of learning opportunities tend to be more available to those attempting to build growth-oriented companies.

Differences in personal characteristics and competencies are implied in the classic work of Smith (1967) and Smith and Miner (1983), where they distinguish between the craftsman entrepreneur and the promoter entrepreneur. The former is focused on the present and past, has specialized vocational or technical education, and is less flexible and confident.

The latter is future-oriented, has advanced education and greater social awareness, and is more flexible and opportunistic. This work provides an important foundation for distinguishing the backgrounds of the kinds of individuals who launch each of our four venture types. The promoter is more likely to innovate and build a growth company, while the craftsman more typically creates a survival or lifestyle venture.

PREVIOUS EXPERIENCES

The term "entrepreneurship experience" has been defined in a number of ways. For example, it can be approached as involvement in previous entrepreneurial activities (Baron and Ensley, 2006); the acquired knowledge and skills that result in entrepreneurial know-how (Corbett, 2007); the sum total of career events for a founder (Shane and Khurana, 2003); and finally, direct participation in activities associated with an entrepreneurial context (Cope and Watts, 2000). The most common usage is to describe prior knowledge and skills gained either in business or when creating ventures.

Although many entrepreneurs do quite well despite limited backgrounds, having previous entrepreneurial or managerial experience has a positive effect on venture performance. As an antecedent condition, researchers have emphasized the role of prior experience as a factor in explaining entrepreneurial intentions (Krueger, 2007), self-efficacy (Baron and Ensley, 2006), information processing (Cooper and Folta, 1995), business practices (Cliff et al., 2006); learning from failure (Shepherd, 2003), success of habitual entrepreneurs (Ucbasaran et al., 2006) and metacognition in decision-making (Haynie et al., 2010). Politis (2005) discusses how entrepreneurial experience enhances both the ability to recognize viable opportunities and overcome liability of new-ness challenges as a venture evolves. Others have stressed the role of prior experiences within particular industries as a factor in venture performance (Gimeno et al., 1997).

Again, the research has not tended to differentiate among venture types. However, one study of newly established, knowledge-intensive firms found that individuals with less experience in the core of an organizational field, more experience in its periphery or greater experi-ence in other industries are more likely to act as innovative entrepreneurs (Cliff et al., 2006). By extension, one might expect them to start more growth firms. The study also found that entrepreneurs who more strongly question the functional or ethical legitimacy of prevailing practices are also more likely to do things differently, which again might be associated with starting growth-oriented ventures.

VENTURE CREATION AND STRESS

Some of the goals commonly associated with entrepreneurship include independence, wealth and work satisfaction. Research studies of entre-preneurs show that those who achieve these goals often pay a high price (Hessels et al., 2017; Miller, 2015). A majority of entrepreneurs surveyed had back problems, indigestion, insomnia or headaches. To achieve their goals, however, these entrepreneurs were willing to tolerate these effects of stress.

In general, stress can be viewed as the result of discrepancies between a person's expectations and ability to meet demands, as well as discrep-ancies between the individual's expectations and personality (Buttner, 1992). When an entrepreneur's work expectations and actual job demands exceed his or her abilities to perform new venture tasks, they are likely to experience stress. In an entrepreneurial context, this is a common situation, meaning not only that there is considerable stress, but that it is ongoing.

Initiating and managing a business requires taking meaningful risks. Outcomes are uncertain and there is significant ambiguity about what will happen and what the right course of action is when it comes to addressing a range of issues. Lacking the depth of resources, the individual must bear the cost of any mistakes while playing a multitude of roles, such as salesperson, recruiter, spokesperson and negotiator. Entrepreneurs often lack the support from colleagues that may be available to managers in a large corporation. These simultaneous demands can lead to role overload. Owning and operating a business also requires a large commitment of time and energy, often at the expense of family and social activities.

Understanding stress can help shape the entrepreneur's initial and long-term goals for the venture. Some entrepreneurs find that growth is too stressful to handle. Therefore, the ability to better understand and handle these elements will certainly differentiate many entrepreneurs and the ventures they create.

IMPLICATIONS FOR THE TYPE OF VENTURE SELECTED

While they may generally apply, individual entrepreneurs vary in terms of how much they demonstrate each of these characteristics and competencies. Stated differently, as a group, entrepreneurs might be stronger on these factors than society in general, but within the population of entrepreneurs we can expect significant variance. This point is critical, as it has important implications for the type of venture the individual creates.

Consider risk-taking and stress tolerance. All entrepreneurs take risks when they launch a venture. But they differ in both their proclivities toward risk and their skills at managing risk. At the same time, the amount of financial, technological, competitive, career-related and other forms of risk differs significantly based on the type of venture created. One would expect the lowest risk in a survival venture and the highest in an aggressive growth venture. Entrepreneurs also vary in how much stress they are comfortable with or can tolerate. And while all ventures entail stress, the factors that create stress are much more abundant in an aggressive growth compared to a survival or lifestyle type of enterprise.

Figure 9.1 represents an attempt to characterize the environments within the four venture types in terms of these and other characteristics. The opportunities that present themselves as the venture unfolds, such as entering new and more profitable markets, adding strategic partners, hiring people with unique skill sets, or adding a new revenue driver or product line, become greater the more one is running a business that (a) seeks growth, (b) has the kinds of resources and infrastructure that support growth, and (c) operates in industries and markets that are more dynamic in terms of growth possibilities. As a venture strives to offer more products/services, operate in more markets, utilize a larger array of technologies, or otherwise increase in scale and scope, those involved find that more in the way of systems, structures and controls must be put in place. The complexity of the managerial task is increasing with these developments, necessitating greater skills and capabilities. At the same time, as we saw in Chapter 7, the underlying nature of the resources required is changing as we move from the survival to the aggressive growth venture – becoming more instrumental, robust and complex. Further, the volume, volatility and velocity of novel events encountered by the entrepreneur in day-to-day operations is much lower if we consider survival or lifestyle ventures compared to those that seek meaningful growth and expansion (Morris, et al., 2012).

Logically, then, the individual who is less alert to new opportunities, has more limited managerial or entrepreneurial experience, is unable to access more complex resources, or who works better when things are somewhat more stable and predictable may be more comfortable and successful in a survival or lifestyle venture compared to one seeking managed or aggressive growth. There are, of course, always exceptions. The amount of stress an individual experiences, the riskiness of particular actions taken by the entrepreneur, or perceptions regarding the pace of change could conceivably be as high in any one venture type as in any of the others. Yet, as norm, what one must be prepared for will clearly vary as we move across the four types.

Other variables discussed earlier in this chapter, such as self-efficacy and achievement motivation, can also impact the choice of ventures. One might have strong self-efficacy when it comes to creating a simple enterprise compared to one that is more complicated or diverse in nature. In a related manner, the strong drive to achieve demonstrated by many founders is probably affected by what one is attempting to achieve. Just as someone motivated to achieve success in running a 5K race may not be similarly motivated to excel in a marathon, the achievements associated with aggressive growth can differ from those surrounding a survival venture in terms of how much they motivate an individual.

Lastly, it is important to consider the goals and personal circumstances of the individual who sets out to be an entrepreneur. The person may well have many of the characteristics and capabilities described above, but their own needs take precedence in determining the kind of venture they are most comfortable with. Thus, one's desire for greater work-life

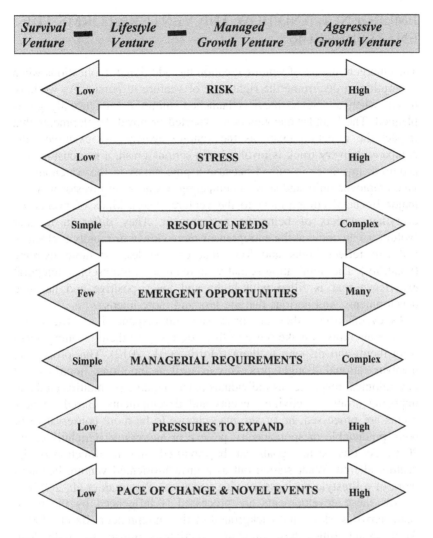

Figure 9.1 Entrepreneurial characteristics and the four types of ventures

balance, need for less stress, commitment to care for a family member, or requirement to be in a particular geographic location could lead them to select a venture type that requires less managerial experience, alertness to new opportunities, or ability to deal with stress than they actually possess.

EMERGENCE AND HOW THE VENTURE FORMS THE ENTREPRENEUR

The emergent nature of venture creation has additional implications when attempting to determine the right type of venture to pursue. As we have noted, when a new business is launched, things do not usually go as planned. The founder encounters unexpected or novel developments that impact the direction taken as the venture evolves. As examples, the company delivery truck is involved in a serious crash, a key customer is acquired, inventory is ruined because a pipe bursts in the warehouse, a vital employee quits and starts a competing business, an investor makes a major financial commitment to the venture. These kinds of events are everyday aspects of being an entrepreneur. They differ in number (volume), can come at the entrepreneur more slowly or rapidly (velocity), and can reflect highs and lows that can be less or more extreme (volatility). The implication is that venture creation represents a temporal experience that is filled with highs and lows, positive and negative developments, and periods that are less and more intense.

As events occur, they are processed and responded to. The entrepreneur attempts to make sense of these events, give them meaning, learn from them, and respond to them (Morris et al., 2012). This processing involves rational thought processes as well as emotions, impulses and physiological responses as individuals react to a diverse, multifaceted and imposing array of activities, events and developments. Based on how events are processed, he or she may choose to be more conservative or bold, predictable or spontaneous, passive or aggressive (Grichnik et al., 2010). As this occurs, goals can be modified, and the direction of the venture altered. What started out as a growth-oriented venture becomes more of a lifestyle business, or vice versa (see Plowman et al., 2007).

How these developments are processed is influenced by the traits, characteristics, skills and background of the entrepreneur (Baron, 2007). At the same time, these ongoing experiences impact the individual, forming him or her into an entrepreneur. For example, the nature of the experience can be quite ambiguous, particularly in the early days of the venture. To survive, the individual learns to be more tolerant of ambiguity. In a similar vein, the sheer need for resources forces the entrepreneur to learn to bootstrap and leverage, while lack of results over a sustained period leads him or her to learn to adapt. Being independent reinforces the desire for independence, and making progress enhances self-efficacy and a feeling of achievement.

To the extent that being in a venture molds one into an entrepreneur over time, the question becomes how differences in the experiences involved with each of our four venture types affect the kind of entrepreneur one becomes. For instance, in an aggressive growth venture, where the volume, velocity and volatility of novel events experienced are generally greater than in a lifestyle venture, the impact on how the individual is formed into an entrepreneur is also likely to be affected. In such a scenario, the individual is reinforced to be proactive, seek new growth opportunities, innovate, operate in a high intensity environment, maximize customer lifetime value, and incorporate the latest technologies to extend reach and scale while enhancing efficiencies. If we instead consider the individual in a lifestyle venture, ongoing conditions reinforce smallness, stability, maintenance of a working model, a local focus, personal relationships with employees and customers, and investment in the community. So, just as the individual forms the venture, the venture forms the individual.

CONCLUSIONS

The entrepreneur's intentions when launching an enterprise determine the kinds of resources he or she seeks, acquires and deploys. Yet, especially in the early days of a business, the founder is one of the most important resources. As such, it is important that there be a reasonable fit between type of venture and type of founder. The ultimate shape taken by the enterprise will often differ from original intentions. However, a significant gap between characteristics, values and skills of the entrepreneur and the requirements involved when building each of our four types of ventures can lead to a much bigger disparity between what the individual hoped to create and what actually emerges. Such a gap is also likely to contribute to frustration on the part of the entrepreneur, and sub-par performance or outright failure of the business.

These possibilities highlight the importance of a rich understanding of the underlying characteristics of the venture types, as discussed in Chapters 3 through 6. The difference between a lifestyle and managed growth venture is not simply one of degree, but instead, they are completely distinct kinds of entities and develop unique identities (see Chapter 8). Just as critical is self-awareness on the part of the entrepreneur regarding one's traits, characteristics, values and skills. Building a successful enterprise is not easy, and it becomes progressively more complicated as one moves across our four venture types. Having a fairly objective sense of one's tolerance of risk, comfort with stress, alertness to opportunity, level of self-efficacy, abilities at resource leveraging, and a host of other variables can serve as a useful guide in selecting the type of venture one seeks to create.

Finally, entrepreneurs do not pre-exist. They emerge as a function of the novel, idiosyncratic and experiential nature of the venture creation process. Venture formation is a lived experience that, as it unfolds, forms the entrepreneur. The characteristics and competencies of the entrepreneur are a major determinant of what sort of venture emerges, but the characteristics of the venture also contribute to what sort of entrepreneur emerges.

REFERENCES

Bandura, A. (1997). *Self-efficacy: The Exercise of Control*. New York: Macmillan.

Baron, R.A. (2007). Behavioral and cognitive factors in entrepreneurship: Entrepreneurs as the active element in new venture creation. *Strategic Entrepreneurship Journal*, *1*(2), 167–182.

Baron, R.A. and Ensley, M. (2006). Opportunity recognition as the detection of meaningful patterns: Novice and experienced entrepreneurs. *Management Science*, *52*(9), 1331–1352.

Bird, B. (1989). *Entrepreneurial Behavior*. London: Scott Foresman.

Buttner, H.E. (1992). Entrepreneurial stress: Is it hazardous to your health? *Journal of Managerial Issues*, *4*(2), 223–240.

Cardon, M.S., Wincent, J., Singh, J., and Drnovsek, M. (2009). The nature and experience of entrepreneurial passion. *Academy of Management Review*, *34*(3), 511–532.

Chen, X.P., Yao, X., and Kotha, S. (2009). Entrepreneur passion and preparedness in business plan presentations: A persuasion analysis of venture capitalists' funding decisions. *Academy of Management Journal*, *52*(1), 199–214.

Cliff, J., Jennings, P., and Greenwood, R. (2006). New to the game and questioning the rules: Experiences and beliefs of founders of imitative vs. innovative firms. *Journal of Business Venturing*, *21*(5), 633–650.

Cooper, A.C. and Folta, T. (1995). Entrepreneurial information search. *Journal of Business Venturing*, *10*(2), 107–122.

Cope, J. and Watts, G. (2000). Learning by doing – an exploration of experience, critical incidents and reflection in entrepreneurial learning. *International Journal of Entrepreneurial Behaviour & Research*, *6*(3), 104–119.

Corbett, A.C. (2007). Learning asymmetries and discovery of entrepreneurial opportunities. *Journal of Business Venturing*, *22*(1), 97–114.

Corbett, A.C. and Katz, J.A. (eds) (2013). *Entrepreneurial Resourcefulness: Competing with Constraints*. Bingley, UK: Emerald Group Publishing.

Gartner, W.B. (1993). Words lead to deeds: Toward an organizational emergence vocabulary. *Journal of Business Venturing*, *8*(3), 231–240.

Gimeno, J., Folta, T., Cooper, A., and Woo, C. (1997). Survival of the fittest? Entrepreneurial human capital and the persistence of underperforming firms. *Administrative Science Quarterly, 42*(4), 750–783.

Grichnik, D., Smeja, A., and Welpe, I. (2010). The importance of being emotional. *Journal of Economic Behavior & Organization, 76*(1), 15–29.

Haynie, J.M., Shepherd, D.A., Mosakowski, E., and Earley, P.C. (2010). A situated metacognitive model of the entrepreneurial mindset. *Journal of Business Venturing, 25*(2), 173–244.

Hessels, J., Rietveld, C.A., and van der Zwan, P. (2017). Self-employment and work-related stress: The mediating role of job control and job demand. *Journal of Business Venturing, 32*(3), 178–196.

Hvide, H.K. and Panos, G.A. (2014). Risk tolerance and entrepreneurship. *Journal of Financial Economics, 111*(1), 200–223.

Krueger, N.F. (2007). What lies beneath: The experiential essence of entrepreneurial thinking. *Entrepreneurship Theory and Practice, 31*(1), 123–142.

Kuratko, D.F. (2020). *Entrepreneurship: Theory, Process, Practice*, 11th edn. Mason, OH: Cengage Publishers.

Lichtenstein, B., Carter, N., Dooley, K., and Gartner, W. (2007). Complexity dynamics of nascent entrepreneurship. *Journal of Business Venturing, 22*(2), 236–253.

McClelland, D.C (1961). *The Achieving Society*. New York: Van Nostrand.

McClelland, D.C. (1986). Characteristics of successful entrepreneurs. *Journal of Creative Behavior, 21*(3), 219–233.

Miller, D. (2015). A downside to the entrepreneurial personality? *Entrepreneurship Theory and Practice, 39*(1), 1–8.

Minniti, M. (2004). Entrepreneurial alertness and asymmetric information in a spin-glass model, *Journal of Business Venturing, 19*(5), 637–658.

Morris, M.H. (1998). *Entrepreneurial Intensity: Sustainable Advantages for Individuals, Organizations, and Societies*. Westport, CT: Greenwood Publishing Group.

Morris, M.H. and Kaplan, J.B. (2014). Entrepreneurial (versus managerial) competencies as drivers of entrepreneurship education. *Annals of Entrepreneurship Education and Pedagogy, 1*, 134–151.

Morris, M.H., Kuratko, D.F., Schindehutte, M., and Spivack, A. (2012). Framing the entrepreneurial experience. *Entrepreneurship Theory and Practice, 36*(1), 11–40.

Morris, M.H., Webb, J.W., Fu, J., and Singhal, S. (2013). A competency-based perspective on entrepreneurship education: Conceptual and empirical insights. *Journal of Small Business Management, 51*(3), 352–369.

Plowman, D., Baker, L., Beck, T., Kulkarni, M., and Villarreal, D. (2007). Radical change accidentally: The emergence and amplification of small change. *Academy of Management Journal, 50*, 515–543.

Politis, D. (2005). The process of entrepreneurial learning: A conceptual framework. *Entrepreneurship Theory and Practice, 29*(4), 399–424.

Rankin, N. (2004). *The New Prescription for Performance: The Eleventh Competency Benchmarking Survey*. Competency & Emotional Intelligence Benchmarking Supplement 2004/2005. London: IRS.

Sánchez, J.C. (2013). The impact of an entrepreneurship education program on entrepreneurial competencies and intention. *Journal of Small Business Management*, *51*(3), 447–465.

Schindehutte, M., Morris, M.H., and Allen, J. (2006). Beyond achievement: Entrepreneurship as extreme experience. *Small Business Economics*, *27*(4), 49–68.

Shane, S. and Khurana, R. (2003). Bringing individuals back in: The effects of career experience on new firm founding. *Industrial and Corporate Change*, *12*(3), 519–543.

Shepherd, D.A. (2003). Learning from business failure: Propositions of grief recovery for the self-employed. *Academy of Management Review*, *28*(2), 318–337.

Shepherd, D.A. and DeTienne, D.R. (2005). Prior knowledge, potential financial reward, and opportunity identification. *Entrepreneurship Theory and Practice*, *29*(1), 91–112.

Smith, N.R. (1967). The entrepreneur and his firm: The relationship between type of man and type of company. *Occasional Papers, Bureau of Business and Economic Research*, Michigan State University, p. 109.

Smith, N.R. and Miner, J.B. (1983). Type of entrepreneur, type of firm, and managerial motivation: Implications for organizational life cycle theory. *Strategic Management Journal*, *4*(4), 325–340.

Tang, J., Kacmar, K.M.M., and Busenitz, L. (2012). Entrepreneurial alertness in the pursuit of new opportunities. *Journal of Business Venturing*, *27*(1), 77–94.

Ucbasaran, D., Westhead, P., and Wright, M. (2006). *Habitual Entrepreneurs*. Cheltenham, UK and Northampton, MA, USA: Edward Elgar Publishing.

Xu, H. and Ruef, M. (2004). The myth of the risk-tolerant entrepreneur. *Strategic Organization*, *2*(4), 331–355.

10. Types within types

INTRODUCTION

Our four types of ventures do not represent a continuum where ventures simply vary by degree – some seeking more growth and some seeking less, or some being more innovative and some being less so. Rather, each is a discrete category of enterprise with its own distinctive properties and identity (see Chapter 8). The kinds of resources and skills involved in each type are unique, such that one could not simply build on the resources of a lifestyle or managed growth venture to create an aggressive growth venture. One would need other kinds of resources and capabilities, and they would need to be bundled and leveraged in new ways.

As a general rule, we believe the differences between any two types of ventures are significantly greater than those among the ventures of a given type. Yet, this is not to suggest that ventures within each category are homogeneous. Considerable variance can be found within the populations of survival, lifestyle, managed growth or aggressive growth businesses. For instance, while both are lifestyle businesses, a small accounting firm has attributes that distinguish it from a local Italian restaurant. The challenge becomes one of placing these businesses into sub-categories that enable us to better understand how they function.

Our purpose in this chapter is to explore underlying differences among ventures of a given type. In effect, we attempt to identify types within types. Our focus is on describing those sub-categories having the greatest potential for enhancing our understanding of new venture creation. We discuss the implications of these sub-categories for how firms of a given type operate, the opportunities open to them, and the obstacles they confront. Finally, we examine how characteristics of these underlying sub-categories tend to reinforce the defining characteristics of each major type of venture.

TYPES OF SURVIVAL FIRMS

As we saw in Chapter 3, survival ventures tend to operate on a hand-to-mouth basis, potentially making enough money to cover current expenses but not much more. They generally do not have premises and have little equipment. These are basic businesses serving as a source of self-employment or supplementary income for the founder. Family members or sources of casual labor might also assist with operations.

Although there are many ways to segment the population of survival businesses, our focus is on breakdowns that have significance for the basic functioning of the enterprise and its relative success, and which include large numbers of enterprises. Table 10.1 presents five sub-categories that help explain key differences among these survivalists.

Table 10.1   Sub-categories of survival ventures

Category One: What they do

- vendors of goods
- people with skills related to a trade or task
- providers of low skilled but broadly demanded tasks
- those pursuing a hobby or personal interest
- individuals owning an under-utilized asset

Category Two: Formal or informal

- formally registered
- unregistered but legitimate informal sector activity
- unregistered but illicit or criminal informal sector activity

Category Three: Where they operate from

- home- or asset-based
- stall- or community site-based
- internet-based

Category Four: Amount of time invested

- full-time
- part-time
- seasonal or periodic

Category Five: Relationship with larger firm or entity

- independent operator
- contractor or sub-contractor to another firm or entity

As these businesses are heavily dependent on the labor of the founder to produce, sell, deliver, keep records and manage cash, among other responsibilities, we first distinguish sub-groups based on what the venture does. With these kinds of businesses, what they do is frequently tied to the capabilities, interests and rudimentary assets of the entrepreneur. Here, we can distinguish ventures that are selling a product or service on the street or at public forums such as fairs and farmers' markets, often that they produce themselves (e.g., fresh vegetables, prepared foods, crafts); people with skills related to the provision of a basic service (e.g., house painter, math tutor, disk jockey); providers of less skilled but broadly demanded tasks (e.g., cleaning homes, lawn care, dog walking); those with a hobby that turns into a business (e.g., sewing quilts, selling things on e-Bay, designing creative screen savers for phones); and individuals owning an under-utilized asset (e.g., person who rents rooms through Airbnb or owns a van and decides to provide transport services or someone who is homebound but offers call center services to small businesses). These sub-categories differ on whether or not any inventory is held, how labor intensive the work is, and the extent to which the entrepreneur can use family members, friends or casual workers to provide the product or service. In different ways, aspects of each sub-type reinforce the simplicity of the businesses, and the struggles involved in differentiating them from competitors, while serving to place capacity constraints on the business, and limiting opportunities for development of the entrepreneur (see Jones et al., 2014).

A second means of grouping survivalists concerns whether they are formally registered as a business or operate in the informal sector. If in the latter, they can be divided based on those offering a good or service that is otherwise legal (e.g., childcare, handyman services) and those engaged in illicit or criminal activities (e.g., selling narcotics, running a prostitution ring, fencing stolen goods). This set of distinctions has implications for who the entrepreneur can do business with, their legitimacy in dealing with potential resource providers, and the ease with which they can get advice and assistance in running the business.

Our third approach to categorizing these ventures centers on where the operations of the business are conducted. The largest group are home-based. They either use their residence as a base of operations, such as with a plumber, graphic designer or cleaning service, or actually provide the service within their home, such as childcare, personal counseling or a gambling parlor. Related to home-based ventures are asset-based ventures. Examples would include a person using his or her personal vehicle as part of a car-sharing service or to offer a delivery service, or someone renting out their power- and hand-tools. Alternatively, many survivalists operate at popular street corners or on the side of the road, from a stall in a farmers' market or in a display area at arts and crafts festivals. Still others use the internet as their base of operations, and can be located anywhere. Each of these options has a different impact on fixed costs (which are generally low), capacity (also generally low), customer perceptions and the perceived legitimacy of the business, and its relative visibility.

Yet another way to segment survival ventures involves levels of commitment of the entrepreneur. There are those that work in the business on a full-time basis, some that may have jobs or other commitments and approach the venture as a side-business or means of augmenting their income, and others who are limited to periodic events (e.g., fairs or festivals), days of the week or month (a vendor selling at a flea market only open on weekends) or times of the year (e.g., a business whose operations are tied to a season, the school calendar or Christmas). The amount of time commitment has implications for the development of the entrepreneur. Without enough time, it is hard for ventures to get traction. Further, the amount of learning and on-the-job development of competencies and skills can suffer.

Lastly, we can distinguish survival ventures that operate independently versus those that operate based on a contractual relationship they have with another firm or organization. A vendor running a hotdog stand and a handyman doing odd jobs for homeowners would be examples of independent operators. However, there are a number of survival entrepreneurs whose business is dependent on another, typically larger and better established, organization. A driver for Uber or Lyft is running his or her own small business, but it is based entirely on the contractual relationship with the ride-sharing company. Similarly, a drywall installer may work as a sub-contractor to some larger construction company. This distinction affects a host of operating variables. For instance, when compared to contractors, independent operators have more responsibility for sales and marketing, more administrative overhead, and a more difficult time establishing legitimacy in the marketplace, but fewer rules and restrictions on how they must operate.

BREAKING DOWN LIFESTYLE FIRMS

Lifestyle ventures are small in size, usually full-time operations with employees, often family-owned, with limited capacity (see Chapter 4). Most have premises or facilities, but many do not. While they are not all profitable, many generate sustained returns. They do not create millionaires, but can produce a very comfortable living for the entrepreneur and his or her family. As a rule, these entrepreneurs seek stability. Once a working business model is uncovered, the focus tends to be on maintenance of that model with periodic improvements to remain competitive.

The businesses that meet this description demonstrate a great deal of diversity. A number of the major sub-categories of lifestyle ventures are identified in Table 10.2. As a generalization, these ventures can be broken down based on what they do, such as professional and technical services, general services, food services & restaurants, small manufacturing & manufacturing services, and retail goods. Perhaps the more relevant question concerns whether what they do involves highly technical or advanced skills or proprietary knowledge (such as a small law firm or manufacturing services business) or, alternatively, if they are doing something that requires more basic or general skills (such as a hardware store or hair salon). The former are often more customized offerings with higher margins, where there may be more potential for differentiation, and less competitive intensity, at least in relative terms. Also, with the former, the potential for expansion may be greater, and not expanding is more of a deliberate choice than one dictated by other factors.

Table 10.2 Sub-categories of lifestyle ventures

Nature of what they sell

- technical or proprietary offering
- general offering

Ownership

- family-owned and operated
- non-family-owned and operated

Independence

- independent operator
- franchisee

Base of operations

- home-based
- premises-based
- internet-based

Number of locations

- single location
- multi-location

Where customers are based

- serve local market
- serve non-local market

Two additional sub-classification approaches concern ownership and independence. The majority of lifestyle businesses are family-owned and operated. This can affect goal setting, decision processes, internal conflicts, time horizons, community engagement, succession plans, and other aspects of the enterprise (Chrisman et al., 2007; Morris et al., 1997). While the evidence is mixed, family ownership can limit the emphasis on growth (Chrisman et al., 2015). And although most lifestyle businesses are independent operators, millions of them are franchisees (Franchise Direct, 2016), with just one or two locations. Those who own franchises have territorial limits and operating restrictions that pre-empt expansion without acquiring another franchise.

A key factor distinguishing lifestyle from survival businesses is the tendency to have physical premises from which the restaurant, auto repair shop or accounting firm operates. This allows for more professionalism and identity building, the adding of employees and equipment, and holding more inventory, as well as greater connectivity to the local community. For their part, home-based ventures are sometimes able to generate the kinds of revenues that support a very comfortable lifestyle, particularly for businesses where little equipment or inventory is needed in their operations. Also, in an age of third party logistics, where other parties will take care of order fulfillment, and where much business can be conducted through a website, social media and apps, the entrepreneur working from home can build a very healthy lifestyle venture.

Once premises are established, most lifestyle entrepreneurs stay with a single location. They may, over time, relocate or expand the facility, but it remains a single site. Some of these entrepreneurs will open a second or third location locally or in the region, but this will be the extent of the growth they can (or are willing to) handle. So, once these locations are established, the business becomes a maintenance operation. Coupled with location is the issue of the customers being served. Businesses such as hair salons and local apparel stores find that over 90 percent of their customer base comes from within five miles of the business location. A variation of this pattern is the lifestyle venture that operates local premises, but serves customers who come from further distances, such as a bed and breakfast. These businesses, and many of those operating online, can concentrate on customers and accounts that are located literally anywhere. There are also those that serve major accounts, such as a landscaping or catering company that contracts with the state or federal government, or a small consultant that works with a limited number of universities or corporate accounts. The localized nature of most lifestyle ventures tends to restrict their potential and the nature of any new opportunities to which these entrepreneurs are exposed.

SUB-CATEGORIES OF MANAGED GROWTH FIRMS

The founder of a managed growth venture seeks ongoing expansion of the business, but in a controlled manner. The nature and scope of the business is being extended, either through adding new locations, expanding the current territory or market reach, entering new markets, creating new products or revenue drivers, developing entirely new lines of business, acquiring other firms, or some combination of these approaches. These ventures confront moderate to high levels of competition, but are more efficient than lifestyle ventures. They usually perform well in local and regional markets, or in a narrowly defined niche within a national or international market. They are adept at building a strong market identity.

Some of the more significant sub-categories of managed growth ventures can be found in Table 10.3. Let us first examine how they achieve growth. These businesses most often succeed in conventional areas of business where the market is well established (i.e., real estate agencies, printing and publishing establishments, financial services firms, transportation companies and other everyday businesses) (see Coltorti et al., 2013; Singla, 2008). They grow and expand based on good management practices, proactive marketing, use of process technologies, and the ability to achieve economies relative to lifestyle competitors. However, there are also those that grow by being early in emergent areas of business such as new forms of medical testing, environmental consulting or third party logistics. Some are tech-based, coming up with technological advances that are not scalable, generally because they apply to a smaller or niche market. Lastly, there are entrepreneurs who diversify, achieving growth by offering a diverse mix of goods and services based on opportunities in different industries and markets. Under one umbrella company, the entrepreneur may be running restaurants, a website development company and a social marketing business.

The role of innovation further serves to distinguish types of managed growth firms. Using our grouping above, a large portion of these ventures are replicating what existing firms are doing, but with improvements, more proactiveness, and/or better management practices. Relatively little in the way of innovation is involved. But there are some of these ventures that produce moderate as well as major product, service and process innovations. They advance technologies and create new sources of intellectual property. Determining the role of innovation becomes a critical strategic decision area, as the nature of these efforts must be consistent with the goals, positioning and resources of these types of

Table 10.3 Sub-categories of managed growth ventures

Strategy for achieving growth

- superior management in established industry
- early mover in emerging industry or new business area
- technological advance in smaller (non-scalable) market
- diversification

Role of innovation

- replicators
- improvers
- innovators

Growth pattern

- steady
- staged
- opportunistic

Ownership

- family-owned and operated
- owned by individuals and partners

Relative independence

- independent operator
- aligned with or strategic partners with other organizations
- multiple location franchisee

Locations or sites

- single location
- head office with multiple locations

Where customers are based

- serve local and regional customers
- serve national and international customers

---

firms. Creating the structures and making the investments needed to support ongoing innovation is costly, while managed growth limits the potential returns.

As controlled growth is the essence of these firms, it is important to segment them based on how they attempt to achieve growth. Any number of patterns can emerge, but three common ones can be highlighted. The first involves relatively stable growth, such as the firm that adds one new location each year. Separately, staged growth finds the entrepreneur expanding a major leap at a time, such as the movement into an entirely new region of the country or a whole new line of business, and then taking time to get the staffing, systems and structures right and consolidate operations before making the next major expansion. And then there are those who grow in a more random fashion, opportunistically exploiting opportunities when they arise or company circumstances permit.

As with lifestyle ventures, managed growth companies are frequently family-owned and operated. However, a growth-oriented firm can be more attractive and better able to financially support successor generations. Family ownership is also consistent with measured growth, a willingness to take moderate risks, and efforts to pursue incremental and dynamically continuous innovation (Zahra, 2005). When not family run, a variety of ownership structures are present, many of which can facilitate financing to support both innovation and ongoing growth.

Related to ownership structures is the question of whether the venture operates independently, is in some way aligned with other organizations, or the entrepreneur has acquired a number of franchises from one or more franchising entities. Although they are most often independent operators (e.g., a regional publishing company), for some their success is tied to a strategic and/or contractual relationship with another firm. An example would be a company that designs, equips and retrofits kitchens exclusively for a national chain of restaurants. With franchising, managed growth companies can own dozens and sometimes hundreds of units.

These organizations can also be distinguished based on whether they operate from a single location, such as a manufacturing facility, or have a head office with locations throughout the served markets, as with a regional bank. These and any other structural approaches have implications for coordination and control of people, cash flows and the consistency of the firm's value offering. The structure can also be driven by the nature of the customer base, with some managed growth firms focused exclusively on local and regional clients, and others serving national and/or international accounts. The latter will usually be niche or specialty markets that do not lend themselves to scaling.

DIFFERENT KINDS OF AGGRESSIVE GROWTH FIRMS

Ventures that experience explosive growth are often disruptive businesses that take on higher risks but can generate much larger financial returns compared to our other three types. Extraordinary amounts of financial, physical, human and relational resources are needed to rapidly scale the enterprise. Systems and structures are continually added, modified, upgraded or expanded to accommodate a growing management team and accelerated expansion of the labor force. Internal work environments are very demanding, while external competitive environments tend to be turbulent.

While far fewer in number than the other types, aggressive growth ventures also have their differences. Table 10.4 highlights some of the key ways in which they can be further broken down. Perhaps the most significant of these concerns technology. Some observers may assume high growth necessarily means high-tech. Yet, as we saw in Chapter 6, two-thirds of these enterprises are not involved in introducing major technological advances. Notable examples over the past few decades include Starbucks, 1-800-GotJunk, Fedex and Nike. These firms use and improve upon available technologies in their internal operations. Some of them take advantage of existing technological platforms. The distinction between these two sub-categories affects where the entrepreneur looks for money, what money is needed for (e.g., the relative spending on research and development versus marketing), how the company is organized, and the kinds of employees hired and skill sets that must be developed. Their market-based strategies can also vary, with the high-tech firms pursuing more of an exploration strategy, and the others relying more on an exploitation strategy (Colombelli et al., 2013).

A related breakdown of these ventures concerns the extent to which their value propositions center on selling a standard offering (e.g., Dell with a range of computer products or Ubreakifix with electronic device repair) or a more diverse mix of items (e.g., Virgin Group, Under Armour). An increasingly prevalent alternative is ventures offering a transactional platform, including ones that bring buyers and sellers together, such as Airbnb, Etsy, eBay and Uber. And lastly, there are those that create high growth through a franchising system, such as Orangetheory Fitness, Fastsigns and 1-800-Got-Junk. These four approaches can be contrasted on a number of bases, of which the most significant may be inventory requirements, fixed cost investments, and the potential for recurring revenue from a customer.

Unlike our other three venture types, aggressive growth ventures can be very attractive to private investors and venture capitalists. This possibility leads to two additional categorizing approaches, each of which affects the other: the nature of ownership and sources of funding. The first of these concerns whether the company is family-owned, privately held but not family-owned, or publicly owned (traded on an open stock exchange). The second involves the extraordinary resource requirements that must be met to fuel aggressive growth. These requirements typically necessitate equity investments from outside parties (angels, private equity

Table 10.4 Sub-categories of aggressive growth ventures

Nature of what they sell (A)

- high-tech
- non-high-tech

Nature of what they sell (B)

- sell fairly standard set of products and/or services
- sell a diverse mix of product and/or service categories
- operate a platform
- operate a franchise system

Ownership

- publicly traded
- privately held, non-family-owned
- family-owned

Funding

- venture capital funded
- funded otherwise

Sustainability of growth

- rapid saturation
- intermediate term
- ten years or longer

Exit strategy

- sell out
- go public
- build/sustain

---

firms, venture capitalists). This can make family ownership more problematic. When these investors include venture capital firms, it often means the loss of considerable control and strong pressures to rapidly scale the business. The venture capitalist demands a meaningful ownership share and seeks high financial returns. This return comes in the form of either seeing the company go public or be acquired by a larger company at some significant multiple of earnings. When not satisfied with progress toward these kinds of outcomes, they can force changes to the business model and leadership team, including moving the founders out.

Aggressive growth is hard to sustain, particularly when measured by the rate of increase in revenue or employees (Acs et al., 2011). As the base size of the company gets progressively larger, maintaining a high rate of growth becomes more difficult. In addition, new market opportunities have eventual limits, and competition increases in response to the success of the aggressive growth firm. Hence, we can distinguish firms that grow aggressively for the short term (e.g., five years or less), those that do so for an intermediate period (e.g., less than ten years), and those able to sustain this kind of growth for ten years or longer. The latter are extremely rare. They can be further sub-divided into sustained high growth that is organically driven (i.e., by adding new products and services and entering new markets) versus acquisition-driven (i.e., by buying up emerging high growth ventures).

Our final classification approach for these ventures concerns their exit strategy, where there are three primary possibilities. The first is to sell the venture to another company. Such acquisitions are especially common with early stage high growth ventures that may not yet be profitable but demonstrate significant potential. The second is to take the company public. The company makes an initial public offering on one of the stock exchanges available across the globe, and this frequently creates a number of billionaires or multi-millionaires among the founders and early employees who by now are ready to exit or play a smaller role. The final exit strategy is for the founders to remain heavily involved on an ongoing basis (even if the company goes public) with the goal of building a company that is sustainable over the long term. Examples would include Amazon and Dell (the latter of which was publicly traded but then was taken private again by the founder).

INTERACTIONS BETWEEN CHARACTERISTICS OF TYPES AND SUB-TYPES

These sub-categories introduce variables that result in unique opportunities and/or challenges for the entrepreneur. They are variables that affect and are affected by the characteristics of the larger category or type of venture. On balance, however, the underlying nature of the sub-categories tends to reinforce the characteristics of the venture type. This tendency can be seen within each of the four venture types.

With a survival venture, the types of things they do, the tendency to not be formally registered, the lack of premises, and limits to the time commitment of the entrepreneur are all consistent with the hand-to-mouth nature of their operations, limits to the volumes of business they can handle, the inability to reinvest in the venture, labor intensity of their operations, high unit costs, and a lack of bargaining power. For lifestyle ventures, to the extent that their offerings are not proprietary, they have few locations or are franchises, and their customers are local, they support the general tendencies to emphasize stability over expansion, and provide for a decent lifestyle over building personal wealth. For managed growth firms, the sub-categories support the potential to differentiate themselves, while also suggesting they operate in competitive markets that have limited untapped potential. And with aggressive growth ventures, sub-categories that center on equity funding, national and global markets, value propositions that lend themselves to scaling, and lucrative potential exits are all consistent with disruptive business models that result in exponential growth.

Also noteworthy is the fact that some of the venture types share similar sub-categories. For example, family ownership is a sub-category for multiple venture types, yet its implications differ. Family business researchers provide mixed evidence regarding the effects of family ownership on the firm's proclivities toward expansion and innovation (Chrisman et al., 2015; Nieto et al., 2015). Hence, it would appear that certain aspects of famliness work against innovation and growth, resulting in a lifestyle business, while other aspects work in favor of innovation and growth, producing managed growth ventures. Another shared sub-category concerns the role of innovation or technology development in producing the firm's value proposition. But the extent to which the innovation is more incremental or discontinuous, and the technology development is more sustaining or disruptive, will tend to vary as one moves from lifestyle to managed growth and then to aggressive growth ventures.

CONCLUSIONS

In this chapter we have examined the heterogeneity that exists among ventures within each of our four general types of ventures. Specific sub-categories of survival, lifestyle, managed growth and aggressive growth ventures have been identified. Although any number of other sub-categories exist for each of these venture types, here we have concentrated on categories that include large numbers of businesses and that have significant implications for differences in the operating conditions of firms.

The factors that define sub-categories of a venture type represent decision variables for the entrepreneur, although some of these can be forced on the business. They are frequently facilitators of success, such as innovation activity, equity funding and having premises, but also factors that introduce complications and constraints. They are often factors that determine resource commitments, such as being a franchise owner, having little product line diversity, or serving only local customers, and these commitments can delimit future options. And they include factors that can play a major role in determining the firm's values, its risk proclivity, or its proactiveness, such as family ownership or operating online.

These sub-categories further highlight the need for theorizing and conceptual tools that move us away from thinking about entrepreneurial ventures as one general category of business organization. Instead, we need to develop theories of lifestyle or aggressive growth ventures that probe deeply into their underlying nature. Further, understanding differences among ventures of a given type has important implications for entrepreneurs, policy makers, educators, economic development professionals, and others trying to foster entrepreneurial behavior. The beginning point is recognizing how the characteristics of the category affect and are affected by characteristics of the sub-categories.

REFERENCES

Acs, Z.J. (2011). High-impact firms: Gazelles revisited. In M. Fritsch (ed.), *Handbook of Research on Entrepreneurship and Regional Development*. Cheltenham, UK and Northampton, MA, USA: Edward Elgar Publishing, Chapter 6.

Chrisman, J.J., Chua, J.H., Kellermanns, F.W., and Chang, E.P. (2007). Are family managers agents or stewards? An exploratory study in privately held family firms. *Journal of Business Research*, *60*(10), 1030–1038.

Chrisman, J.J., Chua, J.H., De Massis, A., Frattini, F., and Wright, M. (2015). The ability and willingness paradox in family firm innovation. *Journal of Product Innovation Management*, *32*(3), 310–318.

Colombelli, A., Krafft, J., and Quatraro, F. (2013). High-growth firms and technological knowledge: Do gazelles follow exploration or exploitation strategies? *Industrial and Corporate Change*, *23*(1), 261–291.

Coltorti, F., Resciniti, R., Tunisini, A., and Varaldo, R. (eds) (2013). *Mid-sized Manufacturing Companies: The New Driver of Italian Competitiveness*. Milan: Springer Science & Business Media.

Franchise Direct (2016). *U.S. Franchise Industry Statistics*. Accessed 1 February, 2019 at https://www.franchisedirect.com/information/usfranchiseindustry statistics/.

Jones, P., Simmons, G., Packham, G., Beynon-Davies, P., and Pickernell, D. (2014). An exploration of the attitudes and strategic responses of sole-proprietor micro-enterprises in adopting information and communication technology. *International Small Business Journal, 32*(3), 285–306.

Morris, M.H., Williams, R.O., Allen, J.A., and Avila, R.A. (1997). Correlates of success in family business transitions. *Journal of Business Venturing, 12*(5), 385–401.

Nieto, M.J., Santamaria, L., and Fernandez, Z. (2015). Understanding the innovation behavior of family firms. *Journal of Small Business Management, 53*(2), 382–399.

Singla, A.R. (2008). Impact of ERP systems on small and mid-sized public sector enterprises. *Journal of Theoretical & Applied Information Technology, 4*(2), 119–131.

Zahra, S.A. (2005). Entrepreneurial risk taking in family firms. *Family Business Review, 18*(1), 23–40.

11. Why all ventures matter: toward a portfolio perspective[1]

INTRODUCTION

New ventures are the lifeblood of an economy. The dynamics of their entry and exit are the key to explaining the long-term welfare of a nation. Whether aggressive growth gazelles or simple lifestyle firms, new ventures contribute to higher levels of competition, create value for customers, employ people, pay taxes, generate wealth, and otherwise contribute to societal well-being (Storey, 1994; Thurik and Wennekers, 2004). As a result, economic development experts and public policy officials around the world are devoting significant effort toward fostering entrepreneurial activity (Acs and Stough, 2008; Acs et al., 2009; Lazear, 2005).

Entrepreneurship is disruptive. Where it flourishes, change is constantly being introduced in the form of new products, services and ways of accomplishing tasks. Efficiencies are enhanced, competition is transformed, and new technologies are capitalized upon. Existing markets are turned upside down, and new markets are created. These new markets present profit opportunities to others, further spurring economic growth. However, do all start-ups provide these kinds of benefits, or is it a select few?

Because most new ventures start small and stay small (Carree and Thurik, 2003), some argue that public policies which encourage more people to become entrepreneurs represent bad policy (Acs and Mueller, 2008; Lerner, 2010; Shane, 2009). They argue that the exclusive focus of our public policies should be only on aggressive growth, high potential ventures that are introducing major product and process innovations. Yet, as we shall see, to discourage all other types of ventures actually harms the longer-term economic well-being of society. Robbins et al. (2000) have found that the higher levels of productivity growth (and lower inflation and unemployment rates) in the United States are in those states with higher proportions of very small businesses (fewer than 20 employees).

In this chapter, we examine the relative contributions of each of our different venture types. Relationships and interdependencies among the four types are investigated. The disproportionate benefits produced by aggressive growth ventures are tied to these interdependencies. A series of arguments are presented regarding the need to encourage all types of ventures. Based on these arguments, we encourage the adoption of a portfolio perspective. As with a financial portfolio, risks and returns to society will be maximized when there is a balance across the portfolio of venture types (Morris et al., 2015). Implications are drawn for venture portfolios that are unbalanced, or over-emphasize a particular type of venture.

DO SOME VENTURES MATTER MORE THAN OTHERS?

In recent decades, levels of entrepreneurial activity have surged through-out the world and constitute one of the most potent and positive forces in economic history. Across the globe, more ventures are being started than ever before, creating record amounts of value. As we have seen through-out the chapters of this book, these ventures take different forms and represent a heterogeneous population (Davidsson, 2005). In addition to fostering innovation and creating value, they are transforming lives, uplifting families and stabilizing communities (Morris et al., 2018).

There are some who argue that most of these ventures do not matter. The essence of their argument is well captured in the work of Shane (2009), who posits that we should not be encouraging more people to start ventures in general, but rather, the focus should exclusively be on aggressive growth ventures (see also Acs et al., 2009; Lerner, 2010). This argument centers on five assumptions:

- Most start-ups are relatively inefficient and hence represent a less productive use of society's resources.
- Most start-ups do not generate much innovation.
- A relatively small percentage of start-ups are responsible for creating most of the net new jobs in society.
- The wealth created by the majority of start-ups is quite limited.
- On balance, most start-ups do not enhance the competitive land-scape or contribute to the strategic advantage of a nation.

In this view, aggressive growth ventures are viewed as the real contributors to efficiency improvements, innovation, job creation and wealth generation despite their relatively small numbers.

It begins with efficiency. When any new business is launched it is consuming societal resources, but is thought to be relatively inefficient in using those resources, and has a good likelihood of failing (Carree and Thurik, 2003). Entrepreneurs typically make lots of mistakes, and they have an extended learning curve. With survival, lifestyle and even managed growth firms, they tend to integrate old technologies (or no technology), and are often more labor-intensive work environments, which means unit costs are higher. Not only are aggressive growth ventures incorporating newer technologies into their operations (and sometimes introducing new technologies), they are disrupting markets by bringing new value propositions that represent better solutions and hence a better use of societal resources.

Beyond this, the majority of start-ups are not generating significant innovations and have relatively little that is proprietary in terms of intellectual property. The typical new restaurant, clothing store, small machine shop or real estate business is operating in an existing market with solutions not that different from those that currently exist. If any innovation exists in their approach or offerings, it represents incremental improvements over the status quo. Alternatively, aggressive growth firms are more focused on breakthrough innovation, completely redefining value propositions and creating new markets. Despite their small numbers, they account for an impressive number of patents. The innovativeness of aggressive growth companies can be seen by considering Uber. The company did not introduce a slightly better version of a taxi service. While it is still moving customers from point A to point B in an automobile, Uber's business model completely changes who is served, how they are served, when they are served, and how they interact with the company and the driver.

As most new ventures start small and stay small, each employs few people. In the United States, 92 percent of them employ fewer than ten people, and 80 percent are solo entrepreneurs (US Small Business Administration, 2015). In any given year, their aggregate impact on new job creation is fairly nominal (Birley and Westhead, 1990; Wiklund and Shepherd, 2003). Meanwhile, aggressive growth ventures are responsible for more than 50 percent of the net new jobs (Birch, 1987; Malchow-Moller et al., 2011). As they scale up the enterprise, hundreds if not thousands of jobs are added. Many of these are high quality jobs with considerable room for self-development of employees.

The returns generated by most start-ups are also not very significant. These returns, more often than not, take the form of income and bonuses extracted from the business for the entrepreneur and his or her family. With aggressive growth ventures, huge amounts of wealth are produced, as reflected in dramatic increases in the valuation of their firms. Not only does the entrepreneur potentially become a billionaire, but many other equity holders, including some early employees, become quite wealthy.

Shane (2009) is thus emphasizing the belief that the start-up ventures creating real economic growth are few and far between. For every Amazon or Google or eBay or SpaceX there are thousands of lifestyle ventures that create little in the way of jobs, income, wealth, innovation or infrastructure. He uses terms such as "dangerous" to describe a belief that simply encouraging more start-ups is the key to the future economic vibrancy of society, or to revitalizing stagnant or declining economic regions. The exclusive focus, particularly of our public policies, should be high growth, high potential ventures. His position would actually seem to reflect the dominant perspective within the discipline of entrepreneurship (Brush et al., 2004; Delmar et al., 2003; Stangler, 2010). What we might label the "dogma of high growth ventures" is reflected in the editorial policies of some of the leading scholarly journals, many of the case studies used in teaching entrepreneurship, and a preoccupation with equity funding and venture capital firms (which fund less than 1 percent of start-ups) among scholars and educators.

WHY ALL VENTURES MATTER

There is no question that aggressive growth ventures make invaluable contributions to society. However, other types of ventures are critically important, and there could be no high growth ventures if these other types of ventures did not exist. Let us consider seven counter-arguments that reinforce the importance of all four venture types (see also Box 11.1).

Costs of Entry and Exit

Where size, scale and control of resources were historically important sources of competitive advantage, such advantages have been undermined by an increasingly turbulent and rapidly changing business environment (Chandler, 1990; Hitt et al., 2010). The contemporary environment is one that rewards speed, flexibility and adaptability. At the same time, dynamic changes in technology, social patterns, market structures, labor practices, supply chains, the ability to outsource and related areas have served to lower entry barriers, enabling firms to operate virtually, from home, or from wherever the entrepreneur happens to be, and with relatively little in the way of fixed assets or permanent resources (Contractor et al., 2010; Robinson, 2002). There is more in the way of a "resource sharing" economy. Jobs are of shorter duration and concepts such as lifetime employment with a single employer are increasingly rare. Meanwhile, markets are more heterogeneous, producing many unique niches that represent distinct opportunities for the small venture (Schindehutte et al., 2008).

BOX 11.1　WHY SURVIVAL, LIFESTYLE AND MANAGED GROWTH VENTURES MATTER

Because of their ability to innovate, rapidly scale and create jobs, aggressive growth ventures such as Space-X, Uber, Facebook and Amazon receive a disproportionate amount of attention from scholars, policy experts, economic development professionals and the popular press. However, the vitality of an economy is dependent upon a balanced mix of venture types. Survival, lifestyle and managed growth ventures produce a number of benefits that complement the contributions of aggressive growth ventures. Examples include:

- *Stabilizing local economies.* These businesses employ millions of people and are the backbone of the economy in many cities and towns. They pay sales or value-added, property and income taxes. Many provide health, retirement and disability benefits to their employees. They maintain facilities and the property adjacent to these facilities.
- *Serving market niches.* Survival, lifestyle and managed growth ventures provide an array of goods and services to local market segments, many of which are too small or insufficiently profitable to be served by aggressive growth or large companies. They hold inventory and offer items that reflect the unique tastes, preferences and needs of localized markets.
- *Producing innovations that can be advanced and scaled by others.* While not usually a source of disruptive innovation, these ventures experiment in local markets and develop incremental product and process innovations. Some of these are adapted and improved upon by aggressive growth ventures and large companies that are able to capitalize on the innovations on a larger scale.
- *Enabling people to climb the economic ladder.* Many poor, lower middle class and middle class individuals are able to meaningfully improve their economic lot through the launch of survival, lifestyle and managed growth ventures.
- *Contributing to the fabric of communities.* These ventures tend to be deeply embedded in their local communities. They will maintain employees during periods of economic decline. They actively engage with community groups and organizations, serve as community leaders, volunteer their time and that of their employees, sponsor local events, and support local causes.

- *Directly supporting aggressive growth ventures.* Survival, lifestyle and managed growth firms act as sources of ideas, contract employees, market experience and supply to aggressive growth ventures. Some are spawned by aggressive growth ventures (e.g., eBay), while others are part of the value equation of these ventures (e.g., Uber).

These patterns have occurred in tandem with a shift away from a manufacturing centric or services centric economy to one that is more information and innovation centric. Thurik and Audretsch (2004) suggest this shift has produced a reversal of some longer-term trends. For instance, the average firm is smaller, while the business ownership rate has increased, as has the small business share of total manufacturing revenues. Meanwhile, van Stel et al. (2005) demonstrate how the importance of entrepreneurship for economic growth is increasing, particularly in more advanced economies.

These developments suggest that it can be easier to start ventures, room exists for more ventures, and the relative costs of market entry and exit are lower than has historically been the case. Lowering of entry and exit costs would seem to especially apply to survival, lifestyle and managed growth ventures. Alternatively, with aggressive growth ventures, particularly those that are technology-based, the initial investment required is quite sizeable and increasing, the regulatory barriers are higher, and the windows of opportunity are shorter than has historically been the case (Delmar et al., 2003; Gruber et al., 2012).

The implication is that an economy today may have less to lose and more to gain from efforts to encourage survival, lifestyle and managed growth ventures. With aggressive growth ventures, the picture is less clear. As we have seen with policies where large amounts of public money have been invested into high growth ventures focused on commercializing alternative energy ventures (Mufson, 2015; Schow, 2012), much can be lost with relatively little to show for it. When aggressive growth ventures do succeed, such as with what Amazon has accomplished after years of investment and continued losses, the net benefit to the economy can indeed be dramatic. Yet even here, as we shall see, there are caveats.

Efficiency and Failure

Shane (2009) claims that start-up ventures make sense where they convert less productive to more productive resources. His argument, however, is that early stage firms are less efficient than incumbent firms, and that new ventures become efficient only when they age. He does not allow for the fact that many new firms will make up for early inefficiencies by ultimately becoming much more efficient, on the assumption that the typical start-up fails before this can happen. The problem with this latter argument is that high failure rates are not the norm, as Shane suggests. They are actually much lower (between 45–55 percent), and vary considerably by industry sector (Lowe et al., 1991; Stangler, 2010).

With regard to types of start-ups, aggressive growth firms predicated on scalable business models and innovative technologies that enable dramatic productivity improvements offer far more possibilities in terms of transforming society's utilization of resources. In fact, aggressive growth entrepreneurs have so far been instrumental in staving off the dire Malthusian predictions regarding the resource implications of ongoing population increases. At the same time, while aggressive growth ventures are bringing new efficiencies to the market spaces in which they operate, they may be less efficient if they attempted to operate in the niches where survival, lifestyle and managed growth ventures compete.

These other ventures are not inherently inefficient. A reliance on bootstrapping, bricolage, resource leveraging and guerrilla tactics can enable the survival or lifestyle firm to do far more with relatively little in resources (Baker and Nelson, 2005; Winborg and Landstrom, 2001). Lifestyle ventures also find ways to greatly enhance their efficiencies through cooperatives or other forms of collaboration (cooperative buying among independent hardware stores or shared marketing and reservation systems among local bed and breakfast establishments). In a similar vein, Eddleston et al. (2008) have provided evidence of efficiencies and productivity enhancements within small family-owned firms.

When it comes to survival ventures, where the benefits of capital equipment, production or purchasing economies, and technology are largely non-existent, one might conclude that they are so inefficient as to warrant that we strongly discourage their creation. The reality, from a societal standpoint, may be quite different (Morris and Pitt, 1995; Webb et al., 2009). For many, such ventures convert non-productive resources (people without an economic livelihood) into more productive resources. They lessen poverty rates and the cost to society in terms of social welfare investments (Morris et al., 2018). The survival venture can also serve as a developmental context that teaches the entrepreneur basic business skills and enables him or her to ultimately create sustainable enterprises (Cassar, 2010).

Finally, if we revisit the failure rates of many of these small ventures, what are the implications in the aggregate? It can be argued that failure is inherently good, especially early failures, and that higher failure rates are associated with higher start-up rates. The case could be made that the nations (or communities) with the highest business failure rates over time are most typically the ones with the most robust and dynamic economies. One of the great strengths of the US economy, then, is its venture failure rate, and the associated ease of exiting.

If as many as 45 to 55 percent of new ventures fail, then, this does not necessarily indicate an inefficient use of society's resources. It may actually reflect efficiency. Alternatively, it can be thought of as a type of investment in the future. When one is focused on creating novel or new sources of value, some number of failures is necessary for there to be a major success, and a 50 percent efficiency rate might be quite good at the societal level. Resources of the "failed" ventures can serve as building blocks for existing and new ventures (and other actors in the market-place), lowering costs and thereby improving productivity and survival among the rest. Failure spurs knowledge, learning, adaptation and resilience, while policies that lessen the perceived costs of failure encourage more entrepreneurs to try and then try again (Shepherd, 2003). Failures produce an improved class of entrepreneurs, as the evidence suggests success rates and growth are higher for entrepreneurs on the second or third venture (Sarasvathy et al., 2013). The subsequent payoff to society may well be enhanced global competitiveness based on a larger community of tested entrepreneurs.

In effect, then, the value of the investment in new ventures may actually be understated to the extent that we fail to consider the real options that they represent. Real options theory (McGrath, 1999) suggests, from a societal vantage point, new ventures can be considered as equivalent to projects in a portfolio in which relatively small amounts are invested, and knowledge is generated. Whether or not they fail, they offer potential options for future action that can be quite valuable. McGrath (1999, p. 16) explains, "the key issue is not avoiding failure but containing the cost of failure by limiting exposure to the downside while preserving access to attractive opportunities and maximizing gains." Thus, even a high failure rate can be a positive thing (Lee et al., 2007).

Job Creation and Employment

When it comes to job creation, the economy can be approached at two levels: the sustained level of economic activity and the dynamics of growth. The sustained level of activity is concerned with the general level of employment, the quality of jobs in existence, income levels, the level of competition in different markets, and general rates of inflation. Dynamics focus on rates of growth or decline, patterns in market structures, the pace of change in technology, and modifications to economic policy variables, such as the money supply.

Start-up activity is a key factor in explaining dynamics, particularly with the rate of entrants and exits, or churn, over time. Here, aggressive growth firms are more efficient in creating jobs and account for a disproportionate share of new employment annually. Arguably, they also produce large numbers of higher quality, better paying jobs. This employment impact should be considered with some caveats. These new jobs might be somewhat offset by the sizeable proportion of these firms that get acquired fairly early on. When this occurs, some jobs are eliminated and others are absorbed into an existing entity. Further, as we shall see, job creation by aggressive growth firms does not occur in isolation – it can be facilitated by the efforts of the other three types of ventures.

While survival, lifestyle and managed growth firms play some role in dynamics, they play a more significant role in the sustained economy (Gohmann and Fernandez, 2014). Arguably, they are the backbone of the economy. For every new medical equipment company there are many smaller medical testing labs. In fact, small businesses, most of which have fewer than 20 employees, account for 49.2 percent of private sector employment, and this is a relatively stable percentage (US Small Business Administration, 2015). If these other three types of start-ups are not encouraged, the impact on aggregate employment patterns would be devastating.

Empirical research has produced mixed results with respect to the relationship between unemployment levels and the launch of new ventures (of all types). Gohmann and Fernandez (2014) found that very small firms can reduce long-term unemployment and suggest implementing policies that lessen the costs of starting these kinds of ventures. Acs and Mueller (2008) have demonstrated that employment growth is positively correlated with the amount of diversification among businesses in metropolitan areas.

The job creation impact of survival, lifestyle and managed growth ventures may also be understated due to measurement issues. Shane (2009) claims two million ventures are started in the United States each year, while the Kauffman Foundation places the number at 500,000 (Stangler, 2010). Clearly, sizeable numbers of start-up ventures may not be captured by the statistics. Examples include many sole proprietorships, home-based businesses, unregistered businesses, seasonal enterprises, new ventures operating under the auspices of an already registered small business, and franchises, among others. Beyond this, the job creation numbers are understated to the extent that they do not fully

capture casual labor, employees who are paid but not properly documented, contract labor, part-time labor, and labor that is compensated
through equity or some other non-financial means. The numbers must
also be adjusted to include job destruction. For instance, while Shane
(2009) stresses the jobs created by high growth and larger firms, if we
take a firm such as Walmart and consider the jobs created when a new
store opens, these might be offset by small businesses that are forced to
eliminate similar kinds of jobs in response. Here, Mielach (2012)
concludes that there is a redistribution in sales estimated at $25 million
annually, such that nearly $660,000 in wages is lost per year.

Industry Sector Differences and Labor Displacement

How we interpret the net contribution to an economy of new ventures
may also depend on the industry sector one considers. Industries vary in
their failure rates, how labor intensive and mature they are, their relative
levels of market saturation and competitive intensity, and the nature of
any entry barriers (Auh and Mengue, 2005; Bates, 1995; Brush and
Chaganti, 1999). These and other industry characteristics suggest meaningful differences exist in the risks and rewards involved when starting
any type of venture in a given industry.

As such, to simply conclude that our only focus should be aggressive
growth ventures is to ignore the relative impacts of different types of
ventures across sectors. If we consider a high growth, online venture that
connects car owners with potential buyers, the virtual nature of this
exchange platform may find relatively few jobs are created, and spending
by the company centers on marketing and salaries for website maintenance and customer service staff once the site is up and running.
Alternatively, with a managed growth regional restaurant chain, given
differences in labor intensity, it may be that a greater number of jobs are
created and the venture has a larger spillover economic impact in terms
of all the facilities it builds and its ongoing purchases of equipment, food
and related items.

Within a given sector, new small firms not seeking significant growth
can also be sources of ideas that are transformative for an entire industry
(Agarwal et al., 2007). Do we really want to discourage or ignore the
non-aggressive growth firm that develops a new manufacturing tech-
nique, logistical approach or pricing method that is then mimicked and
expanded upon by other firms to produce major cost savings or new
value propositions? These types of firms can also be market pioneers,
laying the foundation with a small business that inspires and enables a
subsequent entrepreneur to discover a way to scale what the pioneer is

doing. And, of course, it is impossible to know in advance which firms will be the ones with pioneering ideas others can build upon.

At the sector level, we also often see significant job displacement effects and reduced numbers of competitors based on the successes of aggressive growth firms (e.g., the impact of Home Depot on local hardware stores). Such displacement is tied either to the relative efficiency/economic power of the aggressive growth firm compared to incumbent firms, or to an enhanced value proposition based on some kind of innovation. The value of encouraging high growth firms would seem greater where they are able to expand or grow the sector, or create entirely new market opportunities. A related assumption made by Shane (2009) is that the quality of jobs created by the aggressive growth venture are necessarily superior to the jobs they displace. This certainly can be the case, but there are plenty of circumstances where job benefits and the quality of work life may well be comparable or superior in the incumbent enterprise.

Ecosystem and Community Effects

The differential contributions of all four types of ventures to community-based entrepreneurial ecosystems is yet another consideration. These ecosystems are an agglomeration of interconnected individuals, entities and regulatory bodies in a given geographic area that facilitate entre-preneurial activity (Isenberg, 2010; Malecki, 2011). Components include new start-ups, existing small firms, banks, venture capitalists, incubators, accelerators, universities, professional service providers and government agencies that support entrepreneurial activity. The concept of an eco-system is predicated on the dependence of these elements upon one another. Ecosystems are inherently complex, with direct and indirect interactions among the various components.

In this vein, aggressive growth ventures are highly dependent on other venture types. Similar to an ecological ecosystem, where different species form a set of interactions in the so-called food chain (Ives and Carpenter, 2007), different sets of entrepreneurial ventures feed on each other, providing a diverse set of services and products. Removing what some authors characterize as resource-wasting ventures could potentially dam-age the entrepreneurial "food-chain."

Extending existing measures of diversity in economics (inequality, polarization, heterogeneity) (Alesina et al., 2004; Wolfson, 1994) and biology (alpha, beta, gamma, Simpson's Diversity Index, Species Rich-ness Index) (Alatalo, 1981; Spellerberg and Fedor, 2003), our typology of entrepreneurial ventures provides a rudimentary diversity measure for entrepreneurial ecosystems. If we take eBay as a sample aggressive growth venture, the business model and growth rate are built on a community of buyers and sellers, the latter group of which contains a variety of small and so-called "marginal" businesses. Similarly, the business models of Amazon and other large online retailers are built around a set of managed growth, lifestyle and survival businesses.

Another important aspect in this discussion concerns the divergence of financial, social and human capital resources that entrepreneurs have access to in different ecosystems. In comparing early stage entrepreneurs in Silicon Valley to more struggling communities such as Detroit, Michigan or Liverpool, England, one is likely to conclude the latter operate in much more adverse conditions that limit their overall economic productivity. Revisiting our efficiency argument, "marginal" entrepreneurs are often critical to the functioning of lower performing economic systems, demonstrating tremendous ingenuity and resourcefulness (Baker and Nelson, 2005; Gundry et al., 2011; Senyard et al., 2010). With Silicon Valley, which is often used as a benchmark, the critical resources for success have been accumulating since the 1940s (Sturgeon, 2000). The accumulation of these resources has caused a quasi-monopoly when it comes to the use of venture capital to develop and distribute new technologies. This has not come without cost. Research has shown that this "closed" ecosystem produces a high level of inequality with regard to women and minorities (Bochner et al., 2015; Phillips, 2005). Survival, lifestyle and managed growth ventures, on the other hand, are associated with a more diverse set of entrepreneurs that can benefit the overall economy.

The ecosystem argument ultimately reminds us that entrepreneurial firms are embedded in communities. As more ventures of different types are created, they can serve to stabilize local economies, bring down crime rates, support community initiatives, and contribute to the tax base. The value of such contributions is measured not only through social benefits, but in economic returns and potentially more productive use of public monies. The implication is that public policy might be better served if it encourages entrepreneurial ecosystem development rather than exclusively focus on aggressive growth venture development, and this implies encouraging all types of ventures. Such investments can encourage a culture of entrepreneurship, which in turn facilitates even more entrepreneurial activity in a given geographic area.

The Emergent Nature of Venture Creation

Perhaps the greatest flaw in arguments that favor only aggressive growth firms is that they assume we know what kind of venture an entrepreneur is going to create. Yet this is rarely the case. While a given entrepreneur may intend to create a high growth venture, the reality is that what actually emerges is often something quite different (Gartner, 1993; Lichtenstein et al., 2006). What was intended as a lifestyle venture becomes a managed growth firm based on unexpected developments along the way, while the entrepreneur who sought aggressive growth creates a venture that demonstrates nominal growth.

Emergence means that when a venture is started, we cannot be certain it will survive or what form it will take. Even venture capitalists who, as a rule, only invest once a business has established revenues and what appears to be a working and potentially scalable business model have a relatively low success record in terms of picking the winners (Gompers et al., 2009; Michel, 2014). The real implication of emergence may be that we need to encourage a greater number of start-ups of all kinds – not knowing what they will become – as a greater pool is likely to mean more of all four types of ventures.

This conclusion is reinforced when considering Shane's (2009) argument suggesting that creating incentives for people to start ventures will only attract the worst kinds of entrepreneurs. While it is not clear what constitutes the best and worst entrepreneurs, the inference is that responding to an incentive is more likely among those who are unemployed or otherwise experiencing less than full employment when it comes to their skills and capabilities. Further, because these are "less ideal" entrepreneurs, it is assumed they start less attractive or lower potential ventures. Yet, the reality is that, in spite of many years of research, we still know relatively little about the make-up of a successful entrepreneur. We do not have the ability to predict who will succeed or fail, or what kind of venture they will create. We also do not have a well-developed notion of what constitutes higher quality or lower quality entrepreneurs, as the underlying criteria for determining quality are highly debatable. Further, it can be argued that the venture experience is what forms the entrepreneur over time – suggesting that the quality of the entrepreneur that will emerge is situational (Morris et al., 2012). The emergence of the entrepreneur leads to our final counter-argument.

Human Capital Development

The creation of a venture exposes the founder to a large array of novel and unexpected events. To survive, the entrepreneur must engage in creative problem-solving, bootstrapping, adaptation and continuous learning. On-the-job skills are developed, often based on necessity as the individual deals with issues related to procurement, production, order fulfillment, staffing, supervision, record-keeping, money management, resource acquisition and customer service. The individual is being formed into an entrepreneur as a function of the novel, idiosyncratic and experiential nature of the venture creation process. Stated differently, venture creation is a lived experience that, as it unfolds, creates the entrepreneur.

This experiential view of the entrepreneur allows for the fact that the many activities addressed as a venture unfolds are experienced by different entrepreneurs in different ways. Moreover, it acknowledges that venture creation transcends rational thought processes to include emotions, impulses and physiological responses as individuals react to a diverse, multifaceted and imposing array of activities, events and developments.

As a consequence, entrepreneurial ventures of all types represent a rich incubator for developing the human capital of society. Venture experiences of any kind have the potential to enhance self-efficacy, greatly expand one's knowledge base, build new skills, and develop elements of an entrepreneurial mindset that can be applied in all facets of one's life.

THE NEED FOR A PORTFOLIO APPROACH

It becomes clear, based on these counter-arguments, that all venture types provide some level of value to society and should be encouraged, recognizing that they each have fundamentally different roles in the economy. As such, we believe they should be approached from a portfolio approach. The notion of a portfolio is based on achieving a balanced mix of objectives and outcomes (Table 11.1). As with a portfolio approach to financial investments, where the investor is encouraged not to put all their money into a single type of investment, society is best served by having a diverse mix of venture types.

Table 11.1 *Balancing objectives across the venture types*

	Efficiencies Achieved	Risk	Financial Returns	Job Creation	Innovation	Customers Served	Community Benefits
Survival	very low	low	very small	nominal	none	few local customers	employment and learning for lower income citizens
Lifestyle	low	moderate	small	low	little	smaller local markets	stable contributor of jobs, taxes and community engagement
Managed growth	moderate	moderate	moderate	medium	incremental	larger regional markets	significant regional employer
Aggressive growth	high	very high	immense	significant	breakthrough	sizeable global and national markets	dynamic growth, high quality jobs, innovative new sources of value

With the venture portfolio, society (and the communities within society) is able to balance a number of different considerations related to the benefits and costs of new venture creation. Included here are:

- levels of risk undertaken and returns generated
- venture success and failure rates
- income generation versus growth in asset value
- new job creation versus economic stability
- demand for lower- and higher-skilled workers
- incremental and breakthrough innovation
- the ability to create new markets as well as serve existing market niches
- shorter- and longer-term returns to society.

This ability to balance the outcomes can be seen by considering the different roles played by each venture type. Survival ventures can serve to move people out of poverty and joblessness into a mode where they are able to meet basic economic needs. Many lifestyle ventures offer a stabilizing role in local economies, providing markets for locally made goods, paying local taxes, and reinvesting in the community. Together with survival ventures, they service local market niches that might otherwise be ignored. Managed growth firms also help local economies but, because they are focused on growth, their market reach is usually greater with more jobs created and greater potential for innovation. Aggressive growth ventures produce the dynamic breakthroughs and major innovations that open new markets, create large numbers of jobs, and enhance the global competitiveness of a nation (Morris et al., 2015).

The impressive returns that can potentially derive from aggressive growth ventures are offset by the very high risks that are being undertaken. Many of these promising concepts fail, in the process producing huge losses in terms of societal resources. Alternatively, survival ventures may also fail at a high rate, but much less is lost when they fail, and much less is gained when they succeed. Lifestyle and managed growth ventures lie in the middle in terms of both risk and return. A societal approach that emphasizes a portfolio of ventures serves to effectively balance both the risk equation and the mix of benefits that accrue from different types of start-ups.

A portfolio of ventures also better ensures that many more market niches are served. A large number of these niches are too small or not sufficiently profitable to attract aggressive growth ventures. But other types of ventures can do quite well serving them, while also making important local community contributions (e.g., taxes paid, volunteerism, sponsorship of events). The result is a more competitive economy, greater consumer choice, a wider array of prices and quality levels, and more product offerings tailored to reflect local customer preferences. Thus, a portfolio approach helps to ensure the vibrancy of an economy and enhanced quality of life (Nambisan and Baron, 2013).

A portfolio perspective further allows for the fact that different types of ventures fuel one another. This can be seen by considering the contributions of a venture such as Uber. The existence of local taxi companies (lifestyle and managed growth ventures), some of which will ultimately be put out of business by this aggressive growth venture, in effect contributed to the opportunity behind Uber. Survival, lifestyle and managed growth firms may also have provided products, services and resources (including learning) to Uber that proved to be instrumental in the development of the business. As it succeeds, Uber will also motivate adaptation by existing taxi or transport companies and entry of new ones to serve niches and market needs that are inconsistent with the Uber model. Some of these entrants may themselves become aggressive growth ventures, displacing Uber. For its part, Uber creates new jobs for thousands of independent contractors (who are effectively running survival ventures), while also eliminating the jobs of companies being displaced. Further, Uber is made better or declines as new entrants of all types seek to compete with it, sell things to it, and find niches it is not serving.

While the portfolio concept would seem intuitively appealing, we know little about what the mix of ventures should look like. It is believed that survival and lifestyle businesses constitute as much as 85 percent of ventures in developed economies while managed growth and aggressive growth firms represent roughly 15 percent (Acs et al., 2009; Cassar, 2010; Morris et al., 2018). As illustrated in Figure 11.1, a balanced portfolio will consist of different proportions of each of the four venture types. The ranges for each that we have provided are based on patterns over the past few decades. Hence, the implications of doubling the proportion of aggressive growth ventures, or of significantly reducing the proportion of survival ventures, are unknown. However, while such reallocations could mean dynamic economic growth, creation of new markets, and a proliferation of breakthrough innovation, they would also likely result in trade-offs including unacceptable levels of societal risk, huge misallocation of resources, increases in poverty, and other negative externalities at the community and societal levels.

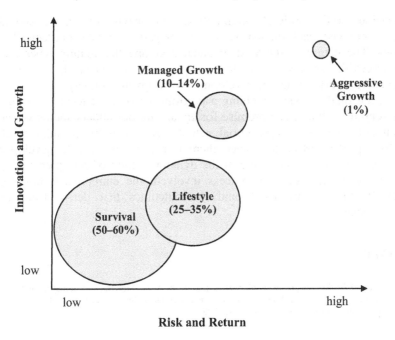

Figure 11.1   A portfolio perspective on venture types

CONCLUSIONS

Entrepreneurial ventures have an indelible impact on the economies in which they are developed. However, not all ventures are the same. They differ in size, growth rates, focus, owner motivations, resource requirements, risks and eventual outcomes for society. In this chapter, we have argued for a portfolio perspective on venture types. Society is best served not simply by improving the total pool of ventures being launched but also the level of diversity among ventures in the entrepreneurial ecosystem.

Each venture type has differing needs and makes unique contributions to the economic vitality and quality of life in society. Further, there are interdependencies among the four types. The disproportionate impact of aggressive growth ventures on innovation and new job creation is complemented by the ability of survival, lifestyle and managed growth firms to employ large numbers of people, help people climb the economic ladder, support local economies, serve market niches, and contribute to the fabric of communities. All four types of ventures should be encouraged, each for reasons tied to its particular roles and contributions. The nature of the kind of balance among the venture types that produces the greatest benefit to society is unclear, but is likely to vary depending on the stage of development of a given economy.

In the final analysis, applying a portfolio perspective to our typology of ventures offers much promise for enhancing our understanding of the rich potential of entrepreneurial activity. As noted by Kuratko et al. (2015, p. 10), "More than ever, there is a pressing need to develop a comprehensive understanding of the dynamic nature of entrepreneurship – the forms it takes, the process involved, the entrepreneur himself/herself, the venture itself, and the outcomes that derive from its occurrence ...".

NOTE

1. Material in this chapter was adapted in part from M.H. Morris, X. Neumeyer, and D.F. Kuratko (2015). A portfolio perspective on entrepreneurship and economic development. *Small Business Economics*, *45*(4), 713–728.

REFERENCES

Acs, Z.J. and Mueller, P. (2008). Employment effects of business dynamics: Mice, gazelles and elephants. *Small Business Economics*, *30*(1), 85–100.

Acs, Z.J. and Stough, R.R. (2008). *Public Policy in an Entrepreneurial Economy: Creating the Conditions for Business Growth*, Vol. 17. New York: Springer Science & Business Media.

Acs, Z.J., Audretsch, D.B., and Strom, R.J. (eds) (2009). *Entrepreneurship, Growth, and Public Policy*. Cambridge: Cambridge University Press.

Agarwal, R., Audretsch, D., and Sarkar, M.B. (2007). The process of creative construction: Knowledge spillovers, entrepreneurship, and economic growth. *Strategic Entrepreneurship Journal*, *7*(3–4), 263–286.

Alatalo, R.V. (1981). Problems in the measurement of evenness in ecology. *Oikos*, *57*(2), 199–204.

Alesina, A., Baqir, R., and Hoxby, C. (2004). Political jurisdictions in heterogeneous communities. *Journal of Political Economy*, *112*(2), 348–396.

Auh, S. and Mengue, B. (2005). Balancing exploration and exploitation: The moderating role of competitive intensity. *Journal of Business Research*, *55*(12), 1652.

Baker, T. and Nelson, R.E. (2005). Creating something from nothing: Resource construction through entrepreneurial bricolage. *Administrative Science Quarterly*, *50*(3), 329–366.

Bates, T. (1995). Analysis of survival rates among franchise and independent small business startups. *Journal of Small Business Management, 55*, 26–36.

Birch, D.G. (1987). *Job Creation in America: How Our Smallest Companies Put the Most People to Work.* Urbana, IL: University of Illinois at Urbana-Champaign's Academy for Entrepreneurial Leadership Historical Research Reference in Entrepreneurship.

Birley, S. and Westhead, P. (1990). Growth and performance contrasts between "types" of small firms. *Strategic Management Journal, 11*(7), 535–557.

Bochner, S., Diaz, F., and Hancock, R. (2015). Silicon Valley index: People, economy, society, place and governance. San Jose, CA: Silicon Valley Institute for Regional Studies.

Brush, C.G. and Chaganti, R. (1999). Businesses without glamour? An analysis of resources on performance by size and age in small service and retail firms. *Journal of Business Venturing, 14*(3), 233–257.

Brush, C., Carter, N., Gatewood, E., Greene, P., and Hart, M. (2004). *Clearing the Hurdles: Women Building High-Growth Enterprises.* New York: Financial Times/Prentice Hall.

Carree, M.A. and Thurik, A.R. (2003). The impact of entrepreneurship on economic growth. In Z.J. Acs and D.B. Audretsch (eds), *Handbook of Entrepreneurship Research.* Boston, MA: Kluwer Academic Publishers, pp. 437–471.

Cassar, G. (2010). Are individuals entering self-employment overly optimistic? An empirical test of plans and projections on nascent entrepreneur expectations. *Strategic Management Journal, 31*(8), 822–840.

Chandler, A. (1990). *Scale and Scope: The Dynamics of Industrial Capitalism.* Cambridge, MA: Harvard University Press.

Contractor, F.J., Kumar, V., Kundu, S.K., and Pedersen, T. (2010). Reconceptualizing the firm in a world of outsourcing and offshoring: The organizational and geographical relocation of high-value company functions. *Journal of Management Studies, 47*(8), 1417–1433.

Davidsson, P. (2005). *Researching Entrepreneurship*, Vol. 5. New York: Springer Science & Business Media.

Delmar, F., Davidsson, P., and Gartner, W.B. (2003). Arriving at the high-growth firm. *Journal of Business Venturing, 18*(2), 189–216.

Eddleston, K.A., Kellermanns, F.W., and Sarathy, R. (2008). Resource configuration in family firms: Linking resources, strategic planning and technological opportunities to performance. *Journal of Management Studies, 45*(1), 26–50.

Gartner, W.B. (1993). Words lead to deeds: Towards an organizational emergence vocabulary. *Journal of Business Venturing, 8*(3), 231–239.

Gohmann, S.F. and Fernandez, J.M. (2014). Proprietorship and unemployment in the United States. *Journal of Business Venturing, 29*(2), 289–309.

Gompers, P., Kovner, A., and Lerner, J. (2009). Specialization and success: Evidence from venture capital. *Journal of Economics & Management Strategy, 18*(3), 817–844.

Gruber, M., MacMillan, I.C., and Thompson, J.D. (2012). From minds to markets: How human capital endowments shape market opportunity identification of technology start-ups. *Journal of Management, 38*(5), 1421–1449.

Gundry, L.K., Kickul, J.R., Griffiths, M.D., and Bacq, S.C. (2011). Creating social change out of nothing: The role of entrepreneurial bricolage in social entrepreneurs' catalytic innovations. *Advances in Entrepreneurship, Firm Emergence and Growth, 13*(7), 1–24.

Hitt, M.A., Takacs, H., and Serpa, R. (2010). Strategic leadership for the 21st century. *Business Horizons, 53*(5), 437.

Isenberg, D.J. (2010). How to start an entrepreneurial revolution. *Harvard Business Review, 88*(6), 40–50.

Ives, A.R. and Carpenter, S.R. (2007). Stability and diversity of ecosystems. *Science, 317*(5834), 58–62.

Kuratko, D.F., Morris, M.H., and Schindehutte, M. (2015). Understanding the dynamics of entrepreneurship through framework approaches. *Small Business Economics, 45*(1), 1–13.

Lazear, E.P. (2005). Entrepreneurship. *Journal of Labor Economics, 23*, 649–680.

Lee, S.H., Peng, M.W., and Barney, J.B. (2007). Bankruptcy law and entrepreneurship development: A real options perspective. *Academy of Management Review, 32*(1), 257–272.

Lerner, J. (2010). The future of public efforts to boost entrepreneurship and venture capital. *Small Business Economics, 35*(3), 255–264.

Lichtenstein, B.B., Dooley, K.J., and Lumpkin, G.T. (2006). Measuring emergence in the dynamics of new venture creation. *Journal of Business Venturing, 21*(2), 153–175.

Lowe, J., Mckenna, J., and Tibbits, G. (1991). Small firm growth and failure: Public policy issues and practical problems. *Economic Papers: A Journal of Applied Economics and Policy, 10*(2), 69–81.

Malchow-Moller, N., Schjerning, B., and Sørensen, A. (2011). Entrepreneurship, job creation and wage growth. *Small Business Economics, 36*(1), 15–32.

Malecki, E.J. (2011). Connecting local entrepreneurial ecosystems to global innovation networks: Open innovation, double networks and knowledge integration. *International Journal of Entrepreneurship and Innovation Management, 14*(1), 36–59.

McGrath, R.G. (1999). Falling forward: Real options reasoning and entrepreneurial failure. *Academy of Management Review, 24*(1), 13–30.

Michel, J.S. (2014). Return on recent VC investment and long-run IPO returns. *Entrepreneurship Theory and Practice, 38*(3), 527–549.

Mielach, D. (2012). What it really costs when Walmart comes to town. *Business News Daily*, April 23. Accessed April 5, 2015 at http://www.businessnews daily.com/2405-real-cost-walmart.html.

Morris, M.H. and Pitt, L.F. (1995). Informal sector activity as entrepreneurship: Insights from a South African township. *Journal of Small Business Management, 33*(1), 78.

Morris, M.H., Kuratko, D.F., Schindehutte, M., and Spivack, A.J. (2012). Framing the entrepreneurial experience. *Entrepreneurship Theory and Practice, 36*(1), 11–40.

Morris, M.H., Neumeyer, X., and Kuratko, D.F. (2015). A portfolio perspective on entrepreneurship and economic development, *Small Business Economics, 45*(4), 713–728.

Morris, M.H., Santos, S.C., and Neumeyer, X. (eds) (2018). *Poverty and Entrepreneurship in Developed Economies.* Cheltenham, UK and Northampton, MA, USA: Edward Elgar Publishing.

Mufson, S. (2015). Before Solyndra, a long history of failed government energy projects. *Washington Post,* November 12.

Nambisan, S. and Baron, R.A. (2013). Entrepreneurship in innovation ecosystems: Entrepreneurs' self-regulatory processes and their implications for new venture success. *Entrepreneurship Theory and Practice, 37*(5), 1071–1097.

Phillips, K.A. (2005). *The Broken Mirror: Understanding and Treating Body Dysmorphic Disorder.* New York: Oxford University Press.

Robbins, D.K., Pantuosco, L.J., Parker, D.F., and Fuller, B.K. (2000). An empirical assessment of the contribution of small business employment to US state economic performance. *Small Business Economics, 15*(4), 293–302.

Robinson, R.B. (2002). Creating a 21st century entrepreneurial organization. *Academy of Entrepreneurship Journal, 8*(1).

Sarasvathy, S.D., Menon, A.R., and Kuechle, G. (2013). Failing firms and successful entrepreneurs: Serial entrepreneurship as a temporal portfolio. *Small Business Economics, 40*(2), 417–434.

Schindehutte, M., Morris, M.H., and Pitt, L. (2008). *Rethinking Marketing: The Entrepreneurial Imperative.* Upper Saddle River, NJ: Pearson Prentice Hall.

Schow, A. (2012). President Obama's taxpayer-backed green energy failures. *The Daily Signal.* Accessed September 6, 2019 at http://dailysignal.com/2012/10/18/president-obamas-taxpayer-backed-green-energy-failures/.

Senyard, J.M., Baker, T., and Steffens, P.R. (2010). Entrepreneurial bricolage and firm performance: Moderating effects of firm change and innovativeness. Queensland University. Accessed September 2019 at http://eprints. qut.edu.au/39755/.

Shane, S. (2009). Why encouraging more people to become entrepreneurs is bad public policy. *Small Business Economics, 33*(2), 141–149.

Spellerberg, I.F. and Fedor, P. J. (2003). A tribute to Claude Shannon (1916–2001) and a plea for more rigorous use of species richness, species diversity and the "Shannon-Wiener" Index. *Global Ecology and Biogeography, 72*(3), 177.

Stangler, D. (2010). *High-Growth Firms and the Future of the American Economy.* Kansas City: Kauffman Foundation.

Storey, D.J. (1994). New firm growth and bank financing. *Small Business Economics, 6*(2), 139–150.

Sturgeon, S. (2000). *Matters of Mind: Consciousness, Reason and Nature.* London: Psychology Press.

Thurik, A.R. and Audretsch, D.B. (2004). A model of the entrepreneurial economy. *International Journal of Entrepreneurship Education, 2*(1), 143–166.

Thurik, A.R. and Wennekers, S. (2004). Entrepreneurship, small business and economic growth. *Journal of Small Business and Enterprise Development, 11*(1), 140–149.

US Small Business Administration (2015). Accessed March 15, 2019 at https://www.sba.gov/content/small-business-trends-impact.

Van Stel, A., Carree, M., and Thurik, R. (2005). The effect of entrepreneurial activity on national economic growth. *Small Business Economics, 24*(3), 311–321.

Webb, J.W., Tihanyi, L., Ireland, R.D., and Sirmon, D.G. (2009). You say illegal, I say legitimate: Entrepreneurship in the informal economy. *Academy of Management Review, 34*(3), 492–510.

Wiklund, J. and Shepherd, D. (2003). Knowledge-based resources, entrepreneurial orientation, and the performance of small and medium-sized businesses. *Strategic Management Journal, 24*(13), 1307–1314.

Winborg, J. and Landstrom, H. (2001), Financial bootstrapping in small businesses: Examining small business managers' resource acquisition behaviors. *Journal of Business Venturing, 16*(3), 235–254.

Wolfson, M. (1994). When inequalities diverge. *American Economic Review, 84*, 353–358.

12. Venture types, public policy and ecosystem support

INTRODUCTION

The portfolio argument presented in Chapter 11 suggests that survival, lifestyle, managed growth and aggressive growth ventures all serve important roles in the economy. They represent interdependent components of a vibrant entrepreneurial ecosystem both at a national and local level, and so it becomes critical that all four be supported. While Shane (2009) is correct in concluding that all entrepreneurs are not created equal in terms of their impact on the economy, the implication should not be that most of them should be ignored in favor of those creating high growth ventures. A goal of public policy, and of support efforts of economic development agencies, educational institutions, non-profits and others in the so-called entrepreneurial ecosystem, should be to "let a thousand flowers bloom" when it comes to new ventures.

The purpose and nature of the four types of ventures differ significantly, suggesting each has unique needs and requirements to be successful. Public policy and community-based initiatives intended to facilitate entrepreneurship should not be put in the position of "picking the winners" as the venture capitalist attempts to do. Those behind these efforts should instead focus on enlarging and improving the total pool of ventures being launched, and encouraging a level of diversity that maximizes interactions among actors in the entrepreneurial ecosystem.

Unfortunately, this tends not to be the case. In a systematic assessment, Mason and Brown (2013) found that public policy efforts tend to be disjointed and piecemeal, and are not well targeted when it comes to entrepreneurial activity. Similarly, the efforts of those constituting entrepreneurial ecosystems at regional or local levels are often uncoordinated, lack clear strategic focus, and fail to serve many of those attempting to start and grow ventures (Neumeyer et al., 2019). Various observers point to a range of needs within early stage ventures, many of which are largely ignored by policy makers and others trying to support entrepreneurship (Audretsch et al., 2007; Dennis, 2011; Lundstrom and Stevenson, 2006). Arguably, one of the most problematic aspects of current policies and programs is their failure to distinguish among the four venture contexts addressed in this book and address the fundamental differences in their needs.

In this chapter, we examine public policies together with support initiatives at the community level that can foster each of the four venture types. Ongoing gaps in policies and programs to foster entrepreneurial activity are identified. Key policy levers and community elements that could be used to support entrepreneurship are then identified. Attention is devoted to describing the elements of a more holistic policy framework – one that reflects the needs and challenges of the different venture types over their stages of development.

GAPS IN POLICY SUPPORT FOR ENTREPRENEURSHIP

Levels of entrepreneurship differ significantly in countries across the globe. These differences are due to a wide range of factors, but the legal system plays an important role (Acs et al., 2008; Chowdhury et al., 2015). For instance, where policies are created to make business entry and exit easier for entrepreneurs, or to democratize financial markets, the impact on entrepreneurial activity is generally positive (Acs and Szerb, 2007).

An array of laws and regulations accumulate over time in response to social, economic, technological, political and ecological developments. Although often created for other purposes, many of them affect those trying to launch and grow new ventures, such as minimum wage laws, health and safety regulations, product liability legislation, affirmative action requirements and environmental protection rules. Other laws and regulations provide a general framework for conducting business, such as limits to the personal liability of business owners, enforcement of contracts, rules governing unfair or anti-competitive business practices, intellectual property protection and bankruptcy provisions. Finally, there are public policies that directly aid or assist the entrepreneur. These can differ depending on the level of government, but examples include tax incentives for starting, growing or investing in entrepreneurial ventures, and government guarantees for bank loans to entrepreneurs.

Stated differently, governments usually have many policies that impact entrepreneurs positively and negatively, but countries generally lack an overall legal and regulatory strategy or framework for fostering entre-preneurial activity. Instead, what emerges is a patchwork of laws, regulations and programs, some of which emphasize existing small- and medium-sized enterprises (SMEs), others of which prioritize scalable, aggressive growth ventures, and still others that focus on spurring entrepreneurial activity in general (Patzelt and Shepherd, 2009). More critically, there does not appear to be any consensus among those formulating policy regarding what entrepreneurship is, the form(s) it takes, or the priority needs of entrepreneurs (Dennis, 2011).

A variety of observers have raised concerns and noted problems when it comes to public policies directed at entrepreneurial ventures. Below are examples of some of their key conclusions:

- Policy makers are not presently equipped (do not have the research evidence or knowledge base) to properly understand the public policy role for entrepreneurship (Audretsch et al., 2007).
- Policies aimed at fostering entrepreneurship in most western democracies do not greatly reduce or solve market failures but instead waste taxpayers' money, encourage those already intent on becoming entrepreneurs, and mostly generate marginal businesses (Acs et al., 2016).
- Responsibility for entrepreneurship policy (as opposed to policy that only supports the established small business community) generally falls across a wide range of agencies and ministries, with no single agency to coordinate and promote entrepreneurial activity (Audretsch, 2004).
- Policy efforts that attempt to "pick the winners" in terms of resource support for high growth firms have been shown to be largely ineffective (Norrman and Bager-Sjögren, 2010), and likely come at the expense of facilitating other forms of entrepreneurial activity (Dahlstrand and Stevenson, 2010).
- There is no clear evidence of success of policies focused exclusively on encouragement of high growth entrepreneurship, possibly because it is hard to predict whether high growth will actually occur when a venture is launched (Mason and Brown, 2013).
- Direct financial and other firm-specific support from government for knowledge-intensive start-ups is less productive than efforts to facilitate supportive and connected ecosystems (Hefferan and Fern, 2018).
- Regulation that is ostensibly favorable toward entrepreneurship in general can have unintended negative consequences for certain types of ventures (Spencer and Gómez, 2004).
- Policy efforts that remove impediments have a much greater impact than those that provide direct support in their impact on new, small and entrepreneurial firms (Dennis, 2011).

Issues such as these have led Dahlstrand and Stevenson (2010) to conclude that a more holistic policy framework is needed, one that considers general entrepreneurial activity and specific forms of entrepreneurial activity, and one that integrates both innovation policy, SME policy and entrepreneurship policy (see also Gilbert et al., 2004). Taking this concept a step further, we advocate for the development of policies and programs that target the distinct needs of survival, lifestyle, managed growth and aggressive growth ventures as they emerge. In addition, a more complete picture is provided if policy elements are coupled with support initiatives emanating from local communities or ecosystems. Such a coordinated yet targeted approach is much more likely to increase levels of entrepreneurial activity while producing a balanced portfolio of ventures that can mutually reinforce one another and collectively contribute to a variety of positive economic outcomes (see Audretsch and Monsen, 2008; Henrekson and Stenkula, 2010). Before introducing such an approach, let us consider the kinds of policy tools and programs that can play contributing roles.

PRINCIPAL POLICY LEVERS TO SUPPORT ENTREPRENEURSHIP

Policy development is a complex process that includes a large set of actors including politicians, lobbyists, domain experts, non-profit organizations, and various interest groups that use a range of tactics and tools to advance their goals. In the United States, policy makers have several levers they can utilize to effect entrepreneurial outcomes. Here, we can distinguish policies that (a) have an indirect effect on entrepreneurship (e.g., tariffs, immigration policies, trade policy, access to foreign technology, investments in science and technology education); (b) those that set the general rules for entrepreneurship (e.g., limited liability, liberal bankruptcy laws); and (c) those directly targeting nascent and early stage entrepreneurs (Acs and Szerb, 2007). Our focus here is on the latter category, and specifically, policy levers that either provide public support for entrepreneurial activity or remove impediments (reduce transaction costs) (Dennis, 2011). Let us consider eight of these levers (see also Table 12.1).

We begin with taxation policies, which provide entrepreneurs and/or their ventures with tax deductions, credits, preferential rates, deferrals or exclusion of income from taxation. Policy makers can also vary capital gains taxes on investments, including stock in entrepreneurial companies. They determine the goods and services that are subject to sales (or

Table 12.1 Supporting entrepreneurship with both public policy and community action

Public Sector Initiatives	Community-based Initiatives
• Tax incentives for private investors to invest in entrepreneurial ventures • Tax incentives and income supplements for entrepreneurs tied to progress in pursuing a venture • Tax incentives to individuals and companies for sharing facilities and equipment with entrepreneurs • Intellectual property protection • Entrepreneurship tracks in high schools • Access to government patents and knowledge resources • Low cost broadband/internet access • Vouchers to attend conferences, trade shows, fairs, workshops, buy equipment, use legal and accounting service providers, get marketing and branding assistance • Easy access to government, industry and company databases • Government procurement contracts directed at entrepreneurial ventures • Support for small business development centers, women's business centers, minority business centers and related support programs • Loan guarantees • Grants for early stage ventures • Regulatory relief or exemption for small businesses up to a certain size • Simplified paperwork reporting for early stage ventures • Waivers for minimum wage requirements • Streamlining and simplifying permitting and licensing processes • Fiscal incentives for investors and platforms to promote participation in peer-to-peer lending to entrepreneurs • Legislation making angel investment, crowdfunding and microcredit programs easier to create and administer • Co-investment with private investors • Support for hubzones • Financial incentives for creating permanent jobs • Regulation that encourages competition	• Develop local ecosystems that support all four types of start-up ventures • Create local clearing house to connect all components of entrepreneurial ecosystem • Provide low cost space for ventures • Banking and financial community that prioritizes investments in ventures, including microcredit and grants • Encouragement of angel networks and matchmaking of angels and entrepreneurs • Support for community development corps. • Local entrepreneurship training bootcamps and specialized training programs • Small business internships • Creation of local library resources and online portals to support venture start-up • Multi-stakeholder networks to support nascent and early stage entrepreneurs, including coaches, mentors and small business sponsors • Expertise pool to address key problem areas confronting emerging ventures • Partnerships with local businesses to enhance capabilities of new ventures • Community events to connect new entrepreneurs to local businesses • Buy local campaigns • Local business plan/pitch competitions • Access to incubators and accelerators • Technology literacy programs • Access to consulting teams and other expertise from local colleges/universities • Support for development of intellectual property with fablabs and makerspaces • Buying cooperatives • Access to low cost technologies • Procurement contracts from local firms • Local financial literacy programs • Cooperative networks that encourage gifting, sharing, renting, selling, and other forms of collaboration – to include businesses, non-profits, churches, others • Peer-to-peer lending networks and community-based self-financing groups • Speaker forums and celebrations of local entrepreneurial excellence

value-added) and excise taxes. They establish rates and exclusions for the taxes on property owned by businesses. And unless the company has equivalent insurance, they assess workers' compensation taxes for workers injured in the course of their employment.

Tax credits allow individuals or businesses to reduce the amount of tax they owe. When it comes to entrepreneurship, they can also be used to encourage people to start particular types of businesses, locate businesses in defined areas, develop innovations and technology, invest in capital equipment, hire employees, improve facilities, and remain in a given locale. The Earned Income Tax Credit is also available for income received through self-employment, which provides entrepreneurs with an opportunity to earn tax credits on their entrepreneurial activities. Another tool is the saver's tax credit, an incentive to help low income micro-business owners save for retirement.

Just as relevant is the availability of tax incentives for people and organizations that invest money, equipment or other resources into ventures, or invest in funding vehicles such as micro-lending programs. An example of the latter is the New Markets Tax Credit (NMTC), which provides individual and corporate investors with a tax credit for making equity investments in Community Development Entities (CDEs) that can then use the funds to invest in the needs of early stage businesses led by local entrepreneurs. These investments enhance local economies, which can create a ripple effect attracting further investments (NMTC Program Fact Sheet, 2017).

Our second lever is subsidy programs. These generally find the government providing direct payments to individuals to augment their income. An example is the Temporary Assistance for Needy Families (TANF) program in the United States. Technically a block grant to individual states, TANF provides cash assistance for up to 60 months, with the explicit goal of incentivizing beneficiaries to find employment. A successful variation of this type of program designed to impact entrepreneurial activity can be found in Germany. The Bridging Allowance was launched as an income-subsidy policy for the unemployed in the mid-1980s with the intention of fostering nascent entrepreneurship. This became the foundation of the Start-up Subsidy program that was active from 2006 to 2011, and its successor, the New Start-Up Subsidy, running from 2012 to the present. The main goal of the program is to provide unemployed people with a monthly subsidy as they make progress with launching a business. The businesses that were subsequently created by the unemployed demonstrated promising survival rates, with 70 percent of the participants in eastern Germany and 68 percent of those in western Germany still in business five years after leaving the program. Between 30 percent and 40 percent of business founders created additional jobs beyond their own (OECD/European Union, 2014). There were persistent positive long-run effects of both the Start-Up Subsidy and Bridging Allowance programs, particularly for individuals at high risk of being excluded from the labor market and joining the ranks of the long-term unemployed (Caliendo and Künn, 2011).

A third lever, loan guarantees, represent yet another policy tool. Here, the loan itself is usually made by a commercial bank or other financial institution, but the government is guaranteeing some proportion of the loan (sometimes 75 percent or more) in the instance that the borrower defaults. This enables the lending institution to loan money to those who otherwise might not qualify, and/or to provide loans at more attractive interest rates. A key use of guarantees is the development of a business. The COSME Program in Europe and the SBA Loan Program in the United States are examples of initiatives that have enabled the development of hundreds of thousands of small businesses over the years. Some programs, such as the 8(a) Business Development Program of the US Small Business Administration, serve disadvantaged small business owners with a range of support, including financial assistance, mentoring, business counseling and collective bidding.

In the United States, capital access programs (CAPs) represent an interesting variation when it comes to lending. CAPs are historically run by the individual states, but are supported by the federal government's State Small Business Credit Initiative (SSBCI). Under these programs, operated by about 27 states, borrowers (small businesses) and lenders (banks) contribute a percentage of the loan or credit (between 2–7 percent) into a reserve fund that insures the loan in case of a default. Since 1986, state CAPs have enabled more than $1.5 billion in small business loans to be made at low cost and low risk, benefiting significant numbers of small business owners, and particularly minorities (Barr, 2008). CAPs were built to supply early stage ventures that do not possess collateral or other resources that are typically needed to receive a conventional loan from a community or private bank. Despite the attractiveness of these loans, borrowers are often unwilling to pay the initial CAP fee, while lenders are reluctant to participate because they need to enroll a large number of loans to build a sufficient loan loss reserve fund.

In a related vein, several European Union countries have introduced policies to support subsidized loan schemes. Italy and France have developed "Honour Loans" (i.e., offered based on the borrower's word of honor, without requiring collateral or other forms of guarantee) as a combination of grants and interest-free loans. They have provided loans to several generations of young and female entrepreneurs as a tool to address the lack of jobs (OECD/European Union, 2014). The Honour Loan program contributes to formalize hidden economic activities and involves local authorities in incentive schemes to address aspects of unemployment. Moreover, there is a commitment that businesses supported by this program remain located in the disadvantaged part of the community for at least five years after receiving program support (OECD/European Union, 2016).

As government agencies at all levels spend billions each year on purchases of products and services, a relatively high impact tool involves buying directly from small businesses. With this fourth lever, the government might mandate that a certain percentage of spending must go to small or earlier stage businesses. So-called set asides enable small firms to get contracts without competing with larger companies. Preferential procurement gives priority in vendor selection to firms that meet certain criteria, such as being minority-owned, woman-owned, based in particular areas (e.g., inner city, rural locations), or under a defined size in terms of sales or employees.

Another policy lever available to support entrepreneurship involves voucher programs. Vouchers are subsidies that recipients use to pay for goods or services. Governments at various levels have implemented voucher programs that target areas such as childcare, food, housing, education and medical assistance programs (Colin, 2005; Steuerle and Twombly, 2002). If we consider venture creation, vouchers can be used to pay for assistance with registering a business, bookkeeping, development of logos and marketing materials, creation of websites, writing a business plan, attending training courses, and paying rent in an incubator, among other business services.

A sixth policy option is to provide grants for particular projects or initiatives (Beam and Conlan, 2002). Grants are effectively free money, although they often come with conditions. They can be made directly to the beneficiary or to intermediate (public, private or non-profit) agencies who then administer smaller grants to beneficiaries, thereby allowing for more flexibility and tailoring of allocations to reflect local circumstances and needs (Beam and Conlon, 2002). With regard to entrepreneurship, grants are used to help entrepreneurs develop products or services that address particular problems or needs of the government, often products incorporating advanced technologies. They can play a role in seeding microcredit funds administered by non-profits and other organizations. Grants can also be designed to support particular actions or behaviors by entrepreneurs, such as retrofitting or upgrading a facility to be used for business purposes, locating in a particular area, investing in technology or hiring an employee.

Our seventh policy lever is regulatory policies and regulatory relief. Regulations affect everything from the licenses necessary to get into business to rules governing safety practices and access by disabled people, employee hiring and firing, and the minimum wage that must be paid. Early stage businesses are disproportionately affected by virtually any law or regulation. The costs of compliance are a higher portion of their available resources, and it can require a disproportionate amount of their scarce time to understand and figure out how to comply with a given regulation. They cannot afford to hire lawyers and other professionals to get them waivers or otherwise find ways around regulations. Beyond making regulations easier to understand and comply with, or hiring government staff to assist small businesses with compliance, regulations can be designed in ways that exempt businesses that are less than three years old, have fewer than five employees or whose revenues do not exceed $100,000. Similarly, where fees must be paid for a license, permit, variance or government exemption, these can be waived for those in poverty.

Regulatory relief can also be directed at organizations that form parts of the entrepreneurial ecosystem. Especially important in this regard is the regulation of financing vehicles. Making it easier to create and administer microcredit, peer-to-peer lending and community-based group lending initiatives could open up large pools of capital to lower income entrepreneurs.

A final lever involves the creation and financial support of government-affiliated or government-run agencies and organizations that directly assist entrepreneurs in particular areas. Small business development centers, women's business centers and organizations like the SCORE chapters in the United States provide free advice and access to other resources. In addition, workforce development programs can promote career opportunities that include self-employment, together with entrepreneurship training and mentoring services. Many other possibilities exist, such as using the postal service as a means of providing vouchers to entrepreneurs or using government office space for community incubators (Baradaran, 2015).

THE OTHER SIDE OF ENTREPRENEURIAL SUPPORT: COMMUNITY-BASED INITIATIVES

Communities can play an even bigger role than government in supporting entrepreneurial activity in its many forms. Non-profit organizations (including churches), private companies (both large and small), financial institutions, private investors, economic development agencies, libraries, schools and universities can work independently and collaboratively with one another in fostering new venture creation and growth. They form what it has become popular to call "entrepreneurial ecosystems," building on the metaphor of a biological ecosystem.

The challenge with these community-based ecosystems is that they typically consist of a disparate set of players, each with a unique purpose and focus, whose efforts often overlap but tend not to be coordinated. Individual components can act in isolation or as silos, and communication among the players can be limited. They frequently do not see themselves or operate as if part of a system. Ecosystems place most of their emphasis on high potential, technology-based ventures, while tending to underserve women, minorities, immigrants, the disadvantaged and lower income entrepreneurs (Neumeyer et al., 2019).

Nonetheless, with quality community leadership, the organizations and individuals that constitute these ecosystems can arguably have a more direct and significant impact on entrepreneurial activity than do government policies and programs. Below are 12 examples of the kinds of community initiatives that can make a difference:

- A clearinghouse that connects nascent and early stage entrepreneurs to all the available resources in the local community.
- Financial and technology literacy initiatives launched by schools, banks, financial service firms, libraries, churches and professional associations.
- Community-oriented training and development programs that focus on entrepreneurship and basic business topics, including those offered by local workforce development and jobs training agencies, chambers of commerce and colleges/universities.
- Microcredit schemes and small grants for entrepreneurs offered through community development financial institutions, community banks, credit unions and community-based self-financing groups.
- Greater availability of loan products and alternative debt finance such as overdrafts, factoring, leasing and trade credit from banks.
- Angel networks and related investor forums that focus on equity investments in locally and regionally based entrepreneurs.
- Supportive physical spaces for entrepreneurs, including hatcheries, incubators, co-working spaces, accelerators, fablabs and makerspaces.
- Mentoring and advice from local business professionals and small business assistance centers, including online resources, as well as consulting from student teams at local colleges.

- Company procurement programs that commit to make a percentage of product and service purchases from small and early stage businesses, and associated mentor-protégé initiatives to help small business learn how to get and retain business from larger companies.
- Internship programs, apprenticeships and shadowing projects in entrepreneurial firms.
- Free or very low cost broadband access subsidized by local utilities and other community partners.
- Broader access to the sharing or collaborative economy, where the entrepreneur is able to take advantage of resource gifting, sharing, renting, co-marketing, and other forms of collaboration from local and online sources.

This is but a partial listing of the kinds of elements that, together with the earlier policy levers, can produce a sustained entrepreneurial renaissance at the local level (see also Table 12.1). These efforts are not an alternative to public policy, but should be pursued in tandem with, and in ways that capitalize upon, policy efforts. It might also be noted that most attempts to map these local ecosystems leave out a number of the elements identified in Table 12.1. All communities are rich in resources, but many of these are often overlooked. Especially critical is the need for creativity in leveraging the many different types of available resources, encouraging novel collaborations and partnerships between individuals and organizations, and promoting highly visible communication efforts that create awareness and connections among the various stakeholders.

PRIORITY ONE: TAILORING SUPPORT EFFORTS TO THE FOUR VENTURE TYPES

As we look to the future, two priorities should guide ongoing efforts to foster entrepreneurial activity. The first of these concerns the need to tailor support efforts in ways that reflect the unique needs of survival, lifestyle, managed growth and aggressive growth ventures. Let us first consider public policy. Table 12.2 provides an example of a partial mix of policies that might resonate across our four categories of ventures. Here, we consider four categories of government engagement: financial investments, non-financial support programs, taxation incentives and regulation.

Table 12.2   *Examples of public policies addressing needs of the four venture types*

	Survival	Lifestyle	Managed Growth	Aggressive Growth
Financial investment	Grants and no or low interest microloan programs supported by different levels of government	Government-funded microloan programs and guarantees on bank loans to entrepreneurs	Government-backed bank loans for expansion	Small business innovation research grants Government-backed seed funding for high growth ventures
Non-financial support program	Community micro incubators Mentoring and counseling for the socioeconomically disadvantaged Vouchers for business services Welfare-to-work programs	Small disadvantaged business certification programs Preferential government procurement programs targeting small businesses Small business consulting centers	Government contracts for a variety of products and services Programs to facilitate export sales Growth-oriented local incubation programs	Support for venture accelerators Programs to give entrepreneurs access to government-owned technologies Programs to build high growth management capacity
Tax policies	Earned income tax credit applied to ventures started by low income entrepreneurs Tax waivers	Home office tax deduction More liberal write-off of current period expenses	Tax credits for job creation Tax incentives for facility expansion Carry forward loss provisions	R&D tax credits Low capital gains taxes Incentives for R&D partnerships Tax credits for job creation Increasing tax write-off on start-up costs
Regulation and regulatory policies	Policies that lower entry barriers such as more liberal licensing	Regulatory exemptions until venture reaches a certain size	Loosening labor market regulatory requirements and ease of terminating employees Liberalizing rules on accredited investors and crowdfunding	Intellectual property protection Liberal bankruptcy laws Support for transfer of university technologies

For the survival venture, programs that make it easy to enter the market and that provide seed grants, government-supported microcredit schemes, basic business training, and inexpensive ways to utilize small business service providers (e.g., vouchers) would be examples of priorities. For the lifestyle venture, government-guaranteed bank loans, small business counseling and mentoring programs, government vouchers and access to small business procurement programs (from federal, provincial or state, and local government agencies) can be valuable. Tax policy becomes more important with the managed growth venture (incentives for expansion and job creation) and even more so with the high growth venture (incentives related to R&D spending, innovation and capital gains). With the managed growth firm, regulatory relief, particularly associated with the cost of employees, can be an important facilitator. The high growth firm needs access to venture accelerators, development of managerial capacity to scale a venture, and greater protection for its intellectual property. There are, further, many policies that affect more than one type of venture, such as the role of government-backed loans with both lifestyle and managed growth ventures, or the impact of limited liability protection and liberal bankruptcy laws especially on ventures that have more downside risk, such as managed growth and high growth businesses.

Community support initiatives can also be tailored in ways that reflect the four venture types, and this may be easier to accomplish than changes to laws and regulations. As illustrated in Table 12.3, community efforts can be organized into training and development activities directed at the entrepreneur, direct personal assistance, financial resources, and means of accessing other business-related resources.

Training programs for survivalists need to focus on basic knowledge and skill levels including competency at functional (reading, writing, numeracy, communication), financial, technological, economic and business literacies. These entrepreneurs need exposure to small business operations, mentors who have run ventures, and information regarding available local resources. They can benefit from community microcredit programs and small grants, as well as vouchers and scholarships from community organizations to cover the costs of training classes and key services such as logo design, help with business plan preparation, and basic bookkeeping. In addition, campaigns to "buy local" and events to connect these entrepreneurs to the larger business community are helpful. They can use co-working spaces in trying to get their ventures organized, while the ability to tap into cooperative community networks where resources can be provided in-kind, shared or used on a temporary basis, and activities can be accomplished collaboratively, is especially valuable.

*Table 12.3   Community programs addressing needs of the four venture
types*

	Survival	Lifestyle	Managed Growth	Aggressive Growth
Training and development	• Training in functional, financial, technical and business literacies • Training in start-up basics	• Training in financial, technical and business literacies • Entrepreneurship training bootcamps	• Specialized training on how to formalize operations, financial management and business technologies • Entrepreneurship bootcamps	• Specialized training in strategic thinking, delegation, staffing, infrastructure development, scaling issues
Personal advice and expertise	• Small business internships for founder • Mentors/ coaches from small business community • Assistance from local non-profits • Local resource portal	• Expertise pools from local business community • Consulting projects from local universities/ colleges • Mentors/ coaches from small business community • Local resource portal	• Expertise pools from local business community • Mentors and coaches from larger, established companies • Board members • Consulting projects from local universities	• Peer mentors with high growth experience • Investment community advisors • Board members • Potential partners/ co-founders • University support for tech development
Financial resources	• Microcredit programs • Small grants programs • Support from community development corporations • Peer-to-peer lending programs • Vouchers for training, basic service providers	• Microcredit programs • Basic bank loan products • Vouchers for basic service providers, equipment, facilities • Peer-to-peer lending • Support from community development corporations	• Range of bank loan products, including lines of credit • Equipment leases • Angel networks • Community investment forums • Crowdfunding	• Range of bank loan products • Convertible debt • Angel networks • Community investment forums • Connections to venture capitalists • Crowdfunding

	Survival	**Lifestyle**	**Managed Growth**	**Aggressive Growth**
Facilities, equipment, other non-financial resources	• Co-working spaces • Buy local campaigns • Cooperative networks that encourage gifting, sharing, renting, joint selling, other forms of collaboration • Events to make connections to local business community • Space inside of existing businesses	• Hatcheries and incubators • Access to low cost technologies • Local business procurement • Buy local campaigns • Cooperative networks that encourage gifting, sharing, renting, joint selling, other forms of collaboration • Events to make connections to local business community	• Incubators • Accelerators • Fablabs • Makerspaces • Events to make connections to local business community • Student interns	• Access to skilled labor force • Strategic partnerships • Accelerators • Fablabs • Makerspaces • Student interns

With lifestyle ventures, they can benefit from most of the same elements as survival ventures. However, emphasis on developing their financial, technical and business literacies must be even greater. The ability to call on expertise pools from the local business community when they confront particular problems, and to utilize student consulting teams and interns from local colleges/universities also become relevant. With financing, they need help in becoming eligible for basic loan products and credit card services from local banks. Community-supported vouchers can be useful here as well, particularly to pay for professional services, equipment and facility rent. Also pertinent are the abilities to access hatcheries and incubators prior to establishing their own premises, tap into low cost technologies for use in business processes, and participate in the small business procurement programs of larger companies in the region.

While managed growth entrepreneurs can capitalize on a number of these community resources, with some nuances, they also have distinct needs. They require specialized training in financial planning and cash flow management, and on how to formalize operations and incorporate newer technologies into business processes. The more appropriate kinds of expertise and coaching will tend to come from executives who have run larger and more complex operations. They need assistance in taking advantage of an array of bank loan and credit products, and may find local investors willing to support their growth plans. Community investment forums can be instrumental in connecting entrepreneurs to sources of money. In their early days, these ventures can take advantage of incubators, accelerators, fablabs and makerspaces.

The aggressive growth entrepreneur has training needs that, beyond exposing them to start-up fundamentals, emphasize strategic thinking and leadership, team building, delegation skills, an understanding of how to build infrastructure that will support a rapidly expanding enterprise, and approaches to addressing other scaling issues. Any mentoring and coaching must come from those with rapid growth experience as well as experts from the investment community. Access to quality board members and potential co-founders are important. The entrepreneur may be able to tap into local colleges and universities for help with technology development. Early on they will benefit from the facilities, equipment and other forms of support in accelerators, fablabs and makerspaces. While these ventures may qualify for various commercial loan products, they also can attract significant equity investment from angels and venture capital firms, and some initial funding through crowdfunding campaigns. Strategic partnerships with other companies can be a valuable means of developing technology, outsourcing aspects of operations and logistics, and accomplishing marketing and distribution tasks, among other possibilities. As they start to grow, these ventures must be able to access a skilled workforce.

Importantly, these and other public policy elements and community-based initiatives can interact with one another to affect entrepreneurial activity over time. They can serve to increase the desirability and ease of launching more entrepreneurial ventures, the demand for the goods and services of these ventures, and the availability of skills, knowledge and resources that these ventures require to succeed (Audretsch, 2002).

PRIORITY TWO: TAILORING SUPPORT EFFORTS TO STAGES OF DEVELOPMENT

The needs of entrepreneurs do not vary just by type of venture, but also by stage of development. One can identify any number of development stages, but for our purposes we focus here on three general stages: pre-start-up, launch-stabilization and growth.

In the pre-start-up stage, the entrepreneur is identifying a market opportunity, developing a business idea, designing a business model, developing prototypes, interviewing potential customers, writing a business plan, and attempting to marshal resources. It is a stage involving considerable research, networking and experimentation. The launch and stabilization stage is concerned with initiating operations, making initial sales, overcoming obstacles, learning from misjudgments and mistakes, adding resources, adapting and/or changing direction, and ultimately arriving at a sustainable business model. Growth is a stage involving expansion of physical facilities, growth of inventories, addition of locations, entry into new markets, and development of new products or lines of business. The entrepreneur is concerned with professionalizing management of the venture and instituting more formal structures, systems and controls.

The goals and priorities of the entrepreneur are changing in each stage, suggesting a need for different kinds of support efforts. As illustrated in Figure 12.1, the combination of public policy and community support initiatives should also be designed with these stages in mind.

At the pre-start-up stage, one is trying to provide individuals with an understanding of entrepreneurship as an option and prepare them for the entrepreneurial journey. The concern becomes educational programs to develop key literacies (functional, financial, economic, business and technological), expand the nascent entrepreneur's opportunity horizon, and providing entrepreneurship-related training. In addition, the availability of small business internships, local business plan competitions and pitches, entrepreneurial role models, coaches from the entrepreneurial community and networking forums are paramount at this stage. Further, income augmentation, vouchers and seed grants, assistance with licensing and permitting, and access to co-working spaces, hatcheries and facilities to develop prototypes can be critical.

In the launch and business stabilization stage, the focus in terms of support efforts should include development of microcredit programs, incentives for bank credit, the provision of space in incubators and accelerators and other buildings, awarding of procurement contracts to emerging ventures, and vouchers to use for professional service providers. Exclusion or relief from regulations and associated reporting requirements, particularly those driving up transaction costs, can be instrumental in allowing the entrepreneur to gain traction in the marketplace. Tax incentives or breaks tied to achieving particular milestones on the path to a sustainable business model can be relevant at this stage. The need in terms of coaches and mentors centers more on finding people

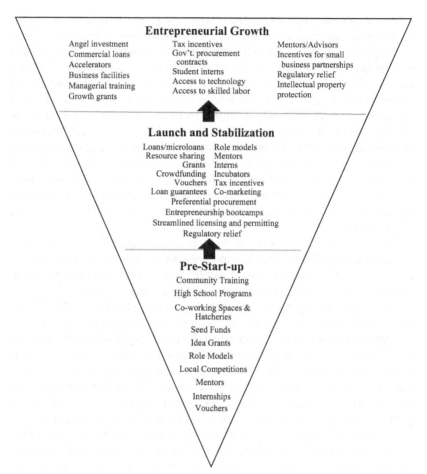

Entrepreneurial Growth

Angel investment	Tax incentives	Mentors/Advisors
Commercial loans	Gov't. procurement	Incentives for small
Accelerators	contracts	business partnerships
Business facilities	Student interns	Regulatory relief
Managerial training	Access to technology	Intellectual property
Growth grants	Access to skilled labor	protection

Launch and Stabilization

Loans/microloans	Role models
Resource sharing	Mentors
Grants	Interns
Crowdfunding	Incubators
Vouchers	Tax incentives
Loan guarantees	Co-marketing

Preferential procurement
Entrepreneurship bootcamps
Streamlined licensing and permitting
Regulatory relief

Pre-Start-up

Community Training

High School Programs

Co-working Spaces &
Hatcheries

Seed Funds

Idea Grants

Role Models

Local Competitions

Mentors

Internships

Vouchers

Figure 12.1   Examples of support needs at different stages of development

with expertise in addressing particular operational problems and resourcing issues as a business takes form and adapts to its competitive context.

Finally, the growth stage has different meanings dependent on venture type. It could entail nominal or incremental sales growth for the survival and lifestyle ventures, steady expansion of locations, products and markets for the managed growth firm, or rapid scaling of the aggressive growth firm. The nature of growth has implications for the kinds of support needed, and these implications are greatest for the managed and aggressive growth firms (Stangler, 2010). Meaningful growth places considerable cash flow pressures on the enterprise, suggesting a need both for advanced financial management skills and access to a range of debt and equity financing sources. Advisors and mentors are required who understand the fundamental changes that become necessary in terms of management skills and styles, the resource pool, organizational systems and structures, culture, and related aspects of the enterprise. Taxation and regulatory policies often penalize growth, when the need is to modify policy levers in ways that incentivize job creation, new product and service development, facility and location expansion, and technological advancements.

CONCLUSIONS

Although policy makers and community leaders increasingly recognize the value of entrepreneurial development, the approaches they rely upon to foster entrepreneurship tend to be piecemeal, disjointed, and of questionable effectiveness. In a time that some have referred to as the "age of entrepreneurship" (Kuratko and Morris, 2013), a more coordinated, integrated and holistic approach is needed, and this can only be accomplished if stakeholders at all levels engage in more strategic and innovative thinking. What is required are public policies and community initiatives that support a balanced portfolio of ventures, and reflect their changing needs over time.

Our purpose in this chapter has not been to advocate for particular policies and approaches, but to provide examples of the kinds of efforts needed to support survival, lifestyle, managed growth and aggressive growth ventures as they are conceptualized, planned, launched, stabilize and grow. It must be kept in mind that when it comes to facilitating entrepreneurship, public policy is a rough and somewhat limited tool. It is more equivalent to shining a floodlight rather than using a laser surgical tool. Community initiatives and local ecosystems, for their part, can play more targeted and specific roles in affecting entrepreneurial outcomes. In the end, it is the ability to formulate unique combinations of government programs and community initiatives that can enable society to tap the empowering and transformative potential of entrepreneurship.

Our recommendations here represent a fertile middle ground between a generic or "one size fits all" approach, and one that attempts to "pick the winners" in terms of policies and programs intended to identify and support only the highest potential ventures. The portfolio approach to policy does not favor any one type of venture, but instead, by reflecting the unique needs of four general categories of ventures, creates an environment favorable for all. Its concern is with encouraging both the overall quantity of start-ups and the quality of ventures created within each category.

REFERENCES

Acs, Z.J. and Szerb, L. (2007). Entrepreneurship, economic growth and public policy. *Small Business Economics*, *28*(2–3), 109–122.

Acs, Z.J., Desai, S., and Hessels, J. (2008). Entrepreneurship, economic development and institutions. *Small Business Economics*, *31*(3), 219–234.

Acs, Z., Åstebro, T., Audretsch, D., and Robinson, D.T. (2016). Public policy to promote entrepreneurship: A call to arms. *Small Business Economics*, *47*(1), 35–51.

Audretsch, D.B. (2002). The dynamic role of small firms: Evidence from the US. *Small Business Economics*, *18*(1–3), 13–40.

Audretsch, D.B. (2004). Sustaining innovation and growth: Public policy support for entrepreneurship. *Industry and Innovation*, *11*(3), 167–191.

Audretsch, D. and Monsen, E. (2008). Entrepreneurship capital: A regional, organizational, team and individual phenomenon. In R. Barrett and S. Mayson (eds), *International Handbook of Entrepreneurship and HRM*. Cheltenham, UK and Northampton, MA, USA: Edward Elgar Publishing, pp. 47–70.

Audretsch, D.B., Grilo, I., and Thurik, A.R. (eds) (2007). Explaining entrepreneurship and the role of policy: A framework. In D.B. Audretsch, I. Grilo, and A.R. Thurik (eds), *Handbook of Entrepreneurship Policy*. Cheltenham, UK and Northampton, MA, USA: Edward Elgar Publishing, pp. 1–17.

Baradaran, M. (2015). *How the Other Half Banks: Exclusion, Exploitation, and the Threat to Democracy*. Cambridge, MA: Harvard University Press.

Barr, M.S. (2008). Policies to expand minority entrepreneurship: Closing comments. In G. Yago, J.R. Barth, and B. Zeidman (eds), *Entrepreneurship in Emerging Domestic Markets: Barriers and Innovation*. The Milken Institute Series on Financial Innovation and Economic Growth, Vol. 7. New York: Springer, pp. 141–150.

Beam, D.R. and Conlan, T.J. (2002). Grants. In L.M. Salamon (ed.), *The Tools of Government: A Guide to the New Governance*. New York: Oxford University Press, pp. 340–380.

Caliendo, M. and Künn, S. (2011). Start-up subsidies for the unemployed: Long-term evidence and effect heterogeneity. *Journal of Public Economics*, *95*(3–4), 311–331.

Chowdhury, F., Terjesen, S., and Audretsch, D. (2015). Varieties of entrepreneurship: Institutional drivers across entrepreneurial activity and country. *European Journal of Law and Economics*, *40*(1), 121–148.

Colin, F. (2005). Public service vouchers. *International Review of Administrative Sciences*, *71*(1), 19–34.

Dahlstrand, A.L. and Stevenson, L. (2010). Innovative entrepreneurship policy: Linking innovation and entrepreneurship in a European context. *Annals of Innovation & Entrepreneurship*, *1*(1), 5602.

Dennis Jr, W.J. (2011). Entrepreneurship, small business and public policy levers. *Journal of Small Business Management, 49*(1), 92–106.

Gilbert, B.A., Audretsch, D.B., and McDougall, P.P. (2004). The emergence of entrepreneurship policy. *Small Business Economics, 22*(3–4), 313–323.

Hefferan, M. and Fern, A. (2018). Questioning the value of government support for start-up, knowledge-intensive companies: Emerging evidence and future options. *The Australasian Journal of Regional Studies, 24*(1), 78.

Henrekson, M. and Stenkula, M. (2010). Entrepreneurship and public policy. In Zoltan J. Acs and David B. Audretsch (eds), *Handbook of Entrepreneurship Research*. New York: Springer, pp. 595–637.

Kuratko, D.F. and Morris, M.H. (eds) (2013). *Entrepreneurship and Leadership*. Cheltenham, UK and Northampton, MA, USA: Edward Elgar Publishing.

Lundstrom, A. and Stevenson, L.A. (2006). *Entrepreneurship Policy: Theory and Practice*. New York: Kluwer Academic Publishers.

Mason, C. and Brown, R. (2013). Creating good public policy to support high-growth firms. *Small Business Economics, 40*(2), 211–225.

Neumeyer, X., Santos, S.C., and Morris, M.H. (2019). Who is left out: Exploring social boundaries in entrepreneurial ecosystems. *The Journal of Technology Transfer, 44*(2), 462–484.

NMTC Program Fact Sheet (2017). *Community Revitalization by Rewarding Private Investment*. US Department of the Treasury. Accessed September 6, 2019 at https://www.cdfifund.gov/programs-training/Programs/new-markets-tax-credit/Pages/default.aspx.

Norrman, C. and Bager-Sjögren, L. (2010). Entrepreneurship policy to support new innovative ventures: Is it effective? *International Small Business Journal, 28*(6), 602–619.

OECD/European Union (2014). *Policy Brief on Access to Business Start-up Finance for Inclusive Entrepreneurship: Entrepreneurial Activities in Europe. European Commission and OECD*. Luxembourg: Publications Office of the European Union.

OECD/European Union (2016). *Inclusive Business Creation: Good Practice Compendium*. Paris: OECD Publishing. http://dx.doi.org/10.1787/978926425 1496-en.

Patzelt, H. and Shepherd, D. (2009). Strategic entrepreneurship at universities: Academic entrepreneurs' assessment of policy programs. *Entrepreneurship Theory and Practice, 33*(1), 319–340.

Shane, S. (2009). Why encouraging more people to become entrepreneurs is bad public policy. *Small Business Economics, 33*(2), 141–149.

Spencer, J.W. and Gómez, C. (2004). The relationship among national institutional structures, economic factors, and domestic entrepreneurial activity: A multicountry study. *Journal of Business Research, 57*(10), 1098–1107.

Stangler, D. (2010), *High-growth Firms and the Future of the American Economy*. Kansas City: Kauffman Foundation.

Steuerle, C.E. and Twombly, E.C. (2002). Vouchers. In Lester M. Salamon (ed.), *The Tools of Government: A Guide to the New Governance*. New York: Oxford University Press, pp. 445–465.

Index

ability to manage growth 70–72
achievement motivation 74, 137, 139, 144
Acs, Z.J. 174
adaptation 81
adaptive tension 7
aggressive growth entrepreneurs 172, 204
aggressive growth firms 86, 119, 156, 159–162, 168, 172, 174, 176, 182, 206
aggressive growth ventures 24, 28–30, 52, 85–86, 109, 115, 147, 167, 170–171
  characteristics of 88–90, 163
  community initiatives for 204
  darker side of 97–98
  decacorns 87
  different kinds of 159–162
  ecosystem 176–177
  efficiencies 172
  entry and exit costs 171
  failing to "crossing the chasm" 92–94
  gazelles 86–87
  identity
    entrepreneurial 125
    organizational 127
  industry sector differences 175–176
  innovation 168, 183
  job creation 174, 183
  job displacement 176
  legitimacy 131
  managerial considerations in 95–97
  new jobs 168
  performance outcomes 119
  portfolio perspective 181–182
  resource 107–109, 118
    bundling for 113

  portfolio 118
  risk and stress in 143
  sub-categories of 161–162
  technology push *versus* market pull 94–95
  unicorn 87
  VRIO and 111–112
  wealth production 169
  see also lifestyle growth ventures; managed growth ventures; survival growth ventures
Airbnb 160
alertness 81
Amazon 87, 89, 129, 169, 171, 177
ambidexterity 81–82
Amit, R. 102
attitudes 11, 70–71
Audretsch, D.B. 171

Bio-clean Medical and Health Specialists (BMHS) 27–29
Birch, D.L. 86
blitzscaling 98
BMHS *see* Bio-clean Medical and Health Specialists (BMHS)
Brännback, M. 125
Bridging Allowance programs 95, 194
Brown, R. 189
Brush, C. 101, 108
Business Development Program of US 195
business idea 3
business (non-financial) literacy 43–45
business model 3, 8

capital access programs (CAPs) 195
Carsrud, A. 125
cash-based businesses 39
cash flow 73, 78, 97

CDEs *see* Community Development
    Entities (CDEs)
Chaganti, R. 101
Charan, R. 96
Churchill, N.C. 75
Clara's cleaning 26, 29
cluster analysis, for organizational
    identity 128
CME *see* Custom Manufacturing &
    Engineering (CME)
Coad, A. 75
co-evolution 7
commodity trap 42–43
Community Development Entities
    (CDEs) 194
community effect 177
community initiatives 197, 201–204,
    207
  examples of 198–199
community investment 204
community obligations 61
competencies, skills and 139–141
competitive advantage 102, 112, 115,
    119, 169
complex resource 108–109, 117, 118
contractual relationship, survival
    ventures 154
control and self-efficacy 138
controlled growth, in managed growth
    venture 158–159
Cooper, A.C. 74, 76
coordinating process 114
corridor principle 8
Cortopassi, Dean (Dino) 68
COSME Program 195
costs of entry and exit 169–171
"crossing the chasm" 92–94
Custom Manufacturing & Engineering
    (CME) 67–68

Dahlstrand, A.L. 192
Davidsson, P. 74
debt 74
decacorns 87
decision-making 10, 53, 58–59
Dell Computer 90
deploying process 114

desire for growth 69–70
differentiation, in lifestyle businesses
    60, 62
diversity 17–18
Dobbs, M. 77
Downing, S. 123
Dunkelberg, W.C. 74
dynamic economy 173–174

Earned Income Tax Credit 194
eBay 160, 169, 177
economic literacy 44, 45
ecosystem 176–177, 198, 204, 207
Eddleston, K.A. 172
efficiency 29, 168, 171–172
emergence 5–6, 9, 178
  properties 7
emergent nature
  of new venture creation 5–9
  of venture creation 146–147, 178
Emerson, Ralph Waldo 94
employment 51–52, 174–175
enriching bundling resource 112, 117
entrepreneur formation, by venture
    146–147
entrepreneurial competencies 140
entrepreneurial ecosystems 198, 207
entrepreneurial firms
  leveraging processes of 114–116
  typologies 18–21
entrepreneurial identity
  dimensions of 124
  motivation and goal 125
  strength and stability 125, 132
  in ventures types 124–129
  see also organizational identity
entrepreneurial journey 2–5, 140
  unique 9–11
entrepreneurial mindset 11
entrepreneurial opportunity strategy
    115
entrepreneurial orientation (EO)
    76–77, 90, 95
entrepreneurial outcomes 181
entrepreneurial process 2–4
entrepreneurial traits
  achievement motivation 137

calculated risk-taking 138
control and self-efficacy 138
opportunity alertness 138
passion 138
perseverance 138
entrepreneurial ventures
bundling processes of 112–114
resource portfolio of 103–104, 112, 113
technology usage 30
typology of 22–25, 32
contrasting the different 26–30
entrepreneurs 1–3, 8
aggressive growth 172, 204
emergence concept 9
identity 123–125
learning 8–9
from mistakes 5
lifestyle *see* lifestyle entrepreneurs
managed growth 203–204
skills and competencies 139–141
survival 44, 119, 125, 154
unique 10
entrepreneurship
community initiatives for 197–199, 201–204
defined 18
emergent nature of 5–9
gaps in policy support for 190–192
myths and misconceptions 13
policy levers for 192–197
understanding 1–2
entrepreneurship experience 141–142, 144, 147, 148
entry costs 169–171
EO *see* entrepreneurial orientation (EO)
equity financing 73–74, 87
Eskimo Joe's 67
ethics 97, 98
Etsy 160
exit costs 169–171
exit strategy, aggressive growth venture 162
Experian 57
experience 141–142, 147, 148
exploitation 96, 99, 117, 160
exploration 96, 99, 160

Facebook 97
failure rates 54, 172–173, 175
family ownership 156, 159–161, 163
Fastsigns 160
Fedex 160
Fernandez, J.M. 174
financial literacy 43–45
firm size 74, 76
fixed cost 61
formative resources 108, 109
franchisees 57, 62
functional literacy 43–45

Gagliardi, P. 129
Gallo, C. 96
Garnsey, E. 75
Gartner, W.B. 18
gazelles 24, 86–87
see also unicorn
Gimeno, J. 124
Glynn, M.A. 126
Gohmann, S.F. 174
Google 87, 89, 129, 169
Go Pro 89
Grameen Bank 47
grants 196–197
Greiner, L. 75
growth determinants 71
growth patterns 75–76
growth potential 69
growth requirements 68
ability 70–72
desire 69–70
potential 69
growth stage 205, 206

Haggerty, A. 86
Hamilton, R.T. 77
hands-on approach 70–71
hand-to-mouth venture 36
Hathaway, I. 89
Henrekson, M. 86
heterogeneity 163
Hoang, H. 124
"hockey stick" pattern 89
Hofer, C.W. 96
Holmes, Elizabeth 97–98

home-based ventures 153, 156
"Honour Loans" program 195–196
human capital 179
human resources
　in lifestyle ventures 104
　in managed growth ventures 107

identity 122
　challenge 133
　and change 126, 128, 130, 133
　defined 123
　entrepreneur 123–125
　fit between personal and
　　organizational 129–130
　and legitimacy 130–131
　organizational 31, 122, 125–128,
　　130–132
　in venture types 124–129, 131–132
inadequate competencies 81–82
industry sector differences 175–176
informal sector, survivalists and
　44–47
infrastructure development, avoidance
　of 79–81
innovation 55, 76–77, 82, 107, 163
　aggressive growth ventures 168,
　　183
　diffusion 93
　in managed growth venture 157
　"newness" 91–92
　process 107, 118
instrumental resources 108, 109
instrumental-robust resource 117, 118
insufficient/ineffective delegation
　78–79
intellectual property (IP) 74
International Franchise Association 62
inventory management 61
IP *see* intellectual property (IP)
irreversibility 7

Jang, Y. 125, 126
job creation 168, 173–175, 183
job displacement 176
Jobs, Steve 96
Johansson, D. 86

Kauffman Foundation 174
Kuratko, D.F. 125, 126, 146, 184

launch-stabilization stage 205
learning opportunities 141
legitimacy 126, 130–132
Lending Club 97
Lewis, V.L. 75
lifestyle entrepreneurs 50, 55–57, 63,
　156
　decisions 58–59
　stability and comfort 58–59
　time horizons of 54
　work-life balance 61–62
lifestyle ventures 23, 24, 29, 30, 50,
　71, 76, 108, 113, 115, 119, 147,
　154–156, 168, 170–171, 172,
　182, 201, 206
　breaking down of lifestyle types
　　154–156
　capacity of businesses 54
　characteristics 52–55
　characteristics of lifestyle types 163
　community initiatives for 203
　decision-making 53
　ecosystem 177
　efficiencies 172
　employment 51–52
　entry and exit costs 171
　financial standpoint of 54
　franchisees as 57, 62
　innovation 55
　job creation 174
　job creation impact 174–175
　key operational challenges 59–61
　legitimacy 131
　myths and misconceptions 55–57
　organizational identity 127
　percentages of 51, 57, 63
　performance outcomes 119
　portfolio perspective 181–182
　resource 104
　　bundling for 113
　　dynamics 117
　riskiness of 54–55
　role in economy 51–52
　role in sustained economy 174

smaller size of 60, 62
sub-categories of lifestyle types
155–156
versus survival ventures 51
venture portfolio 182
VRIO and 110–111
literacy 43–45, 205
loan guarantees 195–196

MacMillan, I.C. 11
Mainstreet Commercial Cleaners
26–29
managed growth entrepreneurs
203–204
managed growth ventures 23–24, 29,
30, 52, 66, 108, 115, 157–159,
163, 168, 170–171, 181, 182,
206
anatomy of 72–74
characteristics of managed growth
firms 73
characteristics of managed growth
types 163
common mistakes
avoidance of infrastructure
development 79–81
failure to stick to the knitting
77–78
inadequate competencies 81–82
insufficient/ineffective delegation
78–79
not understanding cash flow 78
over-reliance 79
community initiatives for 203–204
different patterns of managed
growth firms 75–76
ecosystem 177
efficiencies 172
entrepreneurial orientations 76, 77
entry and exit costs 171
equity financing 73–74
examples 66–68
innovation 76–77, 82
job creation 174
job creation impact 174–175
key characteristics of 72–73
legitimacy 131

organizational identity 126, 127
performance outcomes 119
portfolio perspective 181–182
portfolios development 111
regulatory relief 201
resource 107, 117
bundling for 113
portfolio 118
role in sustained economy 174
sub-categories of managed growth
types 157–159
tax policy 201
venture portfolio 182
VRIO and 111
managerial competencies 140
marginal venture 42, 43
market opportunity strategy 115
market pull 94–95
Martin, K. 126
Mason, C. 189
McClelland, D.C 137
McGrath, R.G. 11, 173
Merry Maids 27–29
microcredit 198, 201, 205
microenterprises 81
micromanager 41
Mielach, D. 175
Miner, J.B. 141
mobilizing process 114
mom and pop 50
Moore, G. 92–94
Morris, M.H. 10, 58, 74, 88, 125–126,
146, 178
literacies in survival ventures 43–44
motivation 125
achievement 74, 137, 139, 144
Mueller, P. 174
Mullainathan, S. 40
myths
in lifestyle venture 55–57
and misconceptions 13

Navis, C. 126
Netflix 89
Neumeyer, X. 125, 126
New Markets Tax Credit (NMTC) 194
"newness" 91–92

New Start-Up Subsidy 194
new technology 91–92
new venture creation, emergent nature
    of 5–9
Nike 160
NMTC *see* New Markets Tax Credit
    (NMTC)
non-financial literacy 43–45

1-800-GotJunk 92, 160
one-person-band syndrome 60
opportunity alertness 138
Orangetheory Fitness 160
organizational identity 31, 122,
    125–128
    fit between personal and 129–130
    in ventures types 131–132
over-reliance 79

Parsons, W. 86
passion 138
perseverance 138
personal identity, fit between
    organizational and 129–130
pioneering bundling resource 112
policy levers
    financial support 197
    government spending 196
    grants 196–197
    loan guarantees 195–196
    regulatory policies 197
    regulatory relief 197
    subsidy programs 194–195
    taxation policies 192, 194
    voucher programs 196
Politis, D. 142
Portfolio perspective, venture types
    and public policy
    potential for growth 69
    pre-start-up stage 205
    previous experience 141–142
    proactiveness 76–77
    process innovation 107, 118
    product innovation 118
    public policy 189
        community action 193
        concerns and problems 191

development 192
    gaps in 190–192
    for venture types 200
    pursuit of opportunity 8

RBV *see* resource-based view (RBV)
real estate agent 66–67
real options theory 173
reciprocal interactions 7
regulations 191
    laws and 190
regulatory policies 197
regulatory relief 197, 201
resource 131
    of aggressive growth ventures
        107–109, 118
    of lifestyle ventures 104
    of managed growth ventures 107,
        117
    of survival ventures 104
    types and their properties 102–103
resource advantage strategy 114–115,
    117
resource-based view (RBV) 101, 102,
    116
resource bundling 115, 117, 118
    for aggressive growth ventures 113
    for lifestyle ventures 113
    for managed growth ventures 113
    processes 112
    for survival ventures 112
resource dynamics 117–118
resource leveraging 118
    processes 114
resource management 102
resource portfolio 103–104, 112, 113,
    118
    characteristics of 105–106
risk-taking 76, 77, 143
Robbins, D.K. 166
robust resources 108, 109
Rogers, E.M. 93

SBA Loan Program 195
scarcity 40
Schein, E.H. 123
Schindehutte, M. 10, 146

Schoemaker, P.J. 102
self-efficacy 138, 144
self-identity 123, 124
Shafir, E. 40
Shah, A.K. 40
Shah, S.K. 123
Shane, S. 86, 167–169, 171–172, 174–176, 178, 189
shorter-term orientation 60
Silicon Valley 177
Sirmon, D. 102
skills 71
    and competencies 139–141
Smith, N.R. 141
social resources, in lifestyle ventures 104
SpaceX 169
Spivack, A. 146
sporadic growth 75–76
stability resource bundling 117
stabilizing bundling resource 112
staged growth 75
stages of development, tailoring support efforts to 204–207
Starbucks 92, 160
start-up activity 174
Start-up Subsidy program 194, 195
steady, consistent growth 75
Stevenson, L. 192
stress 142–143
stress tolerance 143
sub-categories of venture 163–164
    aggressive growth types 161–162
    characteristics of 162–163
    lifestyle types 155–156
    managed growth types 157–159
    survival types 152–153
subsidy programs 194–195
supervenience 7
survival entrepreneurs 44, 119, 125, 154
survival ventures 20, 23, 24, 28–30, 71, 76, 108, 115, 152–154, 168, 170–171, 182, 201, 206
    business operations 37–39
    characteristics of 39–41
    characteristics of survival types 162–163

commodity trap 42–43
community initiatives for 203
continuous struggle 36–37
ecosystem 177
efficiencies 172
entry and exit costs 171
identity 126, 132
    organizational 127
    in informal sector 44–47
job creation 174
job creation impact 174–175
legitimacy 131
lifestyle venture *versus* 51
literacy challenge 43–45
as micromanager 41
performance outcomes 119
portfolio perspective 181–182
resource 104
    bundling for 112
    dynamics 117
    portfolio 118
role in sustained economy 174
stress and risk in 143
sub-categories of survival types 152–153
three examples of 37–39
venture portfolio 182
VRIO and 110
survivalist, and informal sector 44–47
survivalist entrepreneur 39–41
sustainability, in aggressive growth venture 162
sustained economy 173–174
    see also dynamic economy

TANF program *see* Temporary Assistance for Needy Families (TANF) program
tax credits 194
tax incentives 194, 205
tax policy 192, 194, 201
technological literacy 43–45
technology push 94–95
Temporary Assistance for Needy Families (TANF) program 194
Tesla 12, 92
Theranos 97–98

Thurik, A.R. 171
training programs 201
trial-and-error 41, 58–59
Tripsas, M. 123
typologies 18–25
  entrepreneurial firms 18–21
  entrepreneurial ventures 22–25, 32

Uber 160, 168, 182
unicorn 87
utilitarian resources 108

Van Stel, A. 171
Venkatesh, S.A. 46
venture creation 2–5, 9, 13, 179
  competencies in 140
  emergent nature of 5–9, 146–147,
    178
  and stress 142–143
venture diversity 11–12, 17–18, 72
venture portfolio 179–183
venture types 13, 20–25, 32, 47, 71,
  120
  aggressive growth *see* aggressive
    growth ventures
  community programs for 202–203
  contrasting the different 26–30
  entrepreneurial characteristics and
    143–145
  entrepreneurial identity in 124–129
  evolve from one type to another 31,
    128–129, 132

implications for 143–145
  lifestyle growth *see* lifestyle growth
    ventures
  managed growth *see* managed
    growth ventures
  objectives 180
  organizational identity in 131–132
  percent of 182
  portfolio perspective 181–183
  resources and 103–109
  sub-categories of 163–164
  survival growth *see* survival growth
    ventures
  tailoring support efforts to 199–204
  and VRIO 109–112
voucher programs 196
VRIO
  and aggressive growth ventures
    111–112
  characteristics 118
  and lifestyle ventures 110–111
  and managed growth ventures 111
  properties 102, 116–117
  and survival ventures 110
vulnerability 60

Walmart 175
Webb, J.W. 126
WEF *see* World Economic Forum
    (WEF)
work-life balance 61–62
World Economic Forum (WEF) 86–87